TEXTBOOK OF NUTRACEUTICALS AND FUNCTIONAL FOODS

THEORY AND APPLICATIONS

SUDHAKAR KOMMU | THIRUMURUGAN R | BHAVANA MADUPOJU

Contents

Preface

The field of nutraceuticals and functional foods is rapidly evolving, driven by a growing recognition of the critical role that nutrition plays in maintaining health and preventing disease. As educators and researchers in the domain of pharmacognosy and pharmaceutics, we have observed a significant gap in comprehensive, accessible educational resources that integrate the latest scientific advancements with practical applications. This book, "Textbook of Nutraceuticals and Functional Foods," aims to fill this gap by providing a thorough and detailed exploration of the subject, tailored to the needs of students, researchers, and professionals in the field.

This textbook is designed to serve as a definitive resource, offering in-depth knowledge and insights into the diverse aspects of nutraceuticals and functional foods. Our objective is to present complex information in a digestible and engaging manner, ensuring that readers can grasp the fundamental concepts and applications without being overwhelmed by technical jargon.

The content is meticulously organized into chapters that align with the curriculum and syllabus, ensuring comprehensive coverage of essential topics. Each chapter delves into the definitions, classifications, sources, and health benefits of various nutraceuticals and functional foods. We have also included detailed discussions on the mechanisms of action, clinical evidence, and regulatory aspects, providing a holistic understanding of the field.

We extend our gratitude to our colleagues and students, whose feedback and encouragement have been invaluable in shaping this book. We also acknowledge the contributions of the many researchers and practitioners whose work has been instrumental in advancing our knowledge of nutraceuticals and functional foods.

It is our hope that this textbook will not only serve as an essential academic resource but also inspire further research and innovation in the field. We believe that a deeper understanding of nutraceuticals and functional foods will empower future healthcare professionals to make informed decisions, ultimately improving the health and well-being of individuals and communities.

We invite you to embark on this educational journey with us, exploring the fascinating interplay between nutrition and health. May this book be a guiding light in your academic and professional endeavors, helping you to unlock the full potential of nutraceuticals and functional foods.

Mr. Sudhakar Kommu

Mr. R. Thirumurugan

Mrs. Bhavana Madupoju

Textbook Of Nutraceuticals And Functional Foods

Authors

Mr. Sudhakar Kommu
Associate Professor
Department of Pharmacognosy
Anurag Pharmacy College
Ananthagiri, Kodad
Suryapet Dist-508233
Telangana, India

Mr. R. Thirumurugan
Principal
Niveditha College of Pharmacy
Chintamani
Karnataka, India

Mrs. Bhavana Madupoju
Assistant Professor
Department of Pharmaceutics
KL College of Pharmacy
KL Deemed to be University
Guntur
Andhra Pradesh, India

Published by Notion Press
Notion Press, Inc.
800, West El Camino Real #180
California, USA 94040

Notion Press Media Pvt Ltd
#7, Red Cross Road
Egmore, Chennai, Tamil Nadu 600008
Email ID: publish@notionpress.com
Phone Number: +91 44 46315631

ONE

INTRODUCTION TO NUTRACEUTICALS AND FUNCTIONAL FOODS

"Nutraceuticals and Functional Foods: Boosting Health with Nature's Best"

1.1 Definitions

Functional Foods are foods that provide additional health benefits beyond basic nutrition. Unlike conventional foods, which primarily supply essential nutrients and energy, functional foods contain bioactive compounds that can help prevent disease and promote overall health. These foods often include fortified, enriched, or enhanced foods and dietary components that may reduce the risk of chronic diseases such as heart disease, cancer, and diabetes. For example, foods like yogurt with added probiotics, oatmeal with high fiber content, and orange juice fortified with calcium are considered functional foods. The main difference between functional foods and conventional foods lies in their purpose and composition. Conventional foods are primarily consumed to meet basic nutritional needs, while functional foods are specifically designed to deliver additional health benefits, often through the inclusion of specific nutrients or other bioactive compounds.

Nutraceuticals are products derived from food sources that offer extra health benefits in addition to the basic nutritional value found in foods. These products can be used to promote overall health, prevent chronic diseases, delay the aging process, and support the structure or function of the body. Nutraceuticals can be categorized into several types, including dietary supplements, functional foods, and medicinal foods. Common examples of nutraceutical products include omega-3 fatty acids from fish oil, which are known for their cardiovascular benefits, and glucosamine supplements, which are often used to support joint health. Other examples include turmeric extracts containing curcumin for its anti-inflammatory properties, and green tea extracts rich in antioxidants that help protect against cellular damage. The term "nutraceutical" combines the words "nutrition" and "pharmaceutical," highlighting their role in promoting health and preventing disease, much like conventional pharmaceuticals, but with a focus on natural, food-based sources.

Dietary Supplements are products intended to supplement the diet and provide nutrients that may be missing or may not be consumed in sufficient quantities in a person's diet. These supplements can include vitamins, minerals, amino acids, enzymes, herbs, and other botanicals. Dietary supplements come in various forms, such as tablets, capsules, powders, and liquids. The regulation of dietary supplements varies by country, but in many places, they are regulated as a category of food rather than drugs. In the United States, for example, the Food and Drug Administration (FDA) oversees dietary supplements under the Dietary Supplement Health and Education Act (DSHEA) of 1994. Under this act, manufacturers are responsible for ensuring the safety and labeling of their products before they go to market. However, the FDA does not approve dietary supplements for safety or effectiveness before they are sold. Instead, the FDA's role is to take action against any unsafe dietary supplement products after they reach the market. This regulatory approach is different from that of pharmaceuticals, which require rigorous testing and approval processes before they can be made available to consumers. It is important for consumers to use dietary supplements wisely and consult healthcare professionals, as these products can interact with medications or have side effects if not used properly.

1.2 Classification of Nutraceuticals

Classification Based on Source: Nutraceuticals can be classified according to their source of origin. These sources include plants, animals, and microorganisms. **Plant-based nutraceuticals** are derived from fruits, vegetables, grains, nuts, seeds, and herbs. Common examples include polyphenols, flavonoids, and carotenoids, which are found in a variety of fruits and vegetables and are known for their antioxidant properties. **Animal-based nutraceuticals** come from sources such as fish, dairy products, and meat. Omega-3 fatty acids from fish oil and conjugated linoleic acid (CLA) from meat and dairy products are well-known animal-based nutraceuticals with significant health benefits, including cardiovascular health and weight management. **Microorganism-based nutraceuticals** are derived from beneficial bacteria and yeast. Probiotics, which are live microorganisms that provide health benefits when consumed in adequate amounts, are a prime example of this category. These probiotics are often found in fermented foods like yogurt and kefir and are known for their positive effects on gut health.

Chemical Nature Classifications: Nutraceuticals can also be classified based on their chemical nature. This classification includes several categories: **Vitamins** are organic compounds that are essential for normal growth and nutrition and are required in small quantities in the diet because they cannot be synthesized by the body. Examples include vitamin C (ascorbic acid), vitamin E (tocopherol), and the B vitamins. **Minerals** are inorganic elements that play a critical role in various bodily functions, such as calcium for bone health, iron for blood production, and magnesium for muscle and nerve function. **Amino acids and proteins** are the building blocks of proteins and are crucial for the growth, repair, and maintenance of body tissues. Essential amino acids, which cannot be synthesized by the body and must be obtained from the diet, include lysine, tryptophan, and methionine. **Fatty acids** are important for maintaining cell membrane integrity and producing energy. Omega-3 and omega-6 fatty acids are essential fatty acids that must be obtained from the diet and are known for their role in heart health and inflammation regulation. **Phytochemicals** are bioactive compounds found in plants that have health-promoting properties. This category includes polyphenols, flavonoids, carotenoids, and alkaloids. Each of these compounds has unique chemical structures and health benefits. **Probiotics and prebiotics** are another category of nutraceuticals based on their chemical nature. Probiotics are live beneficial bacteria, while prebiotics are non-digestible food ingredients that promote the growth of beneficial bacteria in the gut.

Health Benefits Classification: Nutraceuticals are often classified based on the specific health benefits they provide. **Antioxidants** are compounds that protect the body from oxidative stress and free radical damage. Examples include vitamins C and E, selenium, and various polyphenols. These antioxidants are crucial in preventing chronic diseases such as cancer and heart disease. **Anti-inflammatory agents** help reduce inflammation in the body, which is linked to various chronic conditions, including arthritis, cardiovascular diseases, and metabolic disorders. Omega-3 fatty acids, curcumin from turmeric, and certain polyphenols exhibit strong anti-inflammatory properties. **Cardiovascular health** nutraceuticals support heart health by improving lipid profiles, reducing blood pressure, and enhancing endothelial function. Examples include omega-3 fatty acids, Coenzyme Q10, and plant sterols. **Digestive health** nutraceuticals, such as probiotics and prebiotics, promote a healthy gut microbiome, improve digestion, and enhance nutrient absorption. **Immune system boosters** include vitamins A, C, and D, zinc, and echinacea, which help strengthen the body's defense mechanisms against infections and diseases. **Bone health** nutraceuticals, such as calcium, vitamin D, and magnesium, are essential for maintaining strong bones and preventing osteoporosis. **Weight management** nutraceuticals, including green tea extract, CLA, and fiber supplements, assist in weight loss and weight maintenance by enhancing metabolism and reducing appetite.

By classifying nutraceuticals based on their source, chemical nature, and health benefits, we can better understand their roles and applications in promoting health and preventing diseases. This comprehensive classification helps in identifying specific nutraceuticals suitable for targeted health outcomes, making it easier for healthcare professionals and consumers to select the right products for their needs.

1.3 Health Problems and Diseases Preventable or Manageable by Nutraceuticals

Weight Control: Nutraceuticals play a significant role in weight control by enhancing metabolism, suppressing appetite, and improving fat oxidation. **Green tea extract**, rich in catechins, boosts metabolism and increases fat oxidation, helping to burn calories more efficiently. **Conjugated Linoleic Acid (CLA)**, found in meat and dairy products, helps reduce body fat by inhibiting the formation of fat cells and promoting the breakdown of fats. **Dietary fibers**, such as those found in oats and psyllium husk, promote satiety by increasing the feeling of fullness, thereby reducing overall calorie intake. **Garcinia cambogia** extract contains hydroxycitric acid, which is known to suppress appetite and inhibit fat storage. These nutraceuticals, when combined with a healthy diet and regular exercise, can significantly contribute to weight management and prevent obesity-related complications.

Managing Diabetes: Nutraceuticals play a crucial role in managing diabetes by improving insulin sensitivity, reducing blood glucose levels, and preventing complications associated with diabetes. **Alpha-lipoic acid** is an antioxidant that enhances insulin sensitivity and reduces oxidative stress, which is beneficial for diabetic patients. **Fenugreek seeds** contain soluble fiber and compounds like 4-hydroxyisoleucine that help lower blood sugar levels by slowing carbohydrate absorption and improving insulin secretion. **Chromium picolinate** enhances insulin action and glucose metabolism, thereby reducing blood sugar levels. **Cinnamon** has bioactive compounds that mimic insulin, improving glucose uptake by cells and stabilizing blood sugar levels. **Bitter melon** contains compounds like charantin and polypeptide-p that have insulin-like properties, helping to lower blood glucose levels. These nutraceuticals, along with a balanced diet and regular physical activity, can effectively manage diabetes and its associated risks.

Cancer Prevention and Treatment: Nutraceuticals have shown promise in cancer prevention and treatment due to their antioxidant, anti-inflammatory, and anti-proliferative properties. **Curcumin**, found in turmeric, has potent anti-inflammatory and antioxidant effects, inhibiting the growth of cancer cells and inducing apoptosis (programmed cell death). **Green tea polyphenols**, particularly epigallocatechin gallate (EGCG), have been shown to prevent cancer cell proliferation and metastasis. **Resveratrol**, a polyphenolic compound in grapes and red wine, has anti-cancer properties, inhibiting tumor growth and inducing apoptosis in cancer cells. **Lycopene**, a carotenoid found in tomatoes, has been linked to a reduced risk of prostate cancer and other types of cancer due to its antioxidant activity. **Sulforaphane**, found in cruciferous vegetables like broccoli, activates detoxifying enzymes and protects cells from DNA damage. These nutraceuticals can complement conventional cancer therapies, reducing side effects and enhancing treatment efficacy.

Preventing Cardiovascular Diseases: Nutraceuticals are essential in preventing cardiovascular diseases by improving lipid profiles, reducing inflammation, and enhancing endothelial function. **Omega-3 fatty acids**, found in fish oil, reduce triglyceride levels, lower blood pressure, and decrease inflammation, thereby protecting against heart disease. **Coenzyme Q10 (CoQ10)** improves mitochondrial function and reduces oxidative stress, which is beneficial for heart health. **Plant sterols and stanols** reduce cholesterol absorption in the intestines, lowering LDL cholesterol levels. **Flavonoids**, found in fruits, vegetables, and tea, improve endothelial function and reduce blood pressure. **Magnesium** helps regulate heart rhythm and relaxes blood vessels, reducing the risk of hypertension and heart disease. These nutraceuticals, along with a heart-healthy diet and lifestyle, can significantly reduce the risk of cardiovascular diseases.

Other Health Conditions Managed with Nutraceuticals: Nutraceuticals are also effective in managing various other health conditions. **Bone health** can be supported by calcium, vitamin D, and magnesium, which are essential for maintaining bone density and preventing osteoporosis. **Joint health** benefits from glucosamine and chondroitin, which help maintain cartilage and reduce symptoms of osteoarthritis. **Digestive health** can be improved with probiotics and prebiotics, which promote a healthy gut microbiome and enhance nutrient absorption. **Immune function** is boosted by vitamins A, C, and E, zinc, and echinacea, which help strengthen the body's defenses against infections. **Mental health** can benefit from omega-3 fatty acids, which support brain function and reduce symptoms of depression and anxiety. **Skin health** is enhanced by antioxidants like vitamin C and E, which protect against oxidative damage and promote collagen synthesis. These nutraceuticals provide a holistic approach to health management, addressing various conditions and promoting overall well-being.

By incorporating these nutraceuticals into a balanced diet and lifestyle, individuals can prevent and manage a wide range of health conditions, improving their quality of life and reducing the risk of chronic diseases.

1.4 Benefits and Applications

General Health Benefits of Functional Foods and Nutraceuticals: Functional foods and nutraceuticals offer a wide range of general health benefits that contribute to overall well-being. They are known to enhance **nutritional status** by providing essential vitamins, minerals, and other bioactive compounds that might be lacking in the regular diet. For instance, fortified foods like calcium-enriched orange juice can help meet daily calcium requirements, especially for those who do not consume dairy products. These foods and supplements also play a crucial role in **boosting the immune system**. Nutrients like vitamin C, zinc, and probiotics support immune function, helping the body fend off infections and illnesses. Moreover, functional foods and nutraceuticals are beneficial for **improving digestive health**. Dietary fibers, prebiotics, and probiotics promote a healthy gut microbiome, enhance digestion, and prevent gastrointestinal disorders. They also aid in **enhancing mental health** by providing nutrients that support brain function. Omega-3 fatty acids, B vitamins, and antioxidants like vitamin E can improve cognitive function, reduce the risk of neurodegenerative diseases, and alleviate symptoms of depression and anxiety. Additionally, these foods and supplements contribute to **maintaining healthy skin and hair**. Antioxidants, vitamins A and E, and biotin promote skin health, reduce signs of aging, and improve hair strength and texture. By integrating functional foods and nutraceuticals into the diet, individuals can achieve a balanced nutritional profile, boost their overall health, and enhance their quality of life.

Nutraceuticals in Disease Prevention and Management: Nutraceuticals play a pivotal role in the prevention and management of various chronic diseases, offering therapeutic benefits beyond basic nutrition. They are particularly effective in **preventing cardiovascular diseases**. Omega-3 fatty acids from fish oil, plant sterols, and antioxidants like flavonoids help lower cholesterol levels, reduce blood pressure, and prevent the formation of arterial plaques, thereby protecting against heart disease. In **diabetes management**, nutraceuticals like chromium, alpha-lipoic acid, and fenugreek help regulate blood glucose levels, improve insulin sensitivity, and reduce the risk of complications. For **cancer prevention and treatment**, compounds such as curcumin, resveratrol, and green tea polyphenols exhibit anti-inflammatory, antioxidant, and anti-proliferative properties that inhibit cancer cell growth and promote apoptosis. **Bone health** is another area where nutraceuticals are highly beneficial. Calcium, vitamin D, and magnesium are essential for maintaining bone density and preventing osteoporosis. Nutraceuticals also contribute significantly to **joint health**. Glucosamine and chondroitin sulfate help reduce inflammation, alleviate pain, and improve joint mobility in conditions like osteoarthritis. In the realm of **digestive health**, probiotics and prebiotics support a healthy gut microbiome, enhance nutrient absorption, and prevent digestive disorders such as irritable bowel syndrome. Furthermore, nutraceuticals like antioxidants and vitamins C and E play a crucial role in **skin health**, protecting against oxidative damage, promoting collagen synthesis, and reducing signs of aging. These therapeutic benefits of nutraceuticals make them invaluable in the holistic management of health and prevention of chronic diseases, offering a natural and effective approach to maintaining well-being.

Case Studies and Research Evidence: Numerous studies and clinical trials have demonstrated the efficacy of nutraceuticals in promoting health and managing diseases. For instance, a study published in the **Journal of the American College of Cardiology** highlighted the benefits of omega-3 fatty acids in reducing the risk of cardiovascular events. The research showed that individuals who consumed fish oil supplements had significantly lower levels of triglycerides and a reduced risk of heart attacks and strokes. Another study in the **Journal of Clinical Endocrinology & Metabolism** demonstrated the positive effects of chromium supplementation in managing type 2 diabetes. The participants showed improved insulin sensitivity and better control of blood glucose levels. In the field of oncology, research published in **Cancer Research** indicated that curcumin, a compound found in turmeric, inhibited the growth of various cancer cells, including breast, prostate, and colon cancer, through its anti-inflammatory and antioxidant mechanisms. A clinical trial reported in the **Journal of Bone and Mineral Research** found that calcium and vitamin D supplementation significantly improved bone density in postmenopausal women, reducing the risk of fractures. For joint health, a study in the **Annals of the Rheumatic Diseases** showed that glucosamine and chondroitin supplementation provided relief from osteoarthritis symptoms, improving joint function and reducing pain. Additionally, research on probiotics published in **Gastroenterology** demonstrated their effectiveness in treating irritable bowel syndrome and other gastrointestinal disorders by restoring a healthy balance of gut bacteria. These case studies and research findings provide robust evidence supporting the use of nutraceuticals in various health conditions, underscoring their potential as a complementary approach to conventional medical treatments.

By understanding and leveraging the general health benefits, disease prevention and management capabilities, and robust research evidence, individuals and healthcare professionals can make informed decisions about incorporating functional foods and nutraceuticals into their diets and therapeutic regimens. This approach not only enhances overall health but also provides a natural, effective means of preventing and managing a wide range of health conditions.

Table 1: Differences between Functional Foods, Nutraceuticals, and Dietary Supplements

Aspect	Functional Foods	Nutraceuticals	Dietary Supplements
Definition	Foods that provide additional health benefits beyond basic nutrition	Products derived from food sources with extra health benefits	Products intended to supplement the diet and provide nutrients
Examples	Yogurt with probiotics, fortified orange juice	Omega-3 fish oil, glucosamine supplements	Multivitamins, vitamin D tablets
Purpose	Enhance overall health and prevent disease	Promote health, prevent chronic diseases, support body functions	Fill nutritional gaps in the diet, support specific health needs
Regulation	Often regulated as food with health claims	Varies by country, often less stringent than pharmaceuticals	Regulated as a category of food, less stringent than drugs

Table 2: Classification of Nutraceuticals Based on Source

Source	Examples	Bioactive Compounds	Health Benefits
Plant-based	Fruits, vegetables, herbs	Polyphenols, flavonoids, carotenoids	Antioxidant, anti-inflammatory, cancer prevention
Animal-based	Fish oil, dairy products	Omega-3 fatty acids, CLA	Cardiovascular health, weight management
Microorganism-based	Yogurt, kefir	Probiotics	Gut health, immune support

Table 3: Classification of Nutraceuticals Based on Chemical Nature

Chemical Nature	Examples	Sources	Health Benefits
Vitamins	Vitamin C, Vitamin E	Citrus fruits, nuts	Immune support, antioxidant
Minerals	Calcium, Iron	Dairy products, red meat	Bone health, blood production
Amino Acids	Lysine, Tryptophan	Meat, dairy, legumes	Protein synthesis, muscle repair
Fatty Acids	Omega-3, Omega-6	Fish oil, flaxseed	Cardiovascular health, anti-inflammatory
Phytochemicals	Curcumin, Resveratrol	Turmeric, red grapes	Anti-inflammatory, antioxidant
Probiotics	Lactobacillus, Bifidobacterium	Yogurt, fermented foods	Digestive health, immune support

Table 4: Health Benefits and Uses of Key Nutraceuticals

Nutraceutical	Health Benefits	Uses
Omega-3 Fatty Acids	Reduce triglycerides, lower blood pressure, anti-inflammatory	Heart health, joint health
Curcumin	Anti-inflammatory, antioxidant, anti-cancer	Cancer prevention, arthritis management
Probiotics	Enhance gut health, boost immunity	Digestive disorders, immune support
Calcium	Maintain bone density, prevent osteoporosis	Bone health, fracture prevention
Green Tea Extract	Boost metabolism, antioxidant, anti-cancer	Weight management, cancer prevention
Glucosamine	Maintain cartilage, reduce osteoarthritis symptoms	Joint health, osteoarthritis

Table 5: Key Research Evidence Supporting Nutraceuticals

Nutraceutical	Study Findings	Reference
Omega-3 Fatty Acids	Reduced risk of heart attacks and strokes	Journal of the American College of Cardiology
Chromium	Improved insulin sensitivity in type 2 diabetes	Journal of Clinical Endocrinology & Metabolism
Curcumin	Inhibited growth of cancer cells	Cancer Research
Calcium & Vitamin D	Improved bone density in postmenopausal women	Journal of Bone and Mineral Research
Probiotics	Effective in treating irritable bowel syndrome	Gastroenterology
Glucosamine & Chondroitin	Relief from osteoarthritis symptoms	Annals of the Rheumatic Diseases

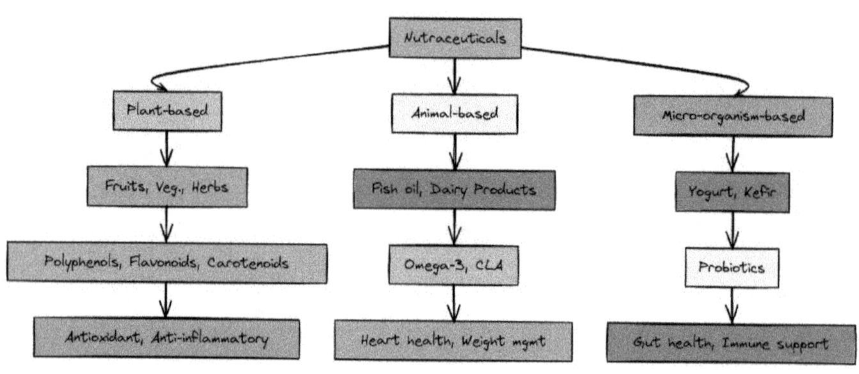

Flowchart 1: Classification of Nutraceuticals Based on Source

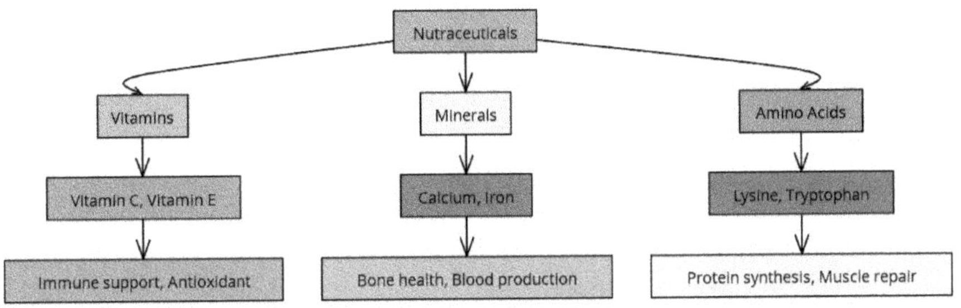

Flowchart 2: Classification of Nutraceuticals Based on Chemical Nature

Fig: Health Benefits and uses of Nutraceuticals

TWO

SOURCES AND BENEFITS OF KEY NUTRACEUTICALS/ FUNCTIONAL FOODS

2.1 Spirulina

Source and Cultivation Process of Spirulina: **Spirulina** is a type of blue-green algae, also known as cyanobacteria, that thrives in warm, alkaline, and high-salt water environments. It is naturally found in lakes and ponds with high pH levels, such as Lake Texcoco in Mexico and Lake Chad in Africa. The cultivation of Spirulina is an intricate process that requires specific environmental conditions to ensure optimal growth and productivity. It is typically grown in open raceway ponds or closed photobioreactors. In the **open raceway pond method**, shallow ponds are constructed with a continuous flow of water to keep the Spirulina in suspension, ensuring uniform exposure to sunlight. The water is mixed and circulated using paddle wheels. Nutrients such as nitrogen, phosphorus, potassium, and trace elements are added to the water to promote growth. The **closed photobioreactor method** involves growing Spirulina in a controlled environment using transparent tubes or flat-panel reactors that provide a sterile environment, protecting the algae from contamination and allowing precise control over light, temperature, and nutrient supply. Once the Spirulina reaches the desired density, it is harvested through filtration, washed to remove impurities, and dried. The dried Spirulina is then processed into various forms such as powder, tablets, and capsules for consumption. The cultivation process is designed to maximize yield and maintain the high nutritional quality of Spirulina, making it a sustainable and efficient source of nutrients.

Marker Compounds Found in Spirulina and Their Chemical Nature: **Spirulina** is rich in a variety of bioactive compounds that contribute to its nutritional and medicinal properties. One of the most important marker compounds is **phycocyanin**, a blue pigment-protein complex that has potent antioxidant and anti-inflammatory properties. Phycocyanin is unique to cyanobacteria and is responsible for the vibrant blue-green color of Spirulina. Another significant compound is **chlorophyll**, the green pigment that plays a crucial role in photosynthesis. Chlorophyll is known for its detoxifying properties and ability to support overall health. **Beta-carotene**, a precursor of vitamin A, is another major compound in Spirulina, contributing to its antioxidant activity and supporting vision and immune health. **Gamma-linolenic acid (GLA)**, an omega-6 fatty acid, is also present in Spirulina, providing anti-inflammatory benefits and supporting cardiovascular health. Additionally, Spirulina contains essential amino acids, vitamins such as B1, B2, B3, B6, and B12, and minerals including iron, calcium, magnesium, and potassium. These compounds collectively enhance the nutritional profile of Spirulina, making it a highly valuable dietary supplement.

Medicinal Uses and Health Benefits of Spirulina: **Spirulina** offers a wide range of medicinal uses and health benefits, making it a popular nutraceutical. One of its primary benefits is its potent **antioxidant** properties, which help protect cells from oxidative damage caused by free radicals. This antioxidant activity is primarily attributed to phycocyanin, chlorophyll, and beta-carotene, which collectively reduce the risk of chronic diseases such as cancer and cardiovascular diseases. Spirulina is also known for its **anti-inflammatory** effects, which can help reduce inflammation in the body and alleviate symptoms of conditions such as arthritis and asthma. The presence of gamma-linolenic acid (GLA) contributes significantly to its anti-inflammatory properties. Furthermore, Spirulina supports **immune health** by enhancing the production and activity of white blood cells and antibodies, thereby boosting the body's defense mechanisms against infections and illnesses. It is also beneficial for **detoxification**, as chlorophyll helps remove toxins from the blood and supports liver function. Spirulina's high protein content, including all essential amino acids, makes it an excellent supplement for **muscle building and recovery**, particularly for vegetarians and vegans. Additionally, Spirulina has been shown to improve **lipid profiles** by lowering LDL cholesterol and triglycerides while increasing HDL cholesterol, thus promoting cardiovascular health. It also aids in **blood sugar regulation**, making it beneficial for individuals with diabetes or those at risk of developing diabetes. The high iron content in Spirulina helps combat **anemia** by improving hemoglobin levels and enhancing oxygen transport in the blood. Overall, Spirulina is a highly nutritious superfood with diverse health benefits, making it a valuable addition to a healthy diet.

2.2 Soybean

Source and Cultivation Process of Soybeans: **Soybeans** are leguminous plants that belong to the species Glycine max. They are native to East Asia and have been cultivated for thousands of years due to their high nutritional value and versatile applications. Soybeans thrive in well-drained, fertile soils with a pH between 6.0 and 7.0, and they require a warm growing season with temperatures between 20°C and 30°C. The cultivation process begins with **soil preparation**, where fields are plowed and harrowed to create a fine seedbed. **Seeds** are then planted either by drilling or broadcasting, typically in rows spaced about 30 to 90 centimeters apart, depending on the farming method and machinery used. Soybeans are often planted in the spring when soil temperatures reach at least 10°C. The crop requires adequate **water** supply, particularly during the flowering and pod-filling stages. Irrigation may be used in areas with insufficient rainfall. **Weed control** is crucial, especially during the early growth stages, and is typically managed through a combination of mechanical and chemical methods. **Pest and disease management** are also essential to ensure healthy crop development. Common pests include soybean aphids and caterpillars, while diseases like soybean rust and root rot can significantly impact yields. Harvesting usually takes place in late summer or early autumn when the pods have matured, and the seeds have reached full size. The soybeans are then **threshed** to separate the seeds from the pods, followed by **drying** and **storage** to maintain their quality and prevent spoilage. The cultivation of soybeans is integral to sustainable agriculture, as these plants can fix nitrogen in the soil, reducing the need for synthetic fertilizers and improving soil health for subsequent crops.

Marker Compounds and Their Chemical Nature in Soybeans: **Soybeans** are rich in several bioactive compounds that contribute to their nutritional and health-promoting properties. One of the primary marker compounds is **isoflavones**, which are a class of phytoestrogens. The main isoflavones in soybeans include genistein, daidzein, and glycitein. These compounds mimic the activity of estrogen in the body and have been linked to various health benefits, including reduced risk of hormone-related cancers and osteoporosis. Another significant compound is **saponins**, which have a soap-like structure and are known for their cholesterol-lowering and immune-boosting properties. **Phytosterols** are also present in soybeans and play a role in reducing cholesterol absorption in the intestines, thus promoting cardiovascular health. Soybeans are an excellent source of **protein**, containing all essential amino acids, making them a complete protein source suitable for vegetarians and vegans. They also contain **omega-3 fatty acids**, particularly alpha-linolenic acid (ALA), which is beneficial for heart health and reducing inflammation. Additionally, soybeans are rich in **vitamins and minerals**, including B vitamins, vitamin K, calcium, magnesium, iron, and potassium. These compounds collectively enhance the nutritional profile of soybeans, making them a valuable addition to a balanced diet.

Medicinal Uses and Health Benefits of Soybeans: **Soybeans** offer a wide array of medicinal uses and health benefits due to their rich nutrient content and bioactive compounds. One of the most notable benefits is their role in **cardiovascular health**. The isoflavones and phytosterols in soybeans help lower LDL cholesterol levels and improve overall lipid profiles, reducing the risk of heart disease. Soybeans also support **bone health**; the isoflavones, particularly genistein, mimic estrogen's effects and help maintain bone density, which is especially beneficial for postmenopausal women at risk of osteoporosis. **Cancer prevention** is another significant benefit of soybeans. Isoflavones have been shown to inhibit the growth of cancer cells and reduce the risk of hormone-related cancers such as breast and prostate cancer. **Digestive health** is enhanced by the high fiber content in soybeans, which promotes healthy bowel movements and prevents constipation. The **protein** in soybeans supports muscle growth and repair, making them an excellent source of plant-based protein for athletes and individuals engaged in regular physical activity. Soybeans also play a role in **weight management**. The protein and fiber in soybeans increase satiety, helping to control appetite and reduce overall calorie intake. Furthermore, soybeans can help manage **blood sugar levels** due to their low glycemic index, making them beneficial for individuals with diabetes. The **omega-3 fatty acids** in soybeans contribute to reducing inflammation and supporting brain health. Lastly, **menopausal symptom relief** is a well-documented benefit of soy isoflavones, which help alleviate hot flashes and other symptoms associated with menopause. Overall, soybeans are a powerhouse of nutrition and offer numerous health benefits, making them a vital component of a healthy diet.

2.3 Ginseng

Source and Cultivation of Ginseng: Ginseng is a perennial plant belonging to the genus Panax, primarily known for its fleshy roots that are used in traditional medicine. It is native to cooler climates and is commonly found in regions such as Korea, China, and parts of North America. The most well-known varieties are **Asian ginseng** (Panax ginseng) and **American ginseng** (Panax quinquefolius). Ginseng cultivation is a labor-intensive process that requires specific conditions to thrive. It grows best in well-drained, fertile, and slightly acidic soils with a pH between 5.5 and 6.5. The cultivation process begins with the **selection of seeds** or roots for planting, which are usually sown in the autumn to allow for natural stratification during the winter. Ginseng plants require a shaded environment, typically provided by artificial shade structures or natural forest canopies, to mimic their natural habitat and protect them from direct sunlight. **Soil preparation** includes ensuring adequate drainage and incorporating organic matter to support root development. **Planting** is done in raised beds to prevent waterlogging and root rot. Ginseng has a slow growth cycle, typically taking 4 to 6 years to reach maturity, which is when the roots are harvested. During the growth period, careful management is necessary to control **weeds, pests, and diseases**, such as root rot and fungal infections. **Harvesting** usually occurs in the fall when the roots are carefully dug out, cleaned, and dried. The cultivation of ginseng requires patience and precise agricultural practices to yield high-quality roots with potent medicinal properties.

Marker Compounds and Their Chemical Nature in Ginseng: Ginseng contains several bioactive compounds that contribute to its health benefits, with the most notable being **ginsenosides** and **polysaccharides**. **Ginsenosides** are a group of steroidal saponins unique to the Panax genus. These compounds are categorized into two main types based on their chemical structure: **protopanaxadiol (PPD)** and **protopanaxatriol (PPT)**. PPD-type ginsenosides, such as Rb1, Rb2, Rc, and Rd, are known for their sedative and anti-inflammatory effects, while PPT-type ginsenosides, including Re, Rf, Rg1, and Rg2, are associated with stimulating and adaptogenic properties. These ginsenosides interact with various cellular pathways, influencing neurotransmission, immune response, and metabolic processes. **Polysaccharides** in ginseng, such as acidic polysaccharides and neutral polysaccharides, have immunomodulatory and antioxidant activities. These complex carbohydrates support the immune system and protect cells from oxidative stress. Additionally, ginseng contains **peptides**, **polyacetylenes**, **alkaloids**, **phenolic compounds**, and **essential oils** that contribute to its therapeutic effects. The synergy of these compounds makes ginseng a powerful natural remedy with a broad spectrum of health benefits.

Medicinal Uses and Health Benefits of Ginseng: Ginseng is renowned for its wide range of medicinal uses and health benefits, making it a staple in traditional medicine systems, particularly in East Asia. One of the primary benefits of ginseng is its role as an **adaptogen**, helping the body to cope with physical, chemical, and biological stressors. This adaptogenic property enhances overall resilience and vitality. **Cognitive function** is significantly improved by ginseng, as it enhances memory, focus, and mental clarity. Studies have shown that ginsenosides promote the release of acetylcholine, a neurotransmitter important for learning and memory, and protect neurons from oxidative stress. Ginseng also supports **immune health** by modulating immune responses, increasing the production of white blood cells, and enhancing the activity of natural killer cells, which helps protect the body against infections and diseases. Another notable benefit is its **anti-inflammatory** effect, which helps reduce inflammation in conditions like arthritis and other inflammatory diseases. Ginseng has shown potential in **cancer prevention and treatment**. Its bioactive compounds inhibit the growth and proliferation of cancer cells, induce apoptosis, and enhance the efficacy of conventional cancer treatments. Additionally, ginseng is beneficial for **cardiovascular health**. It helps regulate blood pressure, reduce cholesterol levels, and improve blood circulation, thereby reducing the risk of heart disease. Ginseng is also known to enhance **physical performance and endurance**, making it popular among athletes. It improves oxygen uptake and utilization, delays fatigue, and enhances recovery after exercise. In the realm of **metabolic health**, ginseng helps regulate blood sugar levels, making it beneficial for individuals with diabetes or those at risk of developing diabetes. It increases insulin sensitivity and reduces insulin resistance. Furthermore, ginseng is used to

combat fatigue and improve energy levels, making it an effective remedy for chronic fatigue syndrome. **Sexual health** benefits from ginseng as well, as it is traditionally used to enhance libido and treat erectile dysfunction. Lastly, ginseng promotes **skin health** by protecting against UV radiation, improving skin hydration, and reducing signs of aging. Overall, ginseng is a versatile medicinal herb with extensive health benefits, making it a valuable addition to natural health practices.

2.4 Garlic

How is Garlic Cultivated and What are Its Sources?: **Garlic** (Allium sativum) is a widely cultivated plant known for its culinary and medicinal uses. It is grown globally, with China being the largest producer. Garlic thrives in well-drained, fertile soils with a pH between 6.0 and 7.0 and requires a cool growing season for optimal development. The cultivation process begins with selecting healthy **garlic cloves** from a bulb, as garlic is typically propagated vegetatively. These cloves are planted in the fall, about 6 to 8 weeks before the first frost, to allow root development before the ground freezes. **Planting** involves placing each clove pointy end up, 2 to 3 inches deep, and spaced about 6 inches apart in rows. Garlic requires regular **watering**, especially during the bulbing stage in spring, but care must be taken to avoid waterlogging, which can lead to root rot. **Weed management** is crucial since garlic does not compete well with weeds. This can be managed through mulching or hand weeding. **Pest and disease control** is also important, with common issues including onion maggots, thrips, and fungal diseases like white rot and downy mildew. Garlic is usually **harvested** in mid to late summer when the lower leaves turn yellow and start to die back. The bulbs are carefully dug out, dried (cured) in a well-ventilated area for several weeks, cleaned, and stored in a cool, dry place. Proper cultivation practices ensure a high yield of quality garlic bulbs that are rich in bioactive compounds.

Marker Compounds in Garlic and Their Chemical Nature: **Garlic** contains several bioactive compounds that are responsible for its health benefits. The primary marker compound in garlic is **allicin**, a sulfur-containing compound that is formed when garlic is chopped or crushed, converting alliin (a sulfoxide) through the action of the enzyme alliinase. Allicin is known for its potent antimicrobial, antifungal, and antioxidant properties. Another significant compound is **ajoene**, derived from allicin, which has been shown to have antithrombotic and antimicrobial effects. **Diallyl disulfide** and **diallyl trisulfide** are other sulfur-containing compounds found in garlic that contribute to its characteristic odor and therapeutic properties. **S-allylcysteine** is a water-soluble sulfur compound formed during the aging process of garlic and is known for its antioxidant and cardioprotective effects. Additionally, garlic contains **flavonoids** such as quercetin and **selenium**, which enhance its antioxidant capacity. The synergy of these compounds makes garlic a powerful natural remedy with a broad spectrum of health benefits.

Medicinal Uses and Health Benefits of Garlic: **Garlic** is renowned for its extensive medicinal uses and health benefits, making it a staple in traditional and modern medicine. One of the most well-known benefits of garlic is its role in **cardiovascular health.** Garlic has been shown to lower blood pressure, reduce cholesterol levels, and improve overall lipid profiles, which helps in the prevention and management of heart disease. The sulfur compounds, particularly allicin, help relax blood vessels and improve blood flow, reducing the risk of atherosclerosis and hypertension. **Antimicrobial properties** of garlic make it effective against a wide range of bacteria, viruses, fungi, and parasites. Allicin and other sulfur compounds in garlic inhibit the growth of pathogens, making it a valuable natural antibiotic. Garlic is also beneficial for **immune health.** It enhances the function of the immune system by stimulating the activity of white blood cells and increasing the production of antibodies, helping the body to fend off infections. The **antioxidant properties** of garlic help protect cells from oxidative stress and reduce inflammation. This is particularly important in preventing chronic diseases such as cancer. Studies have shown that garlic can inhibit the growth of cancer cells and reduce the risk of various cancers, including stomach, colon, and prostate cancer. **Anti-inflammatory effects** of garlic help alleviate symptoms of inflammatory conditions such as arthritis and asthma. Garlic's sulfur compounds inhibit inflammatory pathways and reduce the production of inflammatory cytokines. **Blood sugar regulation** is another benefit of garlic. It improves insulin sensitivity and helps regulate blood glucose levels, making it beneficial for individuals with diabetes or at risk of developing diabetes. **Detoxification** is enhanced by garlic, as it supports liver function and helps eliminate heavy metals from the body. **Digestive health** benefits from garlic's ability to promote healthy gut flora and prevent gastrointestinal infections. Garlic also has **anti-thrombotic properties**, which help prevent blood clots and improve circulation, reducing the risk of stroke and other thrombotic events. Additionally, garlic has been shown to have **anti-aging** effects, protecting against cognitive decline and promoting overall longevity. Lastly, **skin health** is improved with garlic, as its antimicrobial and anti-inflammatory properties help treat acne and other skin conditions. Overall, garlic is a highly versatile and potent natural remedy with numerous health benefits, making it an essential component of a healthy diet.

2.5 Broccoli

Source and Cultivation Process of Broccoli: Broccoli (Brassica oleracea var. italica) is a cool-season vegetable that belongs to the Brassicaceae family, which also includes cabbage, cauliflower, and kale. It is native to the eastern Mediterranean and Asia Minor regions but is now widely cultivated around the world, particularly in temperate climates. Broccoli thrives in well-drained, fertile soils with a pH between 6.0 and 7.0 and requires full sunlight. The cultivation process begins with **seed selection** and **sowing**. Seeds are usually started indoors in seed trays about 6 to 8 weeks before the last expected frost date. Once the seedlings have developed a few true leaves and the danger of frost has passed, they are transplanted into the garden or field, spaced about 18 to 24 inches apart to allow for proper growth and air circulation. **Soil preparation** involves incorporating organic matter, such as compost, to enhance soil fertility and structure. **Irrigation** is critical, especially during dry periods, as broccoli requires consistent moisture for optimal growth. Drip irrigation is often used to provide a steady supply of water while minimizing water waste and disease risk. **Weed control** is important, and can be managed through mulching and hand weeding. **Pest and disease management** is also essential, with common pests including aphids, cabbage worms, and flea beetles, and diseases such as downy mildew and clubroot. **Harvesting** typically occurs 60 to 100 days after transplanting when the central head is fully developed but before the yellow flowers start to open. The central head is cut with a portion of the stalk, and side shoots can continue to produce smaller heads for several weeks. Proper post-harvest handling, including cooling and storage, ensures the quality and nutritional value of the broccoli.

Marker Compounds and Their Chemical Nature in Broccoli: Broccoli is rich in several bioactive compounds that contribute to its health benefits. The primary marker compounds include **glucosinolates**, **sulforaphane**,

indole-3-carbinol, **flavonoids**, and **vitamins**. **Glucosinolates** are sulfur-containing compounds that are hydrolyzed by the enzyme myrosinase to form bioactive compounds like **sulforaphane** and **indole-3-carbinol**. **Sulforaphane** is a potent antioxidant and anti-inflammatory compound that has been shown to have anticancer properties. **Indole-3-carbinol** is another breakdown product of glucosinolates that modulates estrogen metabolism and has anticancer effects, particularly against hormone-related cancers. **Flavonoids**, such as kaempferol and quercetin, are also present in broccoli and contribute to its antioxidant and anti-inflammatory properties. **Vitamins** in broccoli include high levels of vitamin C, which acts as an antioxidant, and vitamin K, which is essential for blood clotting and bone health. Broccoli also contains **fiber**, **minerals** like potassium, calcium, and magnesium, and other phytonutrients that enhance its nutritional profile.

Medicinal Uses and Health Benefits of Broccoli: Broccoli offers numerous medicinal uses and health benefits, making it a highly nutritious and beneficial vegetable. One of the most significant benefits of broccoli is its role in **cancer prevention**. The glucosinolates in broccoli are converted into bioactive compounds like sulforaphane and indole-3-carbinol, which have been shown to inhibit the growth of cancer cells, induce apoptosis, and prevent the formation of tumors. These compounds also help in the detoxification of carcinogens, further reducing cancer risk. **Antioxidant properties** of broccoli are attributed to its high vitamin C content and flavonoids, which help protect cells from oxidative damage caused by free radicals. This reduces the risk of chronic diseases such as heart disease and cancer. **Anti-inflammatory effects** of broccoli are due to sulforaphane and other phytonutrients that help reduce inflammation in the body, alleviating symptoms of inflammatory conditions such as arthritis and asthma. **Cardiovascular health** benefits from broccoli include improved lipid profiles, reduced blood pressure, and enhanced blood vessel function. The fiber, potassium, and antioxidants in broccoli contribute to these effects. **Digestive health** is supported by the high fiber content in broccoli, which promotes healthy bowel movements, prevents constipation, and supports a healthy gut microbiome. **Bone health** benefits from broccoli are due to its high vitamin K and calcium content, which are essential for maintaining bone density and preventing osteoporosis. **Immune health** is enhanced by the vitamin C in broccoli, which boosts the immune system and helps the body fight off infections. **Detoxification** processes in the body are supported by the glucosinolates in broccoli, which promote the elimination of toxins and carcinogens. **Skin health** benefits from the antioxidants and vitamins in broccoli, which protect the skin from oxidative damage and promote a healthy complexion. Lastly, broccoli has been shown to support **eye health** due to its high levels of lutein and zeaxanthin, which help prevent age-related macular degeneration and cataracts. Overall, broccoli is a highly nutritious vegetable with a wide range of health benefits, making it an essential component of a healthy diet.

2.6 Gingko

Source and Cultivation of Gingko: Gingko biloba, commonly known as gingko, is a unique tree species with no close living relatives, often referred to as a living fossil. It is native to China, where it has been cultivated for thousands of years for its medicinal properties and as an ornamental tree. Gingko trees are exceptionally hardy, capable of growing in various soil types, but they prefer well-drained, sandy soils with a slightly acidic to neutral pH. They thrive in temperate climates and can tolerate pollution and confined urban spaces, making them popular in city landscaping. The **cultivation process** of gingko begins with either **seeds** or **cuttings**. Seeds are harvested from female trees in the fall after the fruit has matured. The seeds require stratification, a period of cold treatment, to break dormancy and stimulate germination. Stratified seeds are sown in well-prepared beds in early spring. Alternatively, propagation through **cuttings** can be done using semi-hardwood cuttings taken in the summer. These cuttings are treated with rooting hormones and planted in a suitable medium to encourage root development. Gingko trees require minimal maintenance once established, with periodic watering during dry spells and occasional pruning to maintain shape and remove dead or diseased branches. **Pests and diseases** are generally not significant problems for gingko, although young trees may be susceptible to fungal infections. Harvesting of gingko leaves, the primary source of medicinal compounds, typically occurs in late summer to early autumn when the leaves have reached peak potency. The leaves are dried and processed for use in various forms, such as extracts, tablets, and capsules.

Marker Compounds and Their Chemical Nature in Gingko: Gingko leaves contain several bioactive compounds that contribute to their therapeutic effects. The primary marker compounds include **flavonoids** and

terpenoids. Flavonoids in gingko, such as quercetin, kaempferol, and isorhamnetin, are known for their antioxidant properties, which help protect cells from oxidative damage. These flavonoids also exhibit anti-inflammatory and vasodilatory effects, contributing to improved blood circulation and reduced inflammation. **Terpenoids**, specifically **ginkgolides** and **bilobalide**, are unique to gingko and have been extensively studied for their pharmacological activities. **Ginkgolides** A, B, C, J, and M, and **bilobalide**, are diterpenes that possess potent platelet-activating factor (PAF) antagonistic properties, which help prevent blood clots and improve microcirculation. These compounds also exhibit neuroprotective effects by protecting neurons from oxidative stress and apoptosis. Additionally, gingko leaves contain **proanthocyanidins**, another group of antioxidants that enhance the overall protective effects of the extract. The combination of these bioactive compounds makes gingko a powerful medicinal plant with diverse health benefits.

Medicinal Uses and Health Benefits of Gingko: Gingko biloba has been used for centuries in traditional medicine, and modern research supports many of its health benefits. One of the most well-documented uses of gingko is in **cognitive health**. Gingko is known to improve memory, enhance cognitive function, and slow the progression of cognitive decline in conditions such as Alzheimer's disease and dementia. The flavonoids and terpenoids in gingko enhance cerebral blood flow, protect neurons from oxidative damage, and improve neurotransmitter function, contributing to its neuroprotective effects. **Circulatory health** is another area where gingko excels. The vasodilatory and anti-inflammatory properties of its compounds improve blood circulation, reduce the risk of blood clots, and alleviate symptoms of peripheral artery disease, such as leg pain and cramping. Gingko is also beneficial for **eye health**, particularly in reducing the risk of age-related macular degeneration and glaucoma. The antioxidant properties protect retinal cells from oxidative damage, and improved blood flow supports overall eye health. **Mental health** benefits from gingko include reduced symptoms of anxiety and depression. Gingko's ability to enhance blood flow to the brain and its neuroprotective effects help stabilize mood and reduce anxiety levels. Additionally, gingko has **anti-inflammatory** properties that help alleviate symptoms of conditions like asthma and arthritis by reducing inflammation and improving respiratory function. **Antioxidant effects** of gingko help neutralize free radicals, reducing oxidative stress and lowering the risk of chronic diseases such as cancer and cardiovascular disease. **Hearing health** is another area where gingko shows promise. It is used to treat tinnitus (ringing in the ears) by improving blood flow to the inner ear and reducing oxidative stress. **Sexual health** can also benefit from gingko, as it improves blood circulation, which may help in cases of erectile dysfunction. Lastly, gingko has potential **anti-aging** effects, as its antioxidant properties protect against cellular damage and its circulation-enhancing effects support overall vitality. Overall, gingko biloba is a versatile and potent medicinal plant with a wide range of health benefits, making it a valuable addition to natural health practices.

2.7 Flaxseeds

Source and Cultivation Process of Flaxseeds: **Flaxseeds** are derived from the flax plant (Linum usitatissimum), which has been cultivated for thousands of years for its seeds and fiber. Flax is a versatile crop that thrives in temperate climates and is grown in regions such as Canada, Russia, and China. The cultivation process begins with **soil preparation**. Flax prefers well-drained, fertile soils with a neutral to slightly acidic pH. Fields are plowed and harrowed to create a fine seedbed. **Seeds** are sown directly into the soil in early spring, once the danger of frost has passed. Planting is done at a depth of about 2 to 3 centimeters, with rows spaced approximately 20 to 30 centimeters apart. Flax is a relatively low-maintenance crop but requires consistent **moisture**, particularly during germination and early growth stages. Proper **irrigation** is essential to ensure uniform growth and high yields. **Weed control** is crucial, especially in the initial stages, and can be managed through mechanical methods or herbicides. **Pest and disease management** is also important, with common pests including aphids and flea beetles, and diseases such as flax wilt and rust. **Harvesting** occurs about 90 to 110 days after planting, when the seed heads turn golden brown. The plants are cut and allowed to dry in the field before threshing to separate the seeds from the stalks. The seeds are then cleaned, dried, and stored in cool, dry conditions to maintain their quality and nutritional value. The cultivation of flax is an integral part of sustainable agriculture, as it improves soil health and reduces the need for synthetic inputs.

Marker Compounds in Flaxseeds and Their Chemical Nature: **Flaxseeds** are rich in several bioactive compounds that contribute to their health benefits. The primary marker compounds include **alpha-linolenic acid (ALA)**, **lignans**, and **fiber**. **Alpha-linolenic acid (ALA)** is an omega-3 fatty acid that plays a crucial role in cardiovascular health and anti-inflammatory processes. It is a polyunsaturated fatty acid that is essential for human health, as it must be obtained from the diet. **Lignans** are phytoestrogens with antioxidant properties. The most notable lignan in flaxseeds is **secoisolariciresinol diglucoside (SDG)**, which is converted by intestinal bacteria into enterolactone and enterodiol, compounds that exhibit weak estrogenic activity and potent antioxidant effects. **Fiber** in flaxseeds is present in both soluble and insoluble forms. Soluble fiber helps regulate blood sugar levels and lower cholesterol, while insoluble fiber aids in digestion and promotes bowel regularity. Additionally, flaxseeds contain **protein**, **vitamins** (such as B1, B6, and E), and **minerals** (including magnesium, potassium, and phosphorus), which enhance their nutritional profile.

Medicinal Uses and Health Benefits of Flaxseeds: Flaxseeds offer a wide range of medicinal uses and health benefits due to their rich nutrient content and bioactive compounds. One of the most significant benefits of flaxseeds is their role in **cardiovascular health**. The alpha-linolenic acid (ALA) in flaxseeds helps reduce inflammation, lower blood pressure, and improve overall lipid profiles by decreasing LDL cholesterol and increasing HDL cholesterol. This reduces the risk of heart disease and stroke. **Digestive health** is another area where flaxseeds excel, thanks to their high fiber content. Soluble fiber helps regulate blood sugar levels and lower cholesterol, while insoluble fiber promotes healthy bowel movements and prevents constipation. **Cancer prevention** is a notable benefit of flaxseeds, particularly in hormone-related cancers such as breast and prostate cancer. The lignans in flaxseeds have antioxidant properties and weak estrogenic activity, which help modulate hormone metabolism and reduce the risk of cancer. **Anti-inflammatory effects** of flaxseeds are due to the presence of ALA and lignans, which help reduce inflammation in the body and alleviate symptoms of inflammatory conditions such as arthritis and asthma. **Weight management** is another benefit of flaxseeds, as their high fiber content promotes satiety and helps control appetite, reducing overall calorie intake. **Blood sugar regulation** is supported by the soluble fiber in flaxseeds, which helps slow the absorption of glucose and improve insulin sensitivity, making them beneficial for individuals with diabetes. **Skin health** benefits from the essential fatty acids in flaxseeds, which help maintain skin hydration and reduce the appearance of wrinkles and other signs of aging. **Hormonal balance** is another area where flaxseeds can be beneficial, particularly for women. The phytoestrogens in flaxseeds help modulate estrogen levels, reducing symptoms of menopause and premenstrual syndrome (PMS). Additionally, flaxseeds support **immune health** due to their antioxidant properties, which help protect cells from oxidative stress and enhance the body's defense mechanisms. **Bone health** is improved by the magnesium and phosphorus content in flaxseeds, which are essential for maintaining bone density and preventing osteoporosis. Overall, flaxseeds are a highly nutritious food with numerous health benefits, making them a valuable addition to a balanced diet.

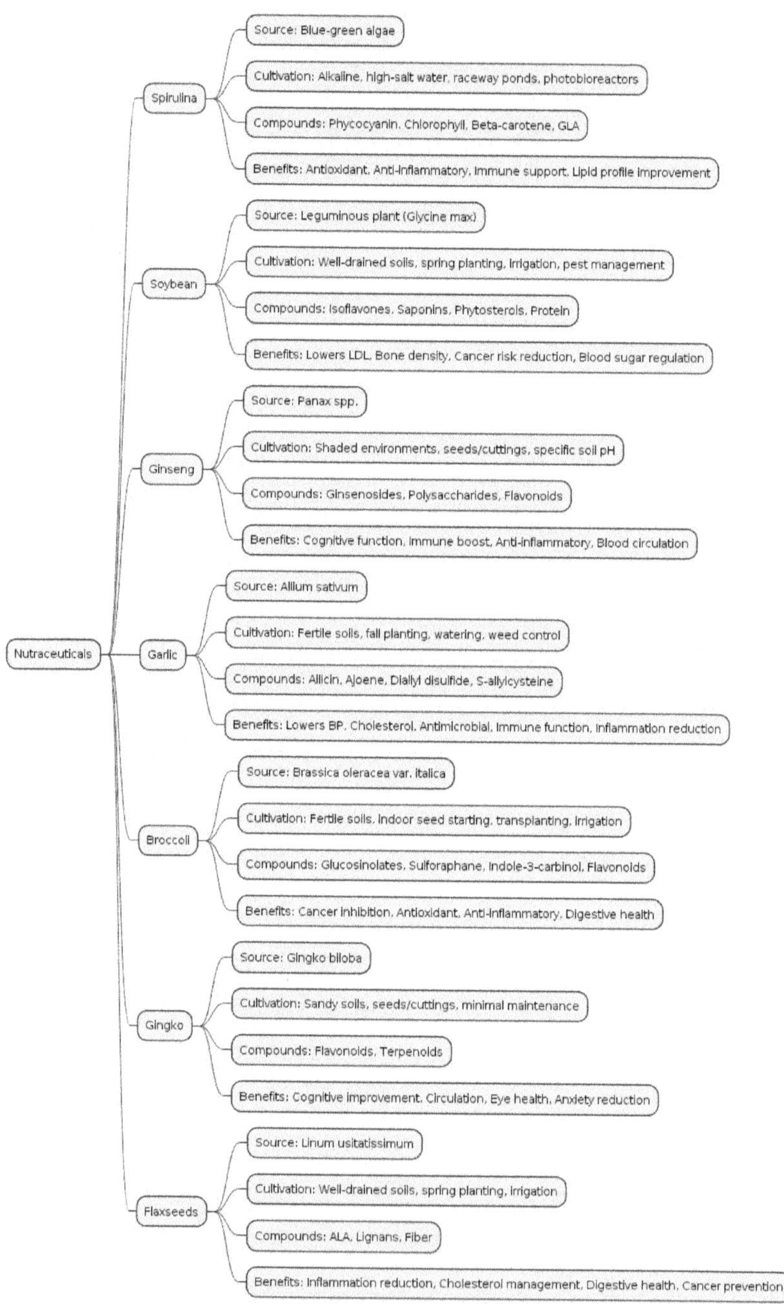

Nutraceuticals: Sources, Marker Compounds, and Health Benefits

Broccoli

Ginseng

Garlic

Soya

Spirulina

Gingko biloba

Flaxseeds

Table 1: Source and Cultivation Process of Nutraceuticals

Nutraceutical	Source	Cultivation Process
Spirulina	Blue-green algae	Grown in alkaline, high-salt water environments; cultivated in open raceway ponds or closed photobioreactors; harvested, washed, dried, and processed.
Soybean	Leguminous plant (Glycine max)	Grown in well-drained, fertile soils; seeds sown in spring; requires irrigation, weed control, pest management; harvested in late summer to early autumn.
Ginseng	Perennial plant (Panax spp.)	Grown in shaded environments; seeds or cuttings planted; requires specific soil pH and climate; harvested after 4-6 years for roots.
Garlic	Allium sativum	Grown in well-drained, fertile soils; cloves planted in fall; requires consistent watering, weed management, pest control; harvested in summer.
Broccoli	Brassica oleracea var. italica	Grown in well-drained, fertile soils; seeds started indoors and transplanted; requires irrigation, weed control, pest management; harvested when heads mature.
Gingko	Gingko biloba tree	Grown in well-drained, sandy soils; seeds or cuttings used; requires minimal maintenance; leaves harvested in late summer to early autumn.
Flaxseeds	Flax plant (Linum usitatissimum)	Grown in well-drained, fertile soils; seeds sown in early spring; requires irrigation, weed control, pest management; harvested when seed heads turn golden brown.

Table 2: Marker Compounds and Their Chemical Nature

Nutraceutical	Marker Compounds	Chemical Nature
Spirulina	Phycocyanin, chlorophyll, beta-carotene, GLA	Phycocyanin: Antioxidant; Chlorophyll: Detoxifying; Beta-carotene: Antioxidant; GLA: Anti-inflammatory
Soybean	Isoflavones, saponins, phytosterols, protein	Isoflavones: Phytoestrogens; Saponins: Cholesterol-lowering; Phytosterols: Reduce cholesterol absorption; Protein: Essential amino acids
Ginseng	Ginsenosides, polysaccharides, flavonoids	Ginsenosides: Adaptogenic; Polysaccharides: Immunomodulatory; Flavonoids: Antioxidant
Garlic	Allicin, ajoene, diallyl disulfide, s-allylcysteine	Allicin: Antimicrobial; Ajoene: Antithrombotic; Diallyl disulfide: Antioxidant; S-allylcysteine: Cardioprotective
Broccoli	Glucosinolates, sulforaphane, indole-3-carbinol, flavonoids	Glucosinolates: Anticancer; Sulforaphane: Antioxidant; Indole-3-carbinol: Hormone modulation; Flavonoids: Antioxidant
Gingko	Flavonoids, terpenoids (ginkgolides, bilobalide)	Flavonoids: Antioxidant; Terpenoids: Platelet-activating factor antagonists, neuroprotective
Flaxseeds	Alpha-linolenic acid (ALA), lignans, fiber	ALA: Omega-3 fatty acid; Lignans: Phytoestrogens, antioxidant; Fiber: Soluble and insoluble for digestion and cholesterol management

Table 3: Medicinal Uses and Health Benefits

Nutraceutical	Medicinal Uses	Health Benefits
Spirulina	Antioxidant, anti-inflammatory, immune support	Protects against oxidative damage, reduces inflammation, enhances immune function, supports muscle recovery, improves lipid profiles
Soybean	Cardiovascular health, bone health, cancer prevention	Lowers LDL cholesterol, maintains bone density, reduces risk of hormone-related cancers, regulates blood sugar, supports weight management
Ginseng	Cognitive function, immune health, anti-inflammatory	Enhances memory, slows cognitive decline, boosts immune function, reduces inflammation, improves blood circulation, supports physical performance
Garlic	Cardiovascular health, antimicrobial, immune support	Lowers blood pressure and cholesterol, fights infections, boosts immune function, reduces inflammation, supports blood sugar regulation
Broccoli	Cancer prevention, antioxidant, anti-inflammatory	Inhibits cancer cell growth, protects against oxidative damage, reduces inflammation, improves cardiovascular health, supports digestive health
Gingko	Cognitive health, circulatory health, eye health	Improves memory and cognitive function, enhances blood circulation, reduces risk of age-related macular degeneration, alleviates symptoms of anxiety and depression
Flaxseeds	Cardiovascular health, digestive health, cancer prevention	Reduces inflammation, lowers blood pressure and cholesterol, promotes healthy bowel movements, reduces risk of hormone-related cancers, supports weight management, regulates blood sugar, improves skin health

THREE

PHYTOCHEMICALS AS NUTRACEUTICALS

3.1 Carotenoids

Carotenoids are a class of pigments naturally occurring in plants, algae, and photosynthetic bacteria. They are responsible for the red, yellow, and orange colors of many fruits and vegetables. Carotenoids play a crucial role in plant health by aiding in the process of photosynthesis and protecting plant tissues from damage by absorbing light energy and quenching free radicals. In the human diet, carotenoids are found in a wide variety of fruits and vegetables. Common sources include carrots, sweet potatoes, spinach, kale, tomatoes, bell peppers, and citrus fruits. There are over 600 known carotenoids, but the most well-known and studied include α-Carotene, β-Carotene, Lycopene, Xanthophylls, and Lutein.

Chemical Nature and Benefits of α and β-Carotene: α-**Carotene** and β-**Carotene** are two of the most important carotenoids, both serving as precursors to vitamin A (retinol) in the human body. They are classified as provitamin A carotenoids because they can be converted into active vitamin A, which is essential for vision, immune function, and skin health.

Chemical Nature:

- **α-Carotene:** α-Carotene has a chemical structure characterized by a long carbon chain with conjugated double bonds and two β-ionone rings at each end. It is less abundant in nature compared to β-Carotene.
- **β-Carotene:** β-Carotene has a similar structure to α-Carotene but differs in the position of one of the double bonds. It is the most abundant provitamin A carotenoid in the diet and has a higher conversion rate to

vitamin A than α-Carotene.

Benefits:

- **Antioxidant Properties:** Both α and β-Carotene are powerful antioxidants, meaning they help neutralize free radicals in the body, reducing oxidative stress and the risk of chronic diseases such as cancer and heart disease.
- **Vitamin A Production:** As precursors to vitamin A, they support essential bodily functions including vision, immune response, and cellular communication.
- **Skin Health:** Vitamin A derived from these carotenoids is crucial for maintaining healthy skin, promoting cell growth, and repairing tissues.

Health Benefits of Lycopene, Xanthophylls, and Lutein:
Lycopene:

- **Chemical Nature:** Lycopene is a non-provitamin A carotenoid with a long chain of conjugated double bonds, giving it strong antioxidant properties. It is responsible for the red color in tomatoes, watermelon, and pink grapefruit.
- **Health Benefits:**

  - **Antioxidant:** Lycopene is one of the most potent antioxidants among carotenoids, protecting cells from oxidative damage.
  - **Cancer Prevention:** Studies have shown that lycopene may reduce the risk of certain cancers, particularly prostate cancer, by inhibiting cancer cell growth and promoting apoptosis.
  - **Cardiovascular Health:** Lycopene helps lower LDL cholesterol and blood pressure, reducing the risk of heart disease.

Xanthophylls (such as Zeaxanthin and Cryptoxanthin):

- **Chemical Nature:** Xanthophylls are oxygenated carotenoids, meaning they contain oxygen in their molecular structure. They are found in green leafy vegetables, corn, and eggs.
- **Health Benefits:**

- ◦ **Eye Health**: Xanthophylls are concentrated in the retina and are crucial for eye health. Zeaxanthin and Lutein help filter harmful blue light and protect against age-related macular degeneration (AMD) and cataracts.
- ◦ **Skin Protection**: Xanthophylls can also protect the skin from UV-induced damage and maintain skin health.

Lutein:

- **Chemical Nature**: Lutein is a xanthophyll with a similar structure to zeaxanthin. It is abundant in green leafy vegetables like spinach, kale, and broccoli.
- **Health Benefits**:

  - ◦ **Eye Health**: Lutein is essential for maintaining healthy vision. It accumulates in the macula, a part of the retina, where it protects against oxidative damage and improves visual acuity.
  - ◦ **Cognitive Function**: Emerging research suggests that lutein may support cognitive function and slow cognitive decline in older adults.
  - ◦ **Skin Health**: Lutein's antioxidant properties help protect the skin from oxidative stress and improve overall skin hydration and elasticity.

3.2 Sulfides

Diallyl sulfides and **allyl trisulfide** are organosulfur compounds found primarily in garlic (Allium sativum). These compounds are part of a larger group of sulfur-containing compounds that contribute to the distinctive aroma, flavor, and health benefits of garlic. **Diallyl sulfides** are a group of compounds that include diallyl disulfide (DADS) and diallyl trisulfide (DATS). **Allyl trisulfide** is a specific type of diallyl sulfide with three sulfur atoms in its structure. These compounds are formed when garlic is chopped, crushed, or chewed, initiating a chemical reaction that converts alliin, a sulfur-containing amino acid, into allicin. Allicin then degrades into various sulfur compounds, including diallyl sulfides and allyl trisulfide, which are responsible for many of garlic's therapeutic properties.

Sources, Chemical Nature, and Health Benefits of Sulfides:

Sources: The primary source of diallyl sulfides and allyl trisulfide is **garlic**. When garlic cloves are crushed or chopped, the enzyme alliinase converts alliin into allicin, which further breaks down into various sulfur-containing compounds, including diallyl sulfides and allyl trisulfide. These compounds can also be found in other Allium vegetables, such as onions, shallots, leeks, and chives, but garlic is the most potent source.

Chemical Nature: The chemical structure of diallyl sulfides includes two allyl groups (CH2=CH-CH2-) attached to a central sulfur atom. **Diallyl disulfide (DADS)**, for instance, has two sulfur atoms between the allyl groups, while **diallyl trisulfide (DATS)** has three sulfur atoms in its chain. The presence of these sulfur atoms gives these compounds their characteristic smell and contributes to their biological activity. **Allyl trisulfide** is more potent than diallyl disulfide due to the additional sulfur atom, which enhances its reactivity and therapeutic effects. The chemical reactions involved in the formation and breakdown of these compounds are complex, but their ability to interact with various biological molecules underlies their health benefits.

Health Benefits: The health benefits of diallyl sulfides and allyl trisulfide are numerous and well-documented.

Antimicrobial Properties: One of the most significant benefits is their **antimicrobial** activity. Diallyl sulfides and allyl trisulfide have been shown to inhibit the growth of a wide range of bacteria, fungi, and viruses. This makes garlic an effective natural remedy for infections and a potential alternative to synthetic antibiotics. Studies have demonstrated that these compounds can disrupt the cell membranes of pathogens, leading to their death.

Cardiovascular Health: Diallyl sulfides and allyl trisulfide also play a crucial role in **cardiovascular health**. They help lower blood pressure by promoting the dilation of blood vessels, improving blood flow, and reducing the workload on the heart. Additionally, these compounds can lower cholesterol levels by inhibiting the synthesis of cholesterol in the liver. They also prevent the formation of blood clots by inhibiting platelet aggregation, reducing the risk of heart attacks and strokes. Research has shown that regular consumption of garlic can significantly reduce blood pressure and cholesterol levels in individuals with hypertension and hyperlipidemia.

Anti-Cancer Properties: Another notable benefit is their **anti-cancer** properties. Diallyl sulfides and allyl trisulfide have been shown to inhibit the growth of cancer cells and induce apoptosis (programmed cell death) in various types of cancer, including colon, breast, lung, and prostate cancers. These compounds work by interfering with the cell cycle, inhibiting angiogenesis (the formation of new blood vessels that supply tumors), and enhancing the immune response against cancer cells. Studies have indicated that individuals who consume garlic regularly have a lower risk of developing certain cancers.

Anti-Inflammatory and Antioxidant Effects: Diallyl sulfides and allyl trisulfide exhibit **anti-inflammatory** and **antioxidant** effects, which help reduce chronic inflammation and oxidative stress, both of which are underlying factors in many chronic diseases, including cardiovascular disease, cancer, and neurodegenerative disorders. These compounds can inhibit the production of pro-inflammatory cytokines and reactive oxygen species (ROS), protecting cells from damage and reducing inflammation. Clinical studies have shown that garlic supplementation can significantly reduce markers of inflammation and oxidative stress in the body.

Neuroprotective Effects: The **neuroprotective** effects of diallyl sulfides and allyl trisulfide are also noteworthy. These compounds have been shown to protect neurons from damage and enhance cognitive function. They achieve this by reducing oxidative stress, improving blood flow to the brain, and modulating neurotransmitter activity. This makes garlic a potential dietary intervention for preventing and managing neurodegenerative diseases such as Alzheimer's and Parkinson's disease. Experimental studies have demonstrated that garlic extracts can improve memory and learning abilities in animal models of neurodegenerative diseases.

Detoxification and Immune Support: Garlic's sulfur compounds also support the body's natural **detoxification** processes by enhancing the activity of liver enzymes responsible for detoxifying harmful substances. This helps in the elimination of toxins and carcinogens from the body. Moreover, diallyl sulfides and allyl trisulfide boost the immune system by stimulating the production of white blood cells and enhancing their ability to fight infections. This immune-modulating effect is beneficial in preventing and managing various infectious diseases.

3.3 Polyphenolics

3.3 Polyphenolics

Introduction to Polyphenolics: **Polyphenolics**, commonly known as **polyphenols**, are a diverse group of naturally occurring compounds found abundantly in plants. They are characterized by the presence of multiple phenol units in their structure. Polyphenols play a crucial role in plants by providing protection against ultraviolet radiation, pathogens, and oxidative stress. In human nutrition, polyphenols are recognized for their potent antioxidant properties and their ability to modulate various biological processes. They are classified into several categories, including **flavonoids**, **phenolic acids**, **stilbenes**, and **lignans**, each with unique structures and health benefits. Foods rich in polyphenols include fruits, vegetables, tea, coffee, red wine, and dark chocolate. These compounds have been extensively studied for their potential in preventing and managing chronic diseases such as cardiovascular diseases, cancers, diabetes, and neurodegenerative disorders.

Resveratrol is a well-known polyphenolic compound that belongs to the stilbene group. It is a type of **phytoalexin**, which are antimicrobial substances synthesized by plants in response to environmental stressors such as pathogen attacks or ultraviolet (UV) radiation. Resveratrol exists in two isomeric forms: **trans-resveratrol** and **cis-resveratrol**, with the trans form being more stable and biologically active.

Sources: The most notable source of resveratrol is the **skin of grapes**, particularly red grapes. This is why red wine is often highlighted as a significant dietary source of resveratrol. The concentration of resveratrol in wine varies depending on factors such as grape variety, geographic location, and winemaking process, typically ranging from 0.1 to 14 milligrams per liter. Besides grapes and red wine, resveratrol is found in several other plant sources. **Berries** like blueberries, cranberries, and mulberries contain resveratrol, contributing to their health-promoting properties. **Peanuts** and **peanut butter** are additional sources, with raw peanuts containing about 0.01 to 0.26 milligrams of resveratrol per gram. **Dark chocolate** and **cocoa** also provide small amounts of resveratrol. One of the richest natural sources is **Japanese knotweed** (Polygonum cuspidatum), a plant used in traditional Chinese medicine and commonly used in dietary supplements due to its high resveratrol content.

Chemical Nature and Synthesis: Resveratrol is chemically composed of two phenol rings connected by a styrene double bond, giving it the formula $C_{14}H_{12}O_3$. This structure allows it to interact with various biological targets, which accounts for its diverse health effects. In plants, resveratrol is synthesized through the **phenylpropanoid pathway**. The synthesis starts with the amino acid **phenylalanine**, which is converted into **cinnamic acid** by the enzyme **phenylalanine ammonia-lyase (PAL)**. Cinnamic acid undergoes further transformations to produce **p-coumaroyl-CoA**, which, through the action of **stilbene synthase (STS)**, combines with malonyl-CoA to form resveratrol. This biosynthetic process is part of the plant's defense mechanism against stress and pathogens.

Extraction and Isolation: The extraction of resveratrol from plant sources typically involves **solvent extraction**. Plant material is ground and mixed with solvents such as ethanol, methanol, or acetone to dissolve the resveratrol. The extract is then filtered and concentrated under reduced pressure. To purify resveratrol, techniques like **column chromatography** and **high-performance liquid chromatography (HPLC)** are used, which separate resveratrol from other compounds based on their chemical properties. The purity and concentration of resveratrol in extracts can be determined using analytical methods such as **mass spectrometry (MS)** and **nuclear magnetic resonance (NMR)** spectroscopy.

Health Benefits and Applications: Resveratrol is widely studied for its extensive health benefits. Its **antioxidant properties** help neutralize free radicals, thereby reducing oxidative stress and the risk of chronic diseases like cardiovascular disease and cancer. The **anti-inflammatory effects** of resveratrol are achieved by inhibiting pro-inflammatory cytokines and enzymes like COX-2, making it beneficial for managing inflammatory conditions such as arthritis.

Cardiovascular Health: Resveratrol is known to improve cardiovascular health by enhancing **endothelial function**, reducing **blood pressure**, and preventing the oxidation of LDL cholesterol. These effects contribute to a lower risk of atherosclerosis and heart disease. Resveratrol also **inhibits platelet aggregation** and promotes vasodilation, improving blood flow and reducing the risk of thrombosis.

Anti-Cancer Properties: Resveratrol has been shown to inhibit the growth of cancer cells and induce **apoptosis** (programmed cell death) in various cancers, including breast, colon, and prostate cancers. It modulates cellular pathways involved in cell growth, apoptosis, and metastasis. Resveratrol also enhances the effectiveness of certain chemotherapy drugs, making it a potential adjunct in cancer treatment.

Neuroprotective Effects: Resveratrol's neuroprotective effects may help prevent and manage neurodegenerative diseases like **Alzheimer's** and **Parkinson's**. It promotes neuronal health by reducing oxidative damage, inhibiting the aggregation of amyloid-beta plaques, and modulating inflammatory responses in the brain. Animal studies have shown that resveratrol supplementation can improve cognitive function and memory.

Metabolic Health: Resveratrol improves metabolic health by enhancing **insulin sensitivity**, reducing inflammation, and modulating lipid metabolism, which can help prevent and manage metabolic disorders such as obesity and type 2 diabetes. Resveratrol activates **SIRT1**, a protein involved in cellular metabolism and longevity, further supporting its role in promoting metabolic health.

Chemical Nature of Resveratrol: Resveratrol is a naturally occurring polyphenolic compound belonging to the stilbene family. Its chemical structure is characterized by two aromatic phenol rings connected by a double bond, forming a 3,5,4'-trihydroxy-trans-stilbene. The molecular formula of resveratrol is $C_{14}H_{12}O_3$, and it exists in two isomeric forms: **trans-resveratrol** and **cis-resveratrol**, with the trans form being more stable and biologically active. This structural configuration allows resveratrol to participate in various biochemical interactions, contributing to its multiple health benefits.

In plants, resveratrol is synthesized via the phenylpropanoid pathway, beginning with the amino acid **phenylalanine**. Phenylalanine is converted into **cinnamic acid** by the enzyme **phenylalanine ammonia-lyase (PAL)**. Cinnamic acid is then transformed into **p-coumaroyl-CoA** through a series of enzymatic reactions. The final step involves the enzyme **stilbene synthase (STS)**, which catalyzes the formation of resveratrol from p-coumaroyl-CoA and malonyl-CoA. This biosynthesis is part of the plant's defense mechanism against stress, pathogens, and UV radiation.

Health Benefits of Resveratrol:

Antioxidant Properties: Resveratrol is a potent antioxidant that helps neutralize free radicals and reduce oxidative stress. This property is crucial in protecting cells from damage caused by oxidative stress, which is linked to chronic diseases such as cancer, cardiovascular diseases, and neurodegenerative disorders. Resveratrol's ability to scavenge free radicals helps in maintaining cellular health and preventing DNA damage.

Cardiovascular Health: Resveratrol has been extensively studied for its cardiovascular benefits. It helps in improving **endothelial function**, which is essential for maintaining the elasticity and health of blood vessels. Resveratrol promotes the production of nitric oxide (NO), a molecule that relaxes blood vessels, improves blood flow, and reduces blood pressure. It also prevents the oxidation of LDL cholesterol, thereby reducing the risk of atherosclerosis. Additionally, resveratrol inhibits platelet aggregation, which prevents blood clots and reduces the risk of heart attacks and strokes.

Anti-Cancer Properties: Resveratrol exhibits significant anti-cancer properties by interfering with various stages of cancer development. It inhibits cancer cell proliferation and induces apoptosis (programmed cell death) in different types of cancer cells, including breast, prostate, colon, and lung cancers. Resveratrol's anti-cancer effects are mediated through multiple mechanisms, such as modulating cell cycle regulators, inhibiting angiogenesis (formation of new blood vessels that supply tumors), and enhancing the body's immune response against cancer cells. Moreover, resveratrol can enhance the efficacy of conventional chemotherapy drugs, making it a potential adjunct in cancer therapy.

Neuroprotective Effects: Resveratrol has shown promise in protecting against neurodegenerative diseases such as Alzheimer's and Parkinson's diseases. It reduces oxidative damage and inflammation in the brain, which are key contributors to neurodegeneration. Resveratrol inhibits the aggregation of amyloid-beta plaques, a hallmark of Alzheimer's disease, and promotes the clearance of these plaques from the brain. Additionally, it enhances cognitive function and memory by supporting neuronal health and improving synaptic plasticity.

Anti-Inflammatory Effects: Resveratrol possesses strong anti-inflammatory properties by inhibiting the activity of pro-inflammatory enzymes like cyclooxygenase (COX) and lipoxygenase (LOX), as well as reducing the production of pro-inflammatory cytokines. These anti-inflammatory effects are beneficial in managing chronic inflammatory conditions such as arthritis, inflammatory bowel disease, and metabolic syndrome. Resveratrol's ability to modulate the inflammatory response helps in reducing pain and swelling associated with these conditions.

Metabolic Health: Resveratrol has been shown to improve metabolic health by enhancing **insulin sensitivity** and modulating lipid metabolism. It activates the SIRT1 gene, which plays a key role in cellular metabolism and energy homeostasis. By activating SIRT1, resveratrol helps in improving glucose uptake and reducing insulin resistance, which is beneficial for individuals with type 2 diabetes or those at risk of developing the condition. Additionally, resveratrol helps in lowering triglycerides and LDL cholesterol levels while increasing HDL cholesterol, thereby improving overall lipid profiles and reducing the risk of metabolic disorders.

Anti-Aging Effects: Resveratrol is often associated with anti-aging effects due to its ability to activate sirtuins, particularly SIRT1, which are proteins involved in cellular longevity and stress resistance. By promoting the activity of sirtuins, resveratrol helps in enhancing DNA repair, improving mitochondrial function, and reducing cellular senescence (aging of cells).

These effects contribute to improved cellular health and longevity, potentially delaying the onset of age-related diseases.

Skin Health: Resveratrol's antioxidant and anti-inflammatory properties also benefit skin health. It helps in protecting the skin from UV-induced damage and oxidative stress, which are major contributors to skin aging. Resveratrol promotes the production of collagen and elastin, enhancing skin elasticity and reducing the appearance of wrinkles and fine lines. Additionally, its anti-inflammatory effects help in managing skin conditions such as acne and eczema.

3.4 Flavonoids

Flavonoids are a large and diverse group of phytonutrients (plant chemicals) that belong to the polyphenolic class of compounds. They are widely recognized for their antioxidant, anti-inflammatory, and anti-carcinogenic properties, contributing to various health benefits. Chemically, flavonoids are characterized by a basic structure consisting of two aromatic rings (A and B rings) connected by a three-carbon bridge that forms a closed pyran ring (C ring). This structure can vary, leading to different subclasses of flavonoids, each with unique properties and health effects. The main subclasses of flavonoids include **flavonols, flavones, flavanones, flavanols, anthocyanins**, and **isoflavones**.

Sources of Flavonoids: Flavonoids are found abundantly in a wide variety of plant-based foods and beverages. They are responsible for the vivid colors in many fruits, vegetables, and flowers, and also contribute to the flavor and nutritional value of these foods. Here are some key sources of flavonoids:

1. **Fruits**: Many fruits are rich in flavonoids. For instance, **citrus fruits** like oranges, lemons, and grapefruits are high in flavanones. **Berries** such as strawberries, blueberries, raspberries, and blackberries are excellent sources of anthocyanins and flavonols. **Apples, grapes**, and **cherries** are also notable for their flavonoid content.

2. **Vegetables**: Vegetables such as **onions, kale, broccoli, spinach**, and **peppers** are rich in various flavonoids, particularly flavonols like quercetin and kaempferol. **Tomatoes** contain flavonoids such as naringenin.

3. **Legumes**: **Soybeans** and other legumes are important sources of isoflavones, which have estrogen-like effects and are studied for their potential benefits in hormone-related conditions.

4. **Tea**: Both **green tea** and **black tea** are rich in flavonoids, especially catechins (a type of flavanol) in green tea and theaflavins in black tea. Tea consumption is associated with numerous health benefits due to these compounds.

5. **Red Wine**: **Red wine** contains significant amounts of flavonoids, particularly anthocyanins and flavonols, derived from the skins of grapes. These compounds contribute to the health benefits attributed to moderate red wine consumption.

6. **Cocoa and Dark Chocolate**: **Cocoa** products and dark chocolate are rich in flavanols, such as epicatechin, which are associated with cardiovascular health benefits.

7. **Herbs and Spices**: Various herbs and spices, including **parsley**, **thyme**, **celery**, and **oregano**, are high in flavonoids. These compounds contribute to the antioxidant and anti-inflammatory properties of these culinary ingredients.

Health Benefits: Flavonoids have been extensively studied for their health-promoting effects. Here are some of the key health benefits associated with flavonoid consumption:

1. **Antioxidant Activity**: Flavonoids are powerful antioxidants that neutralize free radicals, reducing oxidative stress and preventing cellular damage. This helps protect against chronic diseases such as heart disease, cancer, and neurodegenerative disorders.

2. **Anti-Inflammatory Effects**: Flavonoids exhibit anti-inflammatory properties by inhibiting the production of pro-inflammatory cytokines and enzymes. This makes them beneficial in managing inflammatory conditions such as arthritis and inflammatory bowel disease.

3. **Cardiovascular Health**: Flavonoids contribute to cardiovascular health by improving endothelial function, reducing blood pressure, lowering LDL cholesterol levels, and preventing platelet aggregation. These effects help reduce the risk of atherosclerosis, heart attacks, and strokes.

4. **Anti-Cancer Properties**: Flavonoids have shown potential in inhibiting the growth and proliferation of cancer cells, inducing apoptosis, and preventing tumor formation. They modulate various signaling pathways involved in cell cycle regulation and apoptosis, making them potential candidates for cancer prevention and therapy.

5. **Neuroprotective Effects**: Flavonoids support brain health by enhancing cognitive function, protecting neurons from oxidative damage, and reducing the risk of neurodegenerative diseases such as Alzheimer's and Parkinson's. They improve memory and learning by promoting synaptic plasticity and reducing inflammation in the brain.

6. **Immune Support**: Flavonoids enhance immune function by modulating the activity of immune cells, promoting the production of antibodies, and reducing inflammation. This helps in boosting the body's defense mechanisms against infections and diseases.

7. **Metabolic Health**: Flavonoids improve metabolic health by enhancing insulin sensitivity, regulating blood glucose levels, and modulating lipid metabolism. These effects help in preventing and managing metabolic disorders such as obesity and type 2 diabetes.

8. **Skin Health**: Flavonoids protect the skin from UV-induced damage, reduce inflammation, and promote collagen synthesis. This helps in maintaining skin elasticity, reducing the appearance of wrinkles, and preventing skin conditions such as acne and eczema.

3.4 Flavonoids

Chemical Nature and Health Benefits of Rutin, Naringin, Quercetin, Anthocyanidins, Catechins, and Flavones

Rutin: Chemical Nature: Rutin is a glycoside comprising the flavonol quercetin and the disaccharide rutinose. It is chemically known as quercetin-3-rutinoside and is found in many plants, including buckwheat, apples, and citrus fruits. Its molecular formula is $C_{27}H_{30}O_{16}$. **Health Benefits**: Rutin exhibits strong **antioxidant** properties, which help neutralize free radicals and protect cells from oxidative damage. This antioxidant effect is beneficial in reducing the risk of chronic diseases such as heart disease and cancer. Rutin also has **anti-inflammatory** properties, making it useful in managing inflammatory conditions like arthritis. It supports **vascular health** by strengthening blood vessels, improving circulation, and reducing the risk of blood clots. Rutin's ability to inhibit platelet aggregation helps prevent thrombotic events such as heart attacks and strokes. Additionally, rutin has been shown to support **eye health**, reducing the risk of conditions like cataracts and macular degeneration.

Naringin: Chemical Nature: Naringin is a flavanone glycoside found predominantly in citrus fruits, especially grapefruits and oranges. Its molecular formula is $C_{27}H_{32}O_{14}$, and it consists of the flavanone naringenin bound to the disaccharide neohesperidose. **Health Benefits**: Naringin has potent **antioxidant** and **anti-inflammatory** properties. It helps reduce oxidative stress and inflammation, thereby protecting against chronic diseases. Naringin is known to support **cardiovascular health** by lowering cholesterol levels and improving lipid profiles. It inhibits the enzyme HMG-CoA reductase, which is involved in cholesterol synthesis, similar to the action of statin drugs. Naringin also has **anti-cancer** properties, with studies showing its ability to inhibit the proliferation of cancer cells and induce apoptosis. Additionally, naringin supports **metabolic health** by improving insulin sensitivity and regulating blood glucose levels, making it beneficial for individuals with diabetes or metabolic syndrome.

Quercetin: Chemical Nature: Quercetin is a flavonol with a molecular formula of $C_{15}H_{10}O_7$. It is widely distributed in fruits, vegetables, and grains, with high concentrations found in onions, apples, berries, and leafy greens. Quercetin exists in both free and glycosylated forms, with the glycosylated forms being more common in the human diet. **Health Benefits**: Quercetin is known for its strong **antioxidant** properties, which help protect cells from oxidative damage and reduce the risk of chronic diseases such as cardiovascular disease and cancer. It has **anti-inflammatory** effects, inhibiting the production of pro-inflammatory cytokines and enzymes, making it useful in managing conditions like arthritis and asthma. Quercetin supports **immune health** by modulating immune cell function and enhancing the body's defense mechanisms against infections. It also has **anti-cancer** properties, with studies showing its ability to inhibit the growth of cancer cells, induce apoptosis, and prevent metastasis. Additionally, quercetin improves **cardiovascular health** by lowering blood pressure, improving endothelial function, and reducing cholesterol levels.

Anthocyanidins: Chemical Nature: Anthocyanidins are a type of flavonoid responsible for the red, purple, and blue colors in many fruits and vegetables. They have a basic structure consisting of an anthocyanin aglycone (without sugar) and are found in high concentrations in berries, red cabbage, and eggplants. The molecular formula of anthocyanidins varies depending on the specific type, such as cyanidin ($C_{15}H_{11}O_6^+$). **Health Benefits**: Anthocyanidins are powerful **antioxidants** that help neutralize free radicals and protect cells from oxidative damage. This antioxidant activity is associated with a reduced risk of chronic diseases such as cardiovascular disease and cancer. Anthocyanidins have **anti-**

inflammatory properties, which help reduce inflammation and alleviate symptoms of inflammatory conditions. They also support **cardiovascular health** by improving endothelial function, reducing blood pressure, and enhancing blood flow. Studies have shown that anthocyanidins can improve **cognitive function** and protect against neurodegenerative diseases by reducing oxidative stress and inflammation in the brain. Additionally, they promote **eye health**, reducing the risk of conditions like macular degeneration and cataracts.

Catechins: Chemical Nature: Catechins are a type of flavanol found in high concentrations in tea, particularly green tea, as well as in cocoa, berries, and apples. The most well-known catechin is epigallocatechin gallate (EGCG), which has a molecular formula of $C_{22}H_{18}O_{11}$. **Health Benefits**: Catechins are potent **antioxidants** that help reduce oxidative stress and protect cells from damage. This antioxidant activity is linked to a reduced risk of chronic diseases such as cardiovascular disease and cancer. Catechins have **anti-inflammatory** properties, making them beneficial in managing inflammatory conditions. They support **cardiovascular health** by improving lipid profiles, reducing blood pressure, and enhancing blood vessel function. Catechins also have **anti-cancer** properties, with studies showing their ability to inhibit cancer cell growth, induce apoptosis, and prevent metastasis. Additionally, catechins improve **metabolic health** by enhancing insulin sensitivity, regulating blood glucose levels, and promoting weight loss. The neuroprotective effects of catechins help improve **cognitive function** and reduce the risk of neurodegenerative diseases.

Flavones: Chemical Nature: Flavones are a class of flavonoids characterized by a backbone structure of 2-phenylchromen-4-one. Common flavones include apigenin and luteolin, which are found in parsley, celery, and chamomile. The molecular formula of apigenin is $C_{15}H_{10}O_5$. **Health Benefits**: Flavones exhibit strong **antioxidant** properties, helping to neutralize free radicals and protect cells from oxidative damage. This antioxidant activity is associated with a reduced risk of chronic diseases such as cardiovascular disease and cancer. Flavones have **anti-inflammatory** effects, making them useful in managing inflammatory conditions like arthritis and inflammatory bowel disease. They support **cardiovascular health** by improving endothelial function, reducing blood pressure, and preventing platelet aggregation. Flavones also have **anti-cancer** properties, with studies showing their ability to inhibit cancer cell growth, induce apoptosis, and prevent angiogenesis. Additionally, flavones promote **neuroprotective effects**, improving cognitive function and protecting against neurodegenerative diseases by reducing oxidative stress and inflammation in the brain.

3.5 Prebiotics/Probiotics

Fructooligosaccharides (FOS):

Chemical Nature and Sources: **Fructooligosaccharides (FOS)** are a type of carbohydrate belonging to the group of oligosaccharides. They are composed of short chains of fructose molecules, typically linked together by beta(2-1) glycosidic bonds, and often ending with a glucose molecule. The general formula for FOS is GFn, where 'G' stands for glucose, 'F' stands for fructose, and 'n' indicates the number of fructose units. FOS are naturally found in many plants, including **onions, garlic, bananas, wheat, asparagus, leeks**, and **chicory root**. Chicory root, in particular, is a rich source and is often used to extract FOS for commercial purposes.

Prebiotic Properties: FOS are considered **prebiotics**, which means they are non-digestible food ingredients that beneficially affect the host by selectively stimulating the growth and activity of beneficial bacteria in the colon. Unlike regular carbohydrates, FOS resist digestion in the upper gastrointestinal tract and reach the colon intact. Here, they serve as a food source for beneficial gut bacteria, such as **Bifidobacteria** and **Lactobacilli**.

Health Benefits:

1. **Gut Health**: FOS promote the growth of beneficial gut bacteria, which in turn helps maintain a healthy balance of the gut microbiota. This balance is crucial for preventing the overgrowth of pathogenic bacteria and supporting overall digestive health.

2. **Enhanced Mineral Absorption**: FOS can enhance the absorption of minerals like calcium, magnesium, and iron. This is particularly beneficial for bone health and the prevention of conditions like osteoporosis.

3. **Immune Support**: By promoting a healthy gut microbiota, FOS indirectly support the immune system. A healthy gut microbiome plays a key role in the development and function of the immune system.

4. **Digestive Regularity**: FOS increase stool bulk and improve bowel regularity, helping to prevent constipation and improve overall digestive function.

5. **Reduced Risk of Colorectal Cancer**: Some studies suggest that FOS may reduce the risk of colorectal cancer by promoting the production of short-chain fatty acids (SCFAs) like butyrate, which have protective effects on the colon lining.

Lactobacillus:

Chemical Nature and Sources: **Lactobacillus** is a genus of Gram-positive, rod-shaped bacteria that are part of the lactic acid bacteria (LAB) group. These bacteria are characterized by their ability to convert lactose and other sugars into lactic acid through fermentation. Lactobacillus species are commonly found in fermented foods and beverages, such as **yogurt, kefir, sauerkraut, kimchi, pickles, sourdough bread**, and **miso**. They are also naturally present in the human gastrointestinal tract, mouth, and female genital tract.

Probiotic Properties: **Lactobacillus** species are widely recognized as **probiotics**, which are live microorganisms that confer health benefits to the host when administered in adequate amounts. Probiotics work by colonizing the gut and enhancing the natural microbiota, thus promoting various aspects of health.

Health Benefits:

1. **Gut Health**: Lactobacillus species help maintain a healthy balance of gut microbiota, which is essential for proper digestive function. They compete with pathogenic bacteria for nutrients and attachment sites, thus inhibiting the growth of harmful bacteria.

2. **Immune Support**: Lactobacillus species stimulate the immune system by enhancing the production of antibodies and activating immune cells. This helps the body fight off infections and reduce the incidence of diseases.

3. **Digestive Health**: Probiotics like Lactobacillus can alleviate symptoms of gastrointestinal disorders such as irritable bowel syndrome (IBS), inflammatory bowel disease (IBD), and antibiotic-associated diarrhea. They help restore the natural balance of gut bacteria disrupted by antibiotics or illness.

4. **Lactose Intolerance**: Lactobacillus species produce lactase, the enzyme that breaks down lactose, which helps individuals with lactose intolerance digest dairy products more easily.

5. **Skin Health**: Emerging research suggests that Lactobacillus probiotics may have beneficial effects on skin health by reducing inflammation and improving conditions such as eczema and acne.
6. **Urogenital Health**: In women, Lactobacillus species help maintain the natural balance of bacteria in the vaginal microbiota, reducing the risk of infections such as bacterial vaginosis and yeast infections.

Mechanisms of Action:

1. **Colonization and Competition**: Lactobacillus bacteria colonize the gut by adhering to the intestinal lining, where they compete with pathogenic bacteria for nutrients and attachment sites, preventing the growth of harmful microbes.
2. **Production of Antimicrobial Substances**: Lactobacillus species produce lactic acid, hydrogen peroxide, and bacteriocins, which inhibit the growth of pathogenic bacteria.
3. **Modulation of Immune Responses**: Probiotics enhance the immune system by stimulating the production of antibodies, increasing the activity of natural killer (NK) cells, and modulating cytokine production.

3.5 Prebiotics/Probiotics

Sources, Chemical Nature, and Health Benefits of Prebiotics and Probiotics

Prebiotics

Sources: **Prebiotics** are naturally occurring, non-digestible food components that promote the growth and activity of beneficial bacteria in the gut. Common sources of prebiotics include various plant-based foods. The most well-known prebiotics are **fructooligosaccharides (FOS), inulin, galactooligosaccharides (GOS)**, and **resistant starches**. These compounds are found in high concentrations in foods such as:

- **Onions**
- **Garlic**
- **Leeks**
- **Asparagus**
- **Bananas**
- **Chicory root**
- **Jerusalem artichokes**

- **Whole grains** (such as wheat and oats)
- **Soybeans**
- **Legumes**

Chemical Nature: Prebiotics are a category of dietary fibers that the human digestive system cannot digest. They pass through the upper part of the gastrointestinal tract undigested and reach the colon, where they are fermented by the gut microbiota. The fermentation process produces short-chain fatty acids (SCFAs) like butyrate, propionate, and acetate, which provide energy for colon cells and have various health benefits.

Health Benefits:

1. **Gut Health**: Prebiotics selectively stimulate the growth and activity of beneficial bacteria such as Bifidobacteria and Lactobacilli. This helps maintain a healthy balance of gut microbiota, which is crucial for efficient digestion and absorption of nutrients.
2. **Enhanced Mineral Absorption**: Prebiotics improve the absorption of essential minerals like calcium, magnesium, and iron, contributing to better bone health and prevention of conditions like osteoporosis.
3. **Immune Support**: By promoting a healthy gut microbiome, prebiotics help enhance the body's immune response. A healthy gut flora is vital for the development and function of the immune system.
4. **Digestive Regularity**: Prebiotics increase stool bulk and improve bowel regularity, helping prevent constipation and promoting overall digestive health.
5. **Reduced Risk of Colorectal Cancer**: The production of SCFAs during the fermentation of prebiotics has protective effects on the colon lining, reducing the risk of colorectal cancer.

Probiotics

Sources: **Probiotics** are live microorganisms that, when consumed in adequate amounts, confer health benefits to the host. They are naturally found in various fermented foods and beverages. Common sources of probiotics include:

- **Yogurt**
- **Kefir**
- **Sauerkraut**

- **Kimchi**
- **Pickles** (fermented in brine)
- **Miso**
- **Tempeh**
- **Kombucha**
- **Fermented cheeses**

Probiotics are also available in supplement form, which can provide specific strains of beneficial bacteria.

Chemical Nature: Probiotics are primarily bacteria, but some yeasts also serve as probiotics. The most commonly studied and used probiotic bacteria belong to the genera **Lactobacillus** and **Bifidobacterium**. Each species and strain of probiotics has unique properties and health benefits. The chemical nature of probiotics involves their ability to survive the acidic environment of the stomach, adhere to the intestinal lining, and colonize the gut.

Health Benefits:

1. **Gut Health**: Probiotics help maintain a healthy balance of gut microbiota, which is essential for proper digestive function. They compete with pathogenic bacteria for nutrients and attachment sites, thus inhibiting the growth of harmful bacteria.
2. **Immune Support**: Probiotics enhance the immune system by stimulating the production of antibodies, activating immune cells, and modulating immune responses. This helps the body fight off infections and reduce the incidence of diseases.
3. **Digestive Health**: Probiotics can alleviate symptoms of gastrointestinal disorders such as irritable bowel syndrome (IBS), inflammatory bowel disease (IBD), and antibiotic-associated diarrhea. They help restore the natural balance of gut bacteria disrupted by antibiotics or illness.
4. **Lactose Intolerance**: Certain probiotic strains produce lactase, the enzyme that breaks down lactose, which helps individuals with lactose intolerance digest dairy products more easily.
5. **Skin Health**: Emerging research suggests that probiotics may have beneficial effects on skin health by reducing inflammation and improving conditions such as eczema and acne.
6. **Urogenital Health**: In women, probiotics help maintain the natural balance of bacteria in the vaginal microbiota, reducing the risk of infections such as bacterial vaginosis and yeast infections.

Mechanisms of Action:

1. **Colonization and Competition**: Probiotics colonize the gut by adhering to the intestinal lining, where they compete with pathogenic bacteria for nutrients and attachment sites, preventing the growth of harmful microbes.
2. **Production of Antimicrobial Substances**: Probiotic bacteria produce lactic acid, hydrogen peroxide, and bacteriocins, which inhibit the growth of pathogenic bacteria.
3. **Modulation of Immune Responses**: Probiotics enhance the immune system by stimulating the production of antibodies, increasing the activity of natural killer (NK) cells, and modulating cytokine production.

Integration of Prebiotics and Probiotics: The combination of prebiotics and probiotics is referred to as **synbiotics**. This combination can have synergistic effects, enhancing the survival and colonization of probiotics in the gut. Consuming prebiotics and probiotics together supports the growth and activity of beneficial bacteria, promoting a healthy and balanced gut microbiome.

3.6 Phytoestrogens

Phytoestrogens are naturally occurring plant compounds that have the ability to exert estrogen-like effects in the body. They are structurally similar to the hormone **estrogen** and can mimic or modulate the hormone's effects by binding to estrogen receptors. Phytoestrogens can exhibit both **estrogenic** and **anti-estrogenic** activities, depending on the hormonal environment and the concentration of endogenous estrogens. Due to their structural similarity to estrogen, phytoestrogens can influence various physiological processes and are studied for their potential health benefits, particularly in relation to hormonal balance, bone health, and cardiovascular health.

Chemical Nature of Phytoestrogens: Phytoestrogens belong to several classes of compounds, with the most significant being **isoflavones**, **lignans**, and **coumestans**. Each class has distinct chemical structures and sources.

1. **Isoflavones**: Isoflavones are the most well-known and studied phytoestrogens. They have a chemical structure similar to estradiol, the primary form of estrogen in the body. The main isoflavones include **genistein**, **daidzein**, and **glycitein**. Isoflavones can be metabolized into

other compounds with varying degrees of estrogenic activity.

2. **Lignans**: Lignans are polyphenolic compounds that are converted by intestinal bacteria into enterolignans, such as enterodiol and enterolactone, which have estrogen-like activity. The structure of lignans allows them to interact with estrogen receptors and exert biological effects.

3. **Coumestans**: Coumestans, such as **coumestrol**, are less common than isoflavones and lignans but still possess significant estrogenic activity. They are structurally related to both flavonoids and isoflavones.

Sources of Phytoestrogens: Phytoestrogens are found in a variety of plant-based foods. The most significant sources include:

1. **Soybeans and Soy Products**: Soybeans are the richest source of isoflavones, particularly genistein and daidzein. Soy products such as tofu, tempeh, soy milk, and edamame are excellent sources of phytoestrogens.

2. **Flaxseeds**: Flaxseeds are one of the best sources of lignans. They contain high levels of secoisolariciresinol diglucoside (SDG), which is converted into enterolignans in the body.

3. **Legumes**: Other legumes, including chickpeas, lentils, and beans, also contain varying amounts of isoflavones and lignans.

4. **Whole Grains**: Whole grains such as oats, barley, and rye contain lignans and are beneficial sources of phytoestrogens.

5. **Fruits and Vegetables**: Some fruits and vegetables, including berries, apples, carrots, and pomegranates, contain phytoestrogens, though in smaller amounts compared to soy and flaxseeds.

6. **Nuts and Seeds**: In addition to flaxseeds, other nuts and seeds such as sesame seeds, sunflower seeds, and almonds provide phytoestrogens.

7. **Herbs and Spices**: Certain herbs and spices like fenugreek, licorice, and anise also contain phytoestrogens and have been used traditionally for their hormonal effects.

Health Benefits of Phytoestrogens:

1. **Hormonal Balance**: Phytoestrogens can help balance hormone levels, particularly in women during menopause. They can alleviate symptoms such as hot flashes, night sweats, and mood swings by providing a mild

estrogenic effect when endogenous estrogen levels decline.

2. **Bone Health**: Phytoestrogens have been shown to improve bone density and reduce the risk of osteoporosis. Their estrogen-like effects help maintain bone strength and support bone metabolism, which is particularly beneficial for postmenopausal women at risk of bone loss.

3. **Cardiovascular Health**: Consumption of phytoestrogens is associated with improved cardiovascular health. They can help reduce cholesterol levels, improve endothelial function, and reduce the risk of atherosclerosis. Isoflavones, in particular, have been studied for their cardioprotective effects.

4. **Cancer Prevention**: Some studies suggest that phytoestrogens may reduce the risk of certain hormone-related cancers, such as breast and prostate cancer. They can inhibit the growth of cancer cells, induce apoptosis, and modulate hormone metabolism.

5. **Antioxidant Properties**: Phytoestrogens possess antioxidant properties, which help neutralize free radicals and reduce oxidative stress. This contributes to their protective effects against chronic diseases and aging.

6. **Metabolic Health**: Phytoestrogens can improve metabolic health by enhancing insulin sensitivity and regulating blood glucose levels. This is beneficial for individuals with metabolic syndrome or type 2 diabetes.

7. **Skin Health**: The estrogen-like effects of phytoestrogens can improve skin elasticity, hydration, and reduce the appearance of wrinkles. They help maintain collagen production and skin health.

Mechanisms of Action:

1. **Estrogen Receptor Binding**: Phytoestrogens exert their effects by binding to estrogen receptors (ERα and ERβ) in the body. Depending on the concentration of endogenous estrogens and the type of receptor, they can either mimic or modulate estrogenic activity.

2. **Antioxidant Activity**: Phytoestrogens act as antioxidants, protecting cells from oxidative damage and reducing inflammation.

3. **Gene Expression Modulation**: By interacting with estrogen receptors, phytoestrogens can influence the expression of genes involved in cell growth, apoptosis, and metabolism.

3.6 Phytoestrogens

Chemical Nature and Health Benefits of Isoflavones, Daidzein, Genistein, and Lignans

Isoflavones

Chemical Nature: Isoflavones are a class of phytoestrogens, compounds that have a similar structure to the hormone estrogen. They belong to the flavonoid family and are characterized by a 3-phenylchromen-4-one structure. Isoflavones are primarily found in legumes, especially soybeans. The most well-known isoflavones are **daidzein** and **genistein**. Isoflavones can bind to estrogen receptors in the body, exerting either estrogenic or anti-estrogenic effects depending on the hormonal environment.

Health Benefits:

1. **Hormonal Balance:** Isoflavones help regulate hormonal levels, especially in menopausal women. They can reduce symptoms of menopause such as hot flashes, night sweats, and mood swings by mimicking the effects of estrogen.
2. **Bone Health:** Isoflavones have been shown to improve bone density and reduce the risk of osteoporosis. They support bone metabolism and help maintain bone strength, which is particularly beneficial for postmenopausal women.
3. **Cardiovascular Health:** Isoflavones contribute to cardiovascular health by lowering cholesterol levels, improving endothelial function, and reducing the risk of atherosclerosis. They have been associated with a reduced risk of heart disease.
4. **Cancer Prevention:** Some studies suggest that isoflavones may reduce the risk of hormone-related cancers, such as breast and prostate cancer. They can inhibit cancer cell growth, induce apoptosis, and modulate hormone metabolism.

Daidzein

Chemical Nature: Daidzein is an isoflavone found in soybeans and other legumes. Its chemical structure includes a 4H-chromen-4-one backbone with hydroxyl groups attached at specific positions. The molecular formula of daidzein is $C_{15}H_{10}O_4$.

Health Benefits:

1. **Hormonal Effects:** Daidzein can bind to estrogen receptors and exert weak estrogenic effects. It helps alleviate menopausal symptoms and

may support hormonal balance in both men and women.

2. **Bone Health**: Daidzein supports bone health by enhancing bone mineral density and reducing the risk of fractures. It plays a role in bone metabolism and helps maintain bone strength.

3. **Anti-Cancer Properties**: Daidzein has been studied for its potential anti-cancer effects. It can inhibit the growth of cancer cells, induce apoptosis, and reduce the risk of hormone-related cancers such as breast and prostate cancer.

4. **Cardiovascular Health**: Daidzein may improve cardiovascular health by lowering cholesterol levels, reducing oxidative stress, and enhancing endothelial function.

Genistein

Chemical Nature: **Genistein** is another prominent isoflavone found in soybeans and other legumes. Its chemical structure includes a 4H-chromen-4-one backbone with hydroxyl groups at the 5, 7, and 4' positions. The molecular formula of genistein is $C_{15}H_{10}O_5$.

Health Benefits:

1. **Antioxidant Properties**: Genistein is a potent antioxidant that helps neutralize free radicals and reduce oxidative stress. This antioxidant activity protects cells from damage and reduces the risk of chronic diseases.

2. **Hormonal Balance**: Genistein can bind to estrogen receptors and exert estrogenic or anti-estrogenic effects, depending on the hormonal environment. It helps alleviate menopausal symptoms and supports hormonal balance.

3. **Bone Health**: Genistein has been shown to enhance bone mineral density and reduce the risk of osteoporosis. It supports bone metabolism and helps maintain bone strength, particularly in postmenopausal women.

4. **Anti-Cancer Properties**: Genistein exhibits significant anti-cancer properties. It can inhibit cancer cell proliferation, induce apoptosis, and prevent angiogenesis. Studies have shown that genistein may reduce the risk of hormone-related cancers such as breast, prostate, and colon cancer.

5. **Cardiovascular Health**: Genistein contributes to cardiovascular health by lowering cholesterol levels, improving endothelial function, and reducing the risk of atherosclerosis.

Lignans

Chemical Nature: **Lignans** are a group of polyphenolic compounds found in a variety of plant-based foods. They have a complex structure that includes two phenylpropane units linked by a carbon-carbon bond. Lignans are converted by intestinal bacteria into enterolignans, such as **enterodiol** and **enterolactone**, which have estrogen-like activity. Flaxseeds are one of the richest sources of lignans, but they are also found in sesame seeds, whole grains, legumes, and vegetables.

Health Benefits:

1. **Hormonal Effects**: Lignans can mimic or modulate the effects of estrogen in the body, helping to balance hormone levels. This is particularly beneficial for women during menopause, as lignans can reduce symptoms such as hot flashes and night sweats.
2. **Anti-Cancer Properties**: Lignans have been studied for their potential to reduce the risk of hormone-related cancers, such as breast and prostate cancer. They can inhibit cancer cell growth, induce apoptosis, and modulate hormone metabolism.
3. **Cardiovascular Health**: Lignans contribute to cardiovascular health by lowering cholesterol levels, improving blood pressure, and reducing the risk of atherosclerosis. The antioxidant properties of lignans help protect against oxidative stress and inflammation.
4. **Bone Health**: Lignans support bone health by enhancing bone mineral density and reducing the risk of osteoporosis. They play a role in bone metabolism and help maintain bone strength.
5. **Antioxidant Properties**: Lignans are potent antioxidants that help neutralize free radicals and reduce oxidative stress. This antioxidant activity contributes to their protective effects against chronic diseases and aging.

3.7 Tocopherols

Chemical Nature and Types of Tocopherols: **Tocopherols** are a class of organic chemical compounds, many of which have vitamin E activity. They are fat-soluble antioxidants that play a critical role in protecting cell membranes from oxidative damage. The tocopherol molecule consists of a chromanol ring with a long, saturated phytyl side chain. The most common types of tocopherols include **alpha-tocopherol**, **beta-tocopherol**, **gamma-tocopherol**, and **delta-tocopherol**, each differing in the number and position of methyl groups on the chromanol ring.

1. **Alpha-Tocopherol**: This is the most biologically active form of vitamin E in humans and is the predominant form found in supplements and fortified foods. It has a molecular formula of $C_{29}H_{50}O_2$.
2. **Beta-Tocopherol**: Similar in structure to alpha-tocopherol but with one less methyl group on the chromanol ring. Its molecular formula is $C_{28}H_{48}O_2$.
3. **Gamma-Tocopherol**: This form is abundant in the diet, particularly in oils, and has significant antioxidant properties. Its molecular formula is $C_{28}H_{48}O_2$.
4. **Delta-Tocopherol**: This form has the fewest methyl groups and is known for its potent antioxidant activity. Its molecular formula is $C_{27}H_{46}O_2$.

Sources of Tocopherols: Tocopherols are found in a variety of plant-based foods. The richest dietary sources include:

- **Vegetable oils**: such as wheat germ oil, sunflower oil, safflower oil, and olive oil.
- **Nuts and seeds**: such as almonds, sunflower seeds, and hazelnuts.
- **Green leafy vegetables**: such as spinach, kale, and broccoli.
- **Whole grains**: such as wheat germ, barley, and oats.
- **Fortified foods**: such as cereals and dairy products.

Health Benefits of Tocopherols:

1. **Antioxidant Properties**: Tocopherols are powerful antioxidants that protect cells from oxidative damage caused by free radicals. This helps prevent lipid peroxidation in cell membranes, thereby maintaining cellular integrity and function. By neutralizing free radicals, tocopherols reduce the risk of chronic diseases such as cardiovascular diseases, cancer, and neurodegenerative disorders.
2. **Cardiovascular Health**: Tocopherols, especially alpha-tocopherol, play a significant role in promoting cardiovascular health. They help prevent the oxidation of LDL cholesterol, which is a key factor in the development of atherosclerosis. Tocopherols also improve endothelial function, reduce inflammation, and enhance blood flow, thereby reducing the risk of heart attacks and strokes.

3. **Immune Support**: Tocopherols enhance the immune response by protecting immune cells from oxidative damage. They support the production of antibodies and the function of immune cells such as T-cells and natural killer cells. This is particularly important for maintaining a strong immune system, especially in older adults.

4. **Skin Health**: Tocopherols are widely used in skincare products due to their ability to protect the skin from oxidative damage caused by UV radiation and environmental pollutants. They help maintain skin moisture, reduce the appearance of scars and wrinkles, and promote overall skin health. Tocopherols also have anti-inflammatory properties that help soothe irritated skin.

5. **Eye Health**: The antioxidant properties of tocopherols are beneficial for eye health. They help protect the eyes from oxidative damage that can lead to conditions such as cataracts and age-related macular degeneration (AMD). By neutralizing free radicals, tocopherols help maintain healthy vision.

6. **Cancer Prevention**: Some studies suggest that tocopherols may play a role in reducing the risk of certain cancers. Their antioxidant properties help protect DNA from damage that can lead to cancerous changes. Tocopherols may also inhibit tumor growth and promote apoptosis (programmed cell death) in cancer cells.

7. **Neurological Health**: Tocopherols support neurological health by protecting nerve cells from oxidative stress. This is particularly important in preventing neurodegenerative diseases such as Alzheimer's disease and Parkinson's disease. Tocopherols help maintain cognitive function and memory by reducing oxidative damage and inflammation in the brain.

Mechanisms of Action:

1. **Antioxidant Activity**: Tocopherols neutralize free radicals by donating an electron, thus preventing the free radicals from damaging cellular components such as lipids, proteins, and DNA. This action helps reduce oxidative stress and its associated cellular damage.

2. **Anti-Inflammatory Effects**: Tocopherols inhibit the production of pro-inflammatory cytokines and modulate signaling pathways involved in inflammation. This reduces chronic inflammation and its related health risks.

3. **Gene Expression Modulation**: Tocopherols influence the expression of genes involved in antioxidant defense, inflammation, and cell survival. By modulating gene expression, tocopherols contribute to their protective effects against various diseases.

3.7 Tocopherols
Sources and Chemical Nature of Tocopherols

Sources of Tocopherols: Tocopherols are widely distributed in a variety of plant-based foods. The primary dietary sources of tocopherols include:

1. **Vegetable Oils**:

    ◦ **Wheat Germ Oil**: One of the richest sources of tocopherols, particularly alpha-tocopherol.
    ◦ **Sunflower Oil**: High in alpha-tocopherol and gamma-tocopherol.
    ◦ **Safflower Oil**: Contains significant amounts of alpha-tocopherol.
    ◦ **Olive Oil**: Contains alpha-tocopherol and other minor tocopherols.

2. **Nuts and Seeds**:

    ◦ **Almonds**: A rich source of alpha-tocopherol.
    ◦ **Sunflower Seeds**: High in alpha-tocopherol.
    ◦ **Hazelnuts**: Contain significant amounts of alpha-tocopherol.
    ◦ **Pine Nuts**: Provide alpha-tocopherol and gamma-tocopherol.

3. **Green Leafy Vegetables**:

    ◦ **Spinach**: Contains alpha-tocopherol and other tocopherols.
    ◦ **Kale**: A good source of alpha-tocopherol.
    ◦ **Broccoli**: Contains alpha-tocopherol.

4. **Whole Grains**:

    ◦ **Wheat Germ**: Extremely high in alpha-tocopherol.
    ◦ **Barley**: Contains various tocopherols.
    ◦ **Oats**: Provide tocopherols, including alpha-tocopherol.

5. **Fruits**:

- **Avocados**: Rich in alpha-tocopherol.
- **Tomatoes**: Contain alpha-tocopherol and gamma-tocopherol.

6. **Fortified Foods**:

- **Cereals**: Often fortified with alpha-tocopherol.
- **Dairy Products**: Sometimes fortified with vitamin E (tocopherols).

Chemical Nature of Tocopherols:

Structure and Variants: Tocopherols are a family of organic compounds that belong to the vitamin E group. They are characterized by a chromanol ring and a phytyl side chain. The differences among the tocopherol variants are due to the number and position of methyl groups on the chromanol ring. The four main types of tocopherols are:

1. **Alpha-Tocopherol (α-Tocopherol)**:

- **Structure**: Has three methyl groups on the chromanol ring (5, 7, and 8 positions).
- **Molecular Formula**: $C_{29}H_{50}O_2$.
- **Significance**: The most biologically active form in humans and the primary form found in the human body.

2. **Beta-Tocopherol (β-Tocopherol)**:

- **Structure**: Has two methyl groups on the chromanol ring (5 and 8 positions).
- **Molecular Formula**: $C_{28}H_{48}O_2$.
- **Significance**: Less biologically active compared to alpha-tocopherol.

3. **Gamma-Tocopherol (γ-Tocopherol)**:

- **Structure**: Has two methyl groups on the chromanol ring (7 and 8 positions).
- **Molecular Formula**: $C_{28}H_{48}O_2$.
- **Significance**: The most common form found in the diet, particularly in oils, and has unique anti-inflammatory properties.

4. **Delta-Tocopherol (δ-Tocopherol):**

- **Structure**: Has one methyl group on the chromanol ring (8 position).
- **Molecular Formula**: $C_{27}H_{46}O_2$.
- **Significance**: Known for its potent antioxidant activity.

Antioxidant Mechanism: The chemical structure of tocopherols allows them to act as powerful antioxidants. The chromanol ring can donate a hydrogen atom to neutralize free radicals, thereby preventing lipid peroxidation and protecting cell membranes from oxidative damage. The phytyl tail helps tocopherols integrate into cell membranes, where they can exert their protective effects.

Bioavailability and Function: Among the tocopherols, alpha-tocopherol is preferentially maintained in the human body due to its higher bioavailability and specific transport proteins, such as alpha-tocopherol transfer protein (α-TTP). This ensures that alpha-tocopherol is the predominant form of vitamin E in human tissues and is crucial for protecting cells from oxidative stress.

Summary: Tocopherols are essential fat-soluble antioxidants found abundantly in various plant-based foods, including vegetable oils, nuts, seeds, green leafy vegetables, whole grains, fruits, and fortified foods. Their chemical structure, characterized by a chromanol ring and a phytyl side chain, enables them to effectively neutralize free radicals and protect cells from oxidative damage. The different types of tocopherols, namely alpha, beta, gamma, and delta-tocopherol, each have unique properties and contribute to the diverse health benefits of vitamin E. Incorporating tocopherol-rich foods into the diet can significantly enhance antioxidant defenses and promote overall health.

Table 1: Comparison of α-Carotene and β-Carotene

Aspect	α-Carotene	β-Carotene
Chemical Structure	Long carbon chain with conjugated double bonds, two β-ionone rings	Similar to α-Carotene, different position of one double bond
Abundance	Less abundant	Most abundant provitamin A carotenoid
Vitamin A Conversion	Lower conversion rate	Higher conversion rate
Health Benefits	Antioxidant, vision, immune function, skin health	Antioxidant, vision, immune function, skin health

Table 2: Health Benefits of Lycopene, Xanthophylls, and Lutein

Carotenoid	Chemical Nature	Health Benefits
Lycopene	Non-provitamin A, long chain of conjugated double bonds	Antioxidant, cancer prevention, cardiovascular health
Xanthophylls (e.g., Zeaxanthin, Cryptoxanthin)	Oxygenated carotenoids	Eye health, skin protection
Lutein	Xanthophyll, similar to zeaxanthin	Eye health, cognitive function, skin health

Table 3: Sources and Benefits of Sulfides

Compound	Sources	Health Benefits
Diallyl Sulfides, Allyl Trisulfide	Garlic, onions, shallots, leeks, chives	Antimicrobial, cardiovascula[r] inflammatory, antioxidant, [...] immune support

Table 4: Health Benefits of Key Flavonoids

Flavonoid	Sources	Health Benefits
Rutin	Buckwheat, apples, citrus	Antioxidant, anti-inflammato[ry]
Naringin	Grapefruits, oranges	Antioxidant, cardiovascular h[...]
Quercetin	Onions, apples, berries	Antioxidant, anti-inflammato[ry] health, anti-cancer
Anthocyanidins	Berries, red cabbage, eggplants	Antioxidant, anti-inflammato[ry] function, eye health
Catechins	Green tea, cocoa, berries	Antioxidant, anti-inflammato[ry] metabolic health, neuroprote[ctive]
Flavones	Parsley, celery, chamomile	Antioxidant, anti-inflammato[ry] neuroprotective

Table 5: Differences Between Prebiotics and Probiotics

Aspect	Prebiotics	Probiotics
Definition	Non-digestible food components that promote beneficial bacteria growth	Live microorganisms that confer health benefits
Sources	Onions, garlic, leeks, asparagus, bananas, chicory root, whole grains, soybeans	Yogurt, kefir, sauerkraut, kimchi, pickles, miso, tempeh, kombucha, fermented cheeses
Health Benefits	Gut health, enhanced mineral absorption, immune support, digestive regularity, reduced risk of colorectal cancer	Gut health, immune support, digestive health, lactose intolerance management, skin health, urogenital health

Table 6: Health Benefits of Isoflavones, Daidzein, and Genistein

Compound	Sources	Health Benefits
Isoflavones	Soybeans, legumes	Hormonal balance, bone health, cardiovascular health, cancer prevention
Daidzein	Soybeans, legumes	Hormonal effects, bone health, anti-cancer properties, cardiovascular health
Genistein	Soybeans, legumes	Antioxidant properties, hormonal balance, bone health, anti-cancer properties, cardiovascular health

Table 7: Chemical Nature and Types of Tocopherols

Type of Tocopherol	Structure	Molecular Formula	Significance
Alpha-Tocopherol	Three methyl groups on chromanol ring	$C_{29}H_{50}O_2$	Most biologically active, predominant form in supplements
Beta-Tocopherol	Two methyl groups on chromanol ring	$C_{28}H_{48}O_2$	Less biologically active compared to alpha-tocopherol
Gamma-Tocopherol	Two methyl groups on chromanol ring	$C_{28}H_{48}O_2$	Common in diet, unique anti-inflammatory properties
Delta-Tocopherol	One methyl group on chromanol ring	$C_{27}H_{46}O_2$	Potent antioxidant activity

Table 8: Health Benefits of Tocopherols

Health Benefit	Description
Antioxidant Properties	Protect cells from oxidative damage, prevent lipid peroxidation
Cardiovascular Health	Prevent LDL cholesterol oxidation, improve endothelial function, reduce inflammation
Immune Support	Enhance immune response, protect immune cells from oxidative damage
Skin Health	Protect skin from UV damage, maintain skin moisture, reduce scars and wrinkles
Eye Health	Protect eyes from oxidative damage, reduce risk of cataracts and AMD
Cancer Prevention	Protect DNA from damage, inhibit tumor growth, promote apoptosis in cancer cells
Neurological Health	Protect nerve cells from oxidative stress, maintain cognitive function and memory

FOUR

FREE RADICALS AND OXIDATIVE STRESS

4.1 Introduction to Free Radicals

4.1.1 Definitions and Types

Definitions: **Free radicals** are highly reactive molecules with one or more unpaired electrons. This unpaired electron configuration makes them unstable and highly reactive, as they seek to stabilize themselves by capturing electrons from other molecules. Free radicals can cause significant damage to cells, proteins, lipids, and DNA by initiating chain reactions that can lead to cellular dysfunction and contribute to the development of various diseases. They are generated both endogenously, through normal metabolic processes within the body, and exogenously, through environmental factors such as pollution, radiation, tobacco smoke, and certain chemicals.

The most common free radicals in biological systems are derived from oxygen and nitrogen, known as **reactive oxygen species (ROS)** and **reactive nitrogen species (RNS)**, respectively. Free radicals play a dual role in the body; while they are involved in normal cellular functions and signaling, an imbalance leading to excessive free radical production can result in oxidative stress and tissue damage.

Types of Free Radicals:

Reactive Oxygen Species (ROS):

1. **Superoxide Anion (O2·-)**: Superoxide anion is a primary ROS formed when oxygen molecules gain an extra electron. It is generated mainly in the mitochondria during the electron transport chain process. Although

superoxide anion is not highly reactive, it can undergo dismutation, either spontaneously or catalyzed by the enzyme superoxide dismutase (SOD), to form hydrogen peroxide (H2O2).

2. **Hydrogen Peroxide (H_2O_2):** Hydrogen peroxide is a non-radical ROS that is relatively stable compared to other ROS. It can diffuse across cell membranes and generate highly reactive hydroxyl radicals (·OH) in the presence of transition metals like iron or copper through the Fenton reaction. H2O2 is also involved in cell signaling and immune responses.

3. **Hydroxyl Radical (·OH):** Hydroxyl radical is one of the most reactive and damaging ROS. It can be produced from hydrogen peroxide via the Fenton reaction or through the radiolysis of water. The hydroxyl radical can cause extensive damage to proteins, lipids, and DNA, leading to cell death or mutations.

4. **Singlet Oxygen ($^1O2$):** Singlet oxygen is an excited form of oxygen with higher reactivity. It can be generated during photochemical reactions or by the action of certain enzymes. Singlet oxygen can react with lipids, proteins, and nucleic acids, causing oxidative damage.

Reactive Nitrogen Species (RNS):

1. **Nitric Oxide (NO·):** Nitric oxide is a free radical produced by the enzyme nitric oxide synthase (NOS) from the amino acid arginine. It plays a crucial role in various physiological processes, including vasodilation, neurotransmission, and immune defense. However, excessive production of nitric oxide can contribute to oxidative stress and inflammation.

2. **Peroxynitrite (ONOO⁻):** Peroxynitrite is a potent RNS formed by the reaction of nitric oxide with superoxide anion. It is a highly reactive species that can cause nitration and oxidation of proteins, lipids, and DNA, leading to cellular damage and inflammation.

3. **Nitrogen Dioxide (NO_2·):** Nitrogen dioxide is a reactive nitrogen species formed from nitric oxide in the presence of oxygen. It can cause lipid peroxidation and oxidative damage to proteins and nucleic acids.

Sources of Free Radicals:

1. **Endogenous Sources:** Free radicals are produced as a byproduct of normal metabolic processes. The mitochondrial electron transport chain

is a significant source of superoxide anion. Enzymes like xanthine oxidase, NADPH oxidase, and cytochrome P450 also generate ROS during their catalytic cycles. Inflammatory cells, such as macrophages and neutrophils, produce ROS and RNS as part of the immune response to destroy pathogens.

2. **Exogenous Sources**: Environmental factors contribute to the generation of free radicals. Exposure to **ultraviolet (UV) radiation, ionizing radiation, pollutants** (such as ozone and nitrogen dioxide), **tobacco smoke, pesticides**, and **certain chemicals** can increase free radical production. **Dietary factors**, including high-fat diets and consumption of processed foods, can also enhance oxidative stress.

Mechanisms of Damage:

1. **Lipid Peroxidation**: Free radicals attack polyunsaturated fatty acids in cell membranes, initiating a chain reaction that leads to lipid peroxidation. This process results in the formation of lipid peroxides and secondary products such as malondialdehyde (MDA), which can further damage cellular components and disrupt membrane integrity.
2. **Protein Oxidation**: Free radicals can modify amino acid side chains, leading to protein oxidation. This process can alter protein structure and function, impair enzyme activity, and lead to the formation of protein aggregates.
3. **DNA Damage**: Free radicals can cause single and double-strand breaks in DNA, as well as base modifications and cross-linking. These changes can lead to mutations, impaired gene expression, and genomic instability, contributing to cancer development and aging.

Defense Mechanisms: The body has developed several antioxidant defense mechanisms to neutralize free radicals and prevent oxidative damage. These include:

1. **Enzymatic Antioxidants**: Enzymes such as superoxide dismutase (SOD), catalase, and glutathione peroxidase play crucial roles in detoxifying ROS.
2. **Non-Enzymatic Antioxidants**: Small molecules like vitamin C, vitamin E, glutathione, and flavonoids scavenge free radicals and protect cellular components.

3. **Repair Mechanisms**: The body has repair systems to fix oxidative damage, including DNA repair enzymes and proteases that degrade oxidized proteins.

In summary, free radicals are highly reactive molecules with unpaired electrons that can cause significant cellular damage. They are generated from both endogenous metabolic processes and exogenous environmental factors. The body has developed complex antioxidant defense mechanisms to neutralize free radicals and minimize oxidative damage. Understanding the types and sources of free radicals, as well as their mechanisms of action, is crucial for developing strategies to prevent and mitigate their harmful effects.

4.1.2 Reactive Oxygen Species (ROS)

Introduction: Reactive Oxygen Species (ROS) are highly reactive molecules containing oxygen. They are a subset of free radicals and play dual roles in biological systems as both essential signaling molecules and potential agents of cellular damage. The balance between their production and the body's antioxidant defenses is crucial for maintaining cellular homeostasis. An imbalance, often referred to as oxidative stress, can lead to various pathological conditions, including inflammation, cancer, cardiovascular diseases, and neurodegenerative disorders.

Types of ROS:

1. **Superoxide Anion (O2·-)**: Superoxide anion is the primary ROS formed when molecular oxygen (O2) gains an extra electron. This reaction is often catalyzed by enzymes such as NADPH oxidase during cellular respiration. The superoxide anion itself is not highly reactive, but it serves as a precursor for other more reactive ROS. It can undergo spontaneous dismutation or be catalyzed by the enzyme superoxide dismutase (SOD) to form hydrogen peroxide (H2O2).

2. **Hydrogen Peroxide ($H2O_2$)**: Hydrogen peroxide is a non-radical ROS and is more stable compared to other ROS. It can diffuse across cell membranes and acts as a signaling molecule in various physiological processes, including cell growth and immune response. In the presence of transition metals like iron or copper, hydrogen peroxide can generate highly reactive hydroxyl radicals (·OH) through the Fenton reaction:

$$H2O_2 + Fe^{2+} \rightarrow \cdot OH + OH^- + Fe3^+$$

Hydroxyl Radical (·OH): Hydroxyl radical is one of the most reactive and damaging ROS. It can be generated from hydrogen peroxide via the Fenton reaction or from water radiolysis. Due to its high reactivity, the hydroxyl radical can attack and damage nearly all types of macromolecules, including DNA, proteins, and lipids, leading to cell dysfunction and death.

1. **Singlet Oxygen ($^1O_2$)**: Singlet oxygen is an excited form of oxygen with higher reactivity than the ground state molecular oxygen. It is produced during photochemical reactions or by the action of certain enzymes. Singlet oxygen can react with a wide range of biological molecules, causing oxidative damage to lipids, proteins, and nucleic acids.
2. **Peroxyl Radicals (ROO·)**: Peroxyl radicals are formed during the lipid peroxidation process, where they propagate the chain reaction of lipid oxidation. They can damage cellular membranes, leading to loss of membrane integrity and cell death.

Sources of ROS:

1. **Endogenous Sources**: ROS are primarily generated as byproducts of normal cellular metabolism, particularly during mitochondrial oxidative phosphorylation. Key endogenous sources include:

   - **Mitochondria**: The electron transport chain in mitochondria is a major site of superoxide anion production, particularly at complexes I and III.
   - **Peroxisomes**: Enzymes such as xanthine oxidase and D-amino acid oxidase generate hydrogen peroxide during their catalytic cycles.
   - **Endoplasmic Reticulum**: Enzymes involved in protein folding and metabolism produce ROS as byproducts.
   - **Phagocytic Cells**: Immune cells like neutrophils and macrophages generate ROS through NADPH oxidase during the respiratory burst to destroy pathogens.

2. **Exogenous Sources**: Environmental factors contribute to ROS generation and oxidative stress. These include:

   - **Ultraviolet (UV) Radiation**: UV radiation from the sun can generate ROS in skin cells, leading to DNA damage and skin aging.

- ○ **Ionizing Radiation**: Exposure to ionizing radiation (e.g., X-rays) generates ROS through the radiolysis of water, causing cellular damage.
- ○ **Pollutants**: Air pollutants such as ozone and nitrogen dioxide can increase ROS production in the respiratory tract.
- ○ **Tobacco Smoke**: Contains numerous free radicals and chemicals that generate ROS, leading to oxidative damage in the lungs.
- ○ **Chemicals and Drugs**: Certain chemicals, including pesticides, and drugs can enhance ROS production and contribute to oxidative stress.

Mechanisms of ROS Damage:

1. **Lipid Peroxidation**: ROS, particularly hydroxyl radicals, can initiate the peroxidation of polyunsaturated fatty acids in cellular membranes. This leads to the formation of lipid peroxides and secondary products like malondialdehyde (MDA), which further propagate oxidative damage and disrupt membrane integrity and function.
2. **Protein Oxidation**: ROS can modify amino acid side chains in proteins, leading to the formation of carbonyl groups and cross-linking of protein molecules. This can result in altered protein structure and function, impair enzyme activity, and promote the formation of protein aggregates.
3. **DNA Damage**: ROS can cause a variety of modifications to DNA, including single and double-strand breaks, base modifications, and cross-linking. These changes can lead to mutations, impaired gene expression, and genomic instability, contributing to carcinogenesis and other diseases.

Role of Antioxidant Defense Mechanisms: The body has evolved several defense mechanisms to neutralize ROS and minimize oxidative damage. These include:

1. **Enzymatic Antioxidants:**

   - ○ **Superoxide Dismutase (SOD)**: Converts superoxide anion to hydrogen peroxide and oxygen.
   - ○ **Catalase**: Decomposes hydrogen peroxide into water and oxygen.

- **Glutathione Peroxidase**: Reduces hydrogen peroxide and lipid peroxides using glutathione as a substrate.

2. **Non-Enzymatic Antioxidants**:

  - **Vitamin C (Ascorbic Acid)**: A water-soluble antioxidant that scavenges ROS in the aqueous compartments of cells.
  - **Vitamin E (Tocopherols)**: A lipid-soluble antioxidant that protects cell membranes from lipid peroxidation.
  - **Glutathione**: A tripeptide that acts as a major intracellular antioxidant, maintaining the redox state and detoxifying peroxides.
  - **Flavonoids and Polyphenols**: Plant-derived antioxidants that neutralize ROS and enhance the body's antioxidant capacity.

3. **Repair Mechanisms**:

  - **DNA Repair Enzymes**: Correct oxidative damage to DNA.
  - **Proteolytic Systems**: Degrade oxidatively damaged proteins.
  - **Lipid Repair Mechanisms**: Restore oxidized lipids.

Reactive Oxygen Species (ROS) are highly reactive molecules that play essential roles in cell signaling and homeostasis. However, an overproduction of ROS or a deficiency in antioxidant defenses can lead to oxidative stress and subsequent cellular damage. Understanding the sources, types, and mechanisms of ROS is crucial for developing strategies to mitigate oxidative damage and prevent associated diseases. The balance between ROS production and antioxidant defenses is key to maintaining cellular health and preventing oxidative stress-related conditions.

4.1.3 Production of Free Radicals in Cells

Introduction: Free radicals are highly reactive molecules with unpaired electrons, and their production in cells is a natural part of metabolic processes. While free radicals play essential roles in cell signaling and homeostasis, an imbalance leading to excessive free radical production can result in oxidative stress and cellular damage. Understanding the pathways and sources of free radical production is crucial for comprehending their impact on health and disease.

Endogenous Production of Free Radicals:

1. **Mitochondrial Electron Transport Chain (ETC):**

   - **Process**: The mitochondrial electron transport chain (ETC) is the primary source of endogenous free radicals. During oxidative phosphorylation, electrons are transferred through complexes I to IV, generating a proton gradient that drives ATP synthesis. Occasionally, electrons escape from complexes I and III, reacting with molecular oxygen to form superoxide anion ($O_2\cdot^-$).

   Significance: Superoxide anion can be converted to hydrogen peroxide (H_2O_2) by superoxide dismutase (SOD). Hydrogen peroxide can further generate highly reactive hydroxyl radicals ($\cdot OH$) in the presence of transition metals like iron through the Fenton reaction: $H_2O_2 + Fe^{2+} \rightarrow \cdot OH + OH^- + Fe3^+$

   Impact: The production of ROS in mitochondria can lead to oxidative damage to mitochondrial DNA, proteins, and lipids, impairing mitochondrial function and contributing to aging and various diseases.

2. **Peroxisomes:**

   - **Process**: Peroxisomes are cellular organelles involved in lipid metabolism and detoxification. They generate hydrogen peroxide (H_2O_2) as a byproduct of fatty acid oxidation and other metabolic reactions. Enzymes like acyl-CoA oxidase catalyze the initial step in fatty acid β-oxidation, producing hydrogen peroxide.
   - **Significance**: Peroxisomes contain catalase, an enzyme that decomposes hydrogen peroxide into water and oxygen, thus preventing the accumulation of H2O2 and subsequent formation of hydroxyl radicals.
   - **Impact**: Dysregulation of peroxisomal function can lead to excessive ROS production and oxidative damage, contributing to metabolic disorders and neurodegenerative diseases.

3. **Endoplasmic Reticulum (ER):**

   - **Process**: The endoplasmic reticulum (ER) is involved in protein folding and post-translational modifications. During protein folding, disulfide bond formation is facilitated by the enzyme protein disulfide isomerase (PDI) and involves the generation of ROS as byproducts.

- ○ **Significance**: The ER contains enzymes such as ER oxidoreductin 1 (Ero1) that catalyze the oxidation of PDI, producing hydrogen peroxide.
- ○ **Impact**: Excessive ROS production in the ER can lead to ER stress and activation of the unfolded protein response (UPR), which can result in cell death if homeostasis is not restored.

4. **Phagocytic Cells**:

- ○ **Process**: Phagocytic cells, such as neutrophils and macrophages, produce large amounts of ROS as part of the immune response to destroy pathogens. This process, known as the respiratory burst, involves the enzyme NADPH oxidase, which transfers electrons from NADPH to molecular oxygen, generating superoxide anion ($O_2^{\cdot-}$).
- ○ **Significance**: Superoxide anion is further converted to hydrogen peroxide and other reactive species, which contribute to the antimicrobial activity of phagocytes.
- ○ **Impact**: While ROS production by phagocytes is essential for host defense, excessive or prolonged ROS production can cause tissue damage and contribute to chronic inflammatory diseases.

Exogenous Production of Free Radicals:

1. **Ultraviolet (UV) Radiation**:

- ○ **Process**: Exposure to ultraviolet (UV) radiation from the sun can generate ROS in skin cells. UV radiation can directly ionize cellular molecules and generate free radicals, including singlet oxygen ($^1O_2$) and hydroxyl radicals ($\cdot OH$).
- ○ **Significance**: UV-induced ROS can damage DNA, proteins, and lipids, leading to skin aging, sunburn, and an increased risk of skin cancer.
- ○ **Impact**: Chronic exposure to UV radiation and the resulting oxidative stress contribute to photoaging and the development of skin cancers such as melanoma.

2. **Ionizing Radiation**:

- ○ **Process**: Ionizing radiation, such as X-rays and gamma rays, can generate ROS through the radiolysis of water. The interaction of ionizing radiation with water molecules produces hydroxyl radicals ($\cdot$OH), hydrogen atoms (H$\cdot$), and other reactive species.
- ○ **Significance**: The generated ROS can cause extensive damage to cellular components, including DNA, leading to mutations, chromosomal aberrations, and cell death.
- ○ **Impact**: Ionizing radiation is used in medical imaging and cancer therapy but also poses risks of radiation-induced damage to healthy tissues and long-term health effects such as cancer.

3. **Environmental Pollutants**:

- ○ **Process**: Air pollutants such as ozone (O3), nitrogen dioxide (NO2), and particulate matter can increase ROS production in the respiratory tract. These pollutants can directly generate free radicals or induce the production of ROS through inflammatory responses.
- ○ **Significance**: Pollutant-induced ROS can cause oxidative damage to lung tissue, leading to respiratory diseases such as asthma, chronic obstructive pulmonary disease (COPD), and lung cancer.
- ○ **Impact**: Chronic exposure to environmental pollutants and the associated oxidative stress contribute to the development and progression of respiratory and cardiovascular diseases.

4. **Tobacco Smoke**:

- ○ **Process**: Tobacco smoke contains numerous free radicals and reactive chemicals that can generate ROS in the lungs. The inhalation of tobacco smoke results in the direct introduction of ROS and the activation of inflammatory responses that further increase ROS production.
- ○ **Significance**: The ROS generated by tobacco smoke can damage lung tissue, leading to chronic bronchitis, emphysema, and lung cancer.
- ○ **Impact**: Smoking-related oxidative stress is a major risk factor for respiratory diseases, cardiovascular diseases, and various cancers.

5. **Chemicals and Drugs**:

- **Process**: Certain chemicals and drugs can enhance ROS production through metabolic activation. For example, some chemotherapeutic agents generate ROS as part of their mechanism of action, which can damage cancer cells but also affect healthy cells.
- **Significance**: Chemical-induced ROS can cause oxidative damage to cellular components, contributing to drug toxicity and adverse effects.
- **Impact**: The balance between therapeutic benefits and oxidative damage is critical in the use of ROS-generating drugs in clinical settings.

The production of free radicals in cells is a complex process involving various endogenous and exogenous sources. While free radicals are essential for normal cellular functions and immune defense, an imbalance leading to excessive ROS production can result in oxidative stress and cellular damage. Understanding the pathways and sources of free radical production is crucial for developing strategies to mitigate oxidative damage and prevent related diseases. The body's antioxidant defense mechanisms, including enzymatic and non-enzymatic antioxidants, play a vital role in maintaining the balance between ROS production and elimination, ensuring cellular homeostasis and health.

4.2 Damaging Reactions of Free Radicals

4.2.1 On Lipids

Introduction: Free radicals, particularly **reactive oxygen species (ROS)**, can initiate damaging reactions on cellular components, including lipids, proteins, and DNA. Among these, lipid peroxidation is a significant process where free radicals attack lipids in cell membranes, leading to cellular dysfunction and contributing to various diseases. The peroxidation of lipids, especially polyunsaturated fatty acids (PUFAs), is a chain reaction that can cause extensive damage to cell membranes and lipoproteins.

Mechanism of Lipid Peroxidation:

1. **Initiation:**

   - The lipid peroxidation process begins with the abstraction of a hydrogen atom from a polyunsaturated fatty acid (PUFA) by a free radical, such as the hydroxyl radical ($\cdot$OH). This results in the formation of a lipid radical (L$\cdot$).

- **Reaction**: RH+·OH→R·+H2O

  - Here, RH represents a polyunsaturated fatty acid, and R· is the lipid radical.

2. Propagation:

- The lipid radical (L·) reacts with molecular oxygen (O2) to form a lipid peroxyl radical (LOO·).
- **Reaction**: R·+O2→ROO·R· + O2 → ROO·

  - The lipid peroxyl radical can further react with another PUFA, abstracting a hydrogen atom to form a lipid hydroperoxide (LOOH) and another lipid radical, perpetuating the chain reaction.

- **Reaction**: ROO·+RH→ROOH+R·

3. Decomposition:

- Lipid hydroperoxides (LOOH) are relatively unstable and can decompose into various secondary products, including malondialdehyde (MDA), 4-hydroxynonenal (4-HNE), and other reactive aldehydes.
- These decomposition products can further react with proteins, DNA, and other cellular components, causing extensive cellular damage.

4. Termination:

- The chain reaction of lipid peroxidation can be terminated when two radicals react to form a non-radical product.
- **Reaction**: R·+R·→R–R or R·+ROO·→ROOR
- ROORR·+ROO·→ROOR

  - Antioxidants, such as vitamin E (α-tocopherol), can donate an electron to lipid radicals, neutralizing them and preventing the propagation of the chain reaction.

Consequences of Lipid Peroxidation:

1. **Membrane Damage**:

   - Lipid peroxidation disrupts the integrity and fluidity of cell membranes. The incorporation of lipid hydroperoxides and other oxidation products into the membrane bilayer can alter its structure and function.
   - This can lead to increased membrane permeability, loss of membrane potential, and impaired function of membrane-bound proteins, such as receptors, ion channels, and enzymes.
   - Damage to cellular membranes can compromise cellular homeostasis, leading to cell death through necrosis or apoptosis.

2. **Cell Signaling Disruption**:

   - Lipid peroxidation products, such as 4-HNE, can modify signaling proteins and enzymes, disrupting normal cell signaling pathways.
   - These modifications can affect processes such as cell proliferation, differentiation, and apoptosis, contributing to the development and progression of diseases.

3. **Oxidized Low-Density Lipoprotein (OxLDL)**:

   - Lipid peroxidation of low-density lipoprotein (LDL) particles in the bloodstream leads to the formation of oxidized LDL (OxLDL).
   - OxLDL is recognized by scavenger receptors on macrophages, leading to the formation of foam cells and the development of atherosclerotic plaques.
   - The accumulation of atherosclerotic plaques in blood vessels can result in cardiovascular diseases, such as coronary artery disease, heart attacks, and strokes.

4. **Inflammatory Responses**:

   - Lipid peroxidation products, such as MDA and 4-HNE, can act as pro-inflammatory mediators, triggering inflammatory responses.
   - These products can activate transcription factors, such as NF-κB, leading to the expression of inflammatory cytokines and adhesion molecules.

○ Chronic inflammation induced by lipid peroxidation contributes to the pathogenesis of various diseases, including cardiovascular diseases, neurodegenerative disorders, and cancer.

Antioxidant Defense Mechanisms:

1. **Vitamin E (α-Tocopherol):**

   ○ Vitamin E is a lipid-soluble antioxidant that is incorporated into cell membranes and lipoproteins.
   ○ It protects against lipid peroxidation by donating an electron to lipid radicals, neutralizing them and preventing the propagation of the chain reaction.
   ○ **Reaction:** $ROO·+Vitamin\ E \rightarrow ROOH+Vitamin\ E·$

     ▪ The oxidized form of vitamin E (α-tocopheroxyl radical) can be regenerated by other antioxidants, such as vitamin C.

2. **Glutathione Peroxidase (GPx):**

   ○ Glutathione peroxidase is an enzyme that reduces lipid hydroperoxides (LOOH) to their corresponding alcohols (LOH), using glutathione (GSH) as a reducing agent.
   ○ **Reaction:** $ROOH+2GSH \rightarrow ROH+H_2O+GSSG$

     ▪ This reaction helps to neutralize lipid hydroperoxides and prevent their decomposition into more reactive products.

3. **Superoxide Dismutase (SOD) and Catalase:**

   ○ Superoxide dismutase (SOD) converts superoxide anion ($O_2·^-$) to hydrogen peroxide (H_2O_2), which is then decomposed to water and oxygen by catalase.
   ○ These enzymatic antioxidants help to reduce the levels of superoxide anion and hydrogen peroxide, thereby minimizing the initiation of lipid peroxidation.

The damaging reactions of free radicals on lipids, particularly through the process of lipid peroxidation, have significant implications for cellular function and overall health. Lipid peroxidation can disrupt cell membrane integrity, alter cell signaling, contribute to the development of atherosclerosis, and trigger inflammatory responses. The body employs various antioxidant defense mechanisms, including vitamin E, glutathione peroxidase, and enzymatic antioxidants, to protect against lipid peroxidation and mitigate its harmful effects. Understanding the mechanisms and consequences of lipid peroxidation is essential for developing strategies to prevent and manage oxidative stress-related diseases.

4.2.2 On Proteins

Introduction: Free radicals, particularly **reactive oxygen species (ROS)**, can cause extensive damage to proteins, leading to alterations in their structure, function, and interactions. Proteins are critical macromolecules involved in nearly all cellular processes, including enzymatic activity, signal transduction, structural support, and transport. Oxidative modifications of proteins can impair their function and contribute to various diseases, including neurodegenerative disorders, cardiovascular diseases, and aging.

Mechanisms of Protein Oxidation:

1. **Direct Oxidation by ROS:**

   - **Hydroxyl Radicals (·OH):** Hydroxyl radicals are highly reactive and can directly attack amino acid side chains in proteins, leading to the formation of carbonyl groups, such as aldehydes and ketones. This results in protein carbonylation, which is a hallmark of oxidative protein damage.

     - **Reaction:** $R\text{-}CH_2\text{-}R + \cdot OH \rightarrow R\text{-}CHOH\text{-}R \rightarrow R\text{-}CO\text{-}R + H_2O$

   - **Superoxide Anion (O2·-) and Hydrogen Peroxide (H2O2):** These ROS can also contribute to protein oxidation, either directly or indirectly, by generating more reactive species like hydroxyl radicals through the Fenton reaction.

2. **Metal-Catalyzed Oxidation (MCO):**

- Transition metals, such as iron (Fe) and copper (Cu), can catalyze the oxidation of proteins through the Fenton and Haber-Weiss reactions. These reactions generate highly reactive hydroxyl radicals that can attack protein residues.

Fenton Reaction: $H2O_2 + Fe^{2+} \rightarrow \cdot OH + OH^- + Fe3^+$

- **Haber-Weiss Reaction**: $O2 \cdot - + H_2O2 \rightarrow O2 + \cdot OH + OH^-$

- Metal-catalyzed oxidation often targets amino acid residues such as histidine, cysteine, methionine, tyrosine, and tryptophan.

3. **Lipid Peroxidation Products**:

- Secondary products of lipid peroxidation, such as malondialdehyde (MDA) and 4-hydroxynonenal (4-HNE), can form adducts with proteins, leading to cross-linking and modification of protein structure and function.

- **Reaction**: Protein + MDA/4-HNE → Protein-MDA/4-HNE adducts
  Consequences of Protein Oxidation:

1. **Loss of Enzymatic Activity**:

- Oxidative modification of amino acid residues in the active sites of enzymes can impair their catalytic activity. For example, oxidation of cysteine residues can disrupt disulfide bonds, affecting enzyme structure and function.
- **Impact**: This can lead to a decrease in metabolic efficiency and the accumulation of metabolic intermediates, contributing to cellular dysfunction and disease.

2. **Altered Protein Structure and Stability**:

- Oxidation of amino acid residues can lead to protein unfolding or misfolding, resulting in altered secondary and tertiary structures. This can affect protein stability and solubility, leading to aggregation and precipitation.

- ◦ **Impact**: Protein aggregates can disrupt cellular functions and are associated with neurodegenerative diseases such as Alzheimer's disease, Parkinson's disease, and amyotrophic lateral sclerosis (ALS).

3. **Protein-Protein Cross-Linking**:

- ◦ Oxidative modifications can lead to the formation of covalent cross-links between protein molecules. These cross-links can result from direct radical-radical reactions or through the action of bifunctional aldehydes like MDA and 4-HNE.
- ◦ **Impact**: Cross-linked proteins are often resistant to proteolytic degradation, leading to the accumulation of damaged proteins and contributing to cellular stress and apoptosis.

4. **Inhibition of Protein Synthesis**:

- ◦ Oxidative damage to ribosomal proteins and translation factors can impair the protein synthesis machinery, reducing the overall rate of protein production.
- ◦ **Impact**: This can lead to a decline in cellular function and repair mechanisms, exacerbating the effects of oxidative stress and contributing to aging and disease progression.

5. **Impaired Signal Transduction**:

- ◦ Many signaling proteins contain redox-sensitive cysteine residues that are crucial for their function. Oxidative modification of these residues can alter protein-protein interactions and disrupt signal transduction pathways.
- ◦ **Impact**: This can affect cellular processes such as growth, differentiation, and apoptosis, contributing to the development of diseases such as cancer and cardiovascular disorders.

Antioxidant Defense Mechanisms:

1. **Enzymatic Antioxidants**:

- **Superoxide Dismutase (SOD)**: Converts superoxide anion ($O_2^{\cdot-}$) to hydrogen peroxide (H_2O_2), which is further detoxified by catalase and glutathione peroxidase.
- **Catalase**: Decomposes hydrogen peroxide (H_2O_2) into water and oxygen, preventing the formation of hydroxyl radicals.
- **Glutathione Peroxidase (GPx)**: Reduces hydrogen peroxide and lipid hydroperoxides using glutathione (GSH) as a substrate, protecting proteins from oxidative damage.

2. **Non-Enzymatic Antioxidants**:

- **Glutathione (GSH)**: A tripeptide that acts as a major intracellular antioxidant, maintaining the redox state and protecting proteins from oxidative damage.
- **Vitamin C (Ascorbic Acid)**: A water-soluble antioxidant that scavenges ROS in the aqueous compartments of cells and regenerates oxidized vitamin E.
- **Vitamin E (Tocopherols)**: A lipid-soluble antioxidant that protects cell membranes from lipid peroxidation and preserves the integrity of membrane-bound proteins.

3. **Proteolytic Systems**:

- **Proteasome**: Degrades oxidized and misfolded proteins, preventing their accumulation and the formation of toxic aggregates.
- **Lysosomal Autophagy**: Engulfs and degrades damaged organelles and protein aggregates, maintaining cellular homeostasis.

4. **Repair Mechanisms**:

- **Methionine Sulfoxide Reductases (Msr)**: Enzymes that reduce oxidized methionine residues in proteins back to their functional form.
- **Thioredoxin and Glutaredoxin Systems**: Enzymatic systems that reduce oxidized cysteine residues and restore protein function.

The damaging reactions of free radicals on proteins, particularly through oxidative modifications, have significant implications for cellular function and overall health. Protein oxidation can lead to the loss of enzymatic activity, altered protein structure and stability, protein-protein cross-linking, impaired protein synthesis, and disrupted signal transduction. The body employs various antioxidant defense mechanisms, including enzymatic and non-enzymatic antioxidants, proteolytic systems, and repair mechanisms, to protect against protein oxidation and mitigate its harmful effects. Understanding the mechanisms and consequences of protein oxidation is essential for developing strategies to prevent and manage oxidative stress-related diseases.

4.2.3 On Carbohydrates

Introduction: Free radicals, particularly **reactive oxygen species (ROS)**, can also target carbohydrates, causing oxidative damage. While proteins and lipids are often considered primary targets of oxidative stress, carbohydrates, including simple sugars and complex polysaccharides, are also susceptible to modification by free radicals. Carbohydrate oxidation can lead to the formation of advanced glycation end-products (AGEs), which have been implicated in various pathological conditions, including diabetes, cardiovascular diseases, and aging.

Mechanisms of Carbohydrate Oxidation:

1. **Direct Oxidation by ROS:**

   - **Hydroxyl Radicals ($\cdot$OH):** Hydroxyl radicals are highly reactive and can attack carbohydrate molecules, leading to the abstraction of hydrogen atoms and the formation of carbon-centered radicals. These radicals can further react with oxygen to produce peroxyl radicals.
   - **Reaction:** $C\text{-}H + \cdot OH \rightarrow C\cdot + H2O$
   - **Reaction:** $C\cdot + O2 \rightarrow COO\cdot$
   - These reactions can cause fragmentation of carbohydrate chains, altering their structure and function.

2. **Formation of Advanced Glycation End-Products (AGEs):**

   - **Maillard Reaction:** The Maillard reaction involves the non-enzymatic reaction between reducing sugars and amino groups in proteins or lipids, leading to the formation of Schiff bases and Amadori products. These early glycation products can undergo further oxidation and rearrangement to form advanced glycation end-products (AGEs).

- ◦ **Oxidative Glycation**: In the presence of ROS, the glycation process is accelerated, and the formation of AGEs is enhanced. ROS can oxidize intermediate glycation products, leading to the generation of highly reactive dicarbonyl compounds, such as glyoxal, methylglyoxal, and 3-deoxyglucosone.
- ◦ **Reaction**: Glucose+Protein→Schiff Base→Amadori Product→AGEs \
- ◦ **Reaction**: Amadori Product+ROS→Reactive Dicarbonyls→AGEs

3. Metal-Catalyzed Oxidation (MCO):

- ◦ Transition metals, such as iron (Fe) and copper (Cu), can catalyze the oxidation of carbohydrates through Fenton-like reactions. These metals can generate hydroxyl radicals from hydrogen peroxide, which can then oxidize carbohydrates.
- ◦ **Reaction**: $H2O2 + Fe^{2+} → ·OH + OH- + Fe3^{+}$
- ◦ **Impact**: The generated hydroxyl radicals can initiate oxidative damage to carbohydrate molecules, leading to fragmentation and the formation of reactive intermediates.

Consequences of Carbohydrate Oxidation:

1. Alteration of Glycoconjugates:

- ◦ Glycoconjugates, such as glycoproteins and glycolipids, play critical roles in cell signaling, adhesion, and immune response. Oxidative modification of the carbohydrate moieties in glycoconjugates can alter their structure and function.
- ◦ **Impact**: This can disrupt cell-cell and cell-matrix interactions, impairing cellular communication and immune recognition.

2. Formation of Advanced Glycation End-Products (AGEs):

- ◦ AGEs are highly reactive molecules that can cross-link with proteins, lipids, and nucleic acids, leading to the formation of stable and often insoluble complexes.
- ◦ **Impact**: AGEs can accumulate in tissues over time, contributing to the structural and functional changes associated with aging and chronic diseases. They can also induce inflammation and oxidative stress by

interacting with receptors for AGEs (RAGEs) on the cell surface.

3. **Impairment of Cellular Metabolism**:

- Oxidative damage to glycogen, the primary storage form of glucose in cells, can impair its structure and function. This can affect glycogen metabolism and storage, leading to energy imbalances in cells.
- **Impact**: Impaired glycogen metabolism can compromise cellular energy homeostasis, particularly in tissues with high energy demands, such as muscles and the liver.

4. **Inhibition of Enzymatic Activity**:

- Enzymes involved in carbohydrate metabolism, such as glycolytic enzymes, can be modified by ROS and AGEs, leading to alterations in their activity and stability.
- **Impact**: Inhibition of these enzymes can disrupt metabolic pathways, leading to the accumulation of metabolic intermediates and decreased energy production.

Antioxidant Defense Mechanisms:

1. **Enzymatic Antioxidants**:

- **Superoxide Dismutase (SOD)**: Converts superoxide anion ($O_2^{\cdot-}$) to hydrogen peroxide (H_2O_2), which is further detoxified by catalase and glutathione peroxidase.
- **Catalase**: Decomposes hydrogen peroxide (H_2O_2) into water and oxygen, preventing the formation of hydroxyl radicals.
- **Glutathione Peroxidase (GPx)**: Reduces hydrogen peroxide and lipid hydroperoxides using glutathione (GSH) as a substrate, protecting carbohydrates from oxidative damage.

2. **Non-Enzymatic Antioxidants**:

- **Vitamin C (Ascorbic Acid)**: A water-soluble antioxidant that scavenges ROS in the aqueous compartments of cells and regenerates oxidized vitamin E.

- ◦ **Vitamin E (Tocopherols)**: A lipid-soluble antioxidant that protects cell membranes from lipid peroxidation and preserves the integrity of membrane-bound carbohydrates.
- ◦ **Glutathione (GSH)**: A tripeptide that acts as a major intracellular antioxidant, maintaining the redox state and protecting carbohydrates from oxidative damage.

3. **Detoxification Systems**:

- ◦ **Glyoxalase System**: Detoxifies reactive dicarbonyl compounds, such as methylglyoxal, formed during oxidative glycation. The glyoxalase system converts these reactive intermediates into less harmful compounds, preventing the formation of AGEs.
- ◦ **Reaction**: Methylglyoxal+GSH→Hemithioacetal→D-lactate
- ◦ The damaging reactions of free radicals on carbohydrates, particularly through direct oxidation and the formation of advanced glycation end-products (AGEs), have significant implications for cellular function and overall health. Carbohydrate oxidation can alter glycoconjugates, impair glycogen metabolism, inhibit enzymatic activity, and contribute to the accumulation of AGEs, which are associated with aging and chronic diseases. The body employs various antioxidant defense mechanisms, including enzymatic and non-enzymatic antioxidants, as well as detoxification systems, to protect against carbohydrate oxidation and mitigate its harmful effects. Understanding the mechanisms and consequences of carbohydrate oxidation is essential for developing strategies to prevent and manage oxidative stress-related diseases.

4.2.4 On Nucleic Acids

Introduction: Free radicals, particularly **reactive oxygen species (ROS)**, can cause significant damage to nucleic acids, including DNA and RNA. Oxidative damage to nucleic acids is a critical factor in mutagenesis, carcinogenesis, and aging. Understanding the mechanisms by which free radicals damage nucleic acids and the consequences of such damage is crucial for developing strategies to protect against oxidative stress and maintain genomic integrity.

Mechanisms of Nucleic Acid Oxidation:

1. **Direct Attack by ROS**:

   - **Hydroxyl Radicals (·OH)**: Hydroxyl radicals are highly reactive and can directly attack the deoxyribose sugar and nucleotide bases in DNA and RNA. The hydroxyl radical can abstract hydrogen atoms from the sugar-phosphate backbone, leading to strand breaks and base modifications.

     - **Reaction**: $DNA + \cdot OH \rightarrow DNA \cdot + H_2O$

   - **Superoxide Anion (O2·-) and Hydrogen Peroxide** : These ROS can generate hydroxyl radicals in the presence of transition metals through the Fenton reaction, indirectly causing DNA damage.

2. **Base Modifications**:

   - Oxidative stress can lead to the modification of nucleotide bases, resulting in the formation of various oxidative lesions. Common oxidative base modifications include:

     - **8-Oxo-7,8-dihydroguanine (8-oxoG)**: One of the most frequent and mutagenic lesions, formed by the oxidation of guanine.
     - **Thymine Glycol**: Formed by the oxidation of thymine, leading to base pairing errors.
     - **5-Hydroxycytosine** and **5-Hydroxyuracil**: Oxidative products of cytosine and uracil, respectively.

3. **Sugar-Phosphate Backbone Damage**:

   - Free radicals can cause cleavage of the sugar-phosphate backbone, resulting in single-strand breaks (SSBs) and double-strand breaks (DSBs). These breaks can disrupt the continuity of the DNA helix and interfere with replication and transcription.

4. **Cross-Linking**:

   - ROS can induce the formation of covalent cross-links between DNA strands (interstrand cross-links) or between DNA and proteins (DNA-protein cross-links). These cross-links can block replication and transcription, leading to cell death or mutations.

Consequences of Nucleic Acid Oxidation:

1. **Mutagenesis:**

   - Oxidative lesions in DNA can cause base mispairing during replication, leading to mutations. For example, 8-oxoG can pair with adenine instead of cytosine, resulting in G to T transversions.
   - **Impact:** Accumulation of mutations can lead to genomic instability, contributing to carcinogenesis and the development of various cancers.

2. **Replication and Transcription Interference:**

   - Oxidative damage to DNA can impede the progression of DNA polymerase and RNA polymerase, leading to replication fork stalling and transcriptional blocks.
   - **Impact:** This can cause replication stress, incomplete replication, and reduced gene expression, affecting cell proliferation and function.

3. **Apoptosis and Cell Death:**

   - Extensive oxidative damage to DNA can activate cell death pathways, including apoptosis. Cells with severe DNA damage may undergo programmed cell death to prevent the propagation of damaged DNA.
   - **Impact:** Apoptosis triggered by DNA damage is a protective mechanism but can contribute to tissue degeneration and aging.

4. **Cancer Development:**

   - Persistent oxidative stress and DNA damage can lead to the activation of oncogenes or inactivation of tumor suppressor genes. This genomic instability can drive the transformation of normal cells into cancerous cells.
   - **Impact:** Oxidative DNA damage is implicated in the initiation and progression of various cancers, including lung, breast, and colon

cancer.

5. **Aging and Age-Related Diseases**:

   - Accumulation of oxidative DNA damage over time contributes to the aging process and the development of age-related diseases. Mitochondrial DNA (mtDNA) is particularly susceptible to oxidative damage due to its proximity to the electron transport chain and lack of protective histones.
   - **Impact**: Oxidative damage to mtDNA can impair mitochondrial function, leading to reduced energy production and increased production of ROS, creating a vicious cycle of oxidative stress and cellular aging.

Antioxidant Defense Mechanisms:

1. **DNA Repair Mechanisms**:

   - **Base Excision Repair (BER)**: BER is the primary pathway for repairing oxidative base lesions, such as 8-oxoG. The enzyme 8-oxoguanine glycosylase (OGG1) recognizes and excises the damaged base, followed by DNA polymerase and ligase to restore the DNA strand.

     - **Reaction**: 8-oxoG+OGG1→AP site+Base

   - **Nucleotide Excision Repair (NER)**: NER is involved in removing bulky DNA lesions and cross-links. It recognizes the distortion in the DNA helix, excises the damaged segment, and fills the gap with newly synthesized DNA.
   - **Mismatch Repair (MMR)**: MMR corrects base mismatches and insertion/deletion loops that arise during DNA replication. It plays a role in repairing oxidative lesions that result in base mispairing.

2. **Enzymatic Antioxidants**:

   - **Superoxide Dismutase (SOD)**: Converts superoxide anion ($O2^{\cdot-}$) to hydrogen peroxide ($H2O2$), reducing the risk of hydroxyl radical formation.

- ○ **Catalase**: Decomposes hydrogen peroxide (H2O2) into water and oxygen, preventing the formation of hydroxyl radicals.
- ○ **Glutathione Peroxidase (GPx)**: Reduces hydrogen peroxide and lipid hydroperoxides using glutathione (GSH) as a substrate, protecting nucleic acids from oxidative damage.

3. **Non-Enzymatic Antioxidants**:

- ○ **Vitamin C (Ascorbic Acid)**: A water-soluble antioxidant that scavenges ROS in the aqueous compartments of cells and regenerates oxidized vitamin E.
- ○ **Vitamin E (Tocopherols)**: A lipid-soluble antioxidant that protects cell membranes and nucleic acids from oxidative damage.
- ○ **Glutathione (GSH)**: A tripeptide that acts as a major intracellular antioxidant, maintaining the redox state and protecting nucleic acids from oxidative damage.

The damaging reactions of free radicals on nucleic acids, particularly through direct oxidation and the formation of oxidative lesions, have significant implications for genomic integrity and cellular function. Nucleic acid oxidation can lead to mutagenesis, replication and transcription interference, apoptosis, cancer development, and aging. The body employs various antioxidant defense mechanisms, including DNA repair pathways, enzymatic and non-enzymatic antioxidants, to protect against nucleic acid oxidation and maintain genomic stability. Understanding the mechanisms and consequences of nucleic acid oxidation is essential for developing strategies to prevent and manage oxidative stress-related diseases and promote healthy aging.

4.3 Measurement of Free Radicals

4.3.1 Lipid Peroxidation Products

Introduction: Lipid peroxidation is a critical process where free radicals attack polyunsaturated fatty acids (PUFAs) in cell membranes, leading to the formation of lipid peroxidation products. These products serve as biomarkers for oxidative stress and are widely used in research and clinical settings to measure the extent of lipid peroxidation and the presence of free radicals in biological systems. The most commonly measured lipid peroxidation products include malondialdehyde (MDA), 4-hydroxynonenal (4-HNE), and isoprostanes.

Measurement of Lipid Peroxidation Products:

1. **Malondialdehyde (MDA)**:

   ○ **Formation**: MDA is one of the most well-known and widely measured lipid peroxidation products. It is formed as a secondary product during the breakdown of PUFAs, particularly arachidonic acid, by ROS.
   ○ **Detection Methods**:

     - **Thiobarbituric Acid Reactive Substances (TBARS) Assay**: The TBARS assay is a popular method for measuring MDA. In this assay, MDA reacts with thiobarbituric acid (TBA) to form a pink chromogen that can be quantified spectrophotometrically at 532 nm. Despite its popularity, the TBARS assay is not entirely specific for MDA and can react with other aldehydes, leading to potential overestimation.

       - **Procedure**:

         1. Biological samples (e.g., plasma, tissue homogenates) are mixed with TBA reagent.
         2. The mixture is heated to induce the reaction between MDA and TBA.
         3. The resulting chromogen is measured spectrophotometrically.

     - **High-Performance Liquid Chromatography (HPLC)**: HPLC provides a more specific and accurate measurement of MDA. It involves separating MDA from other components in the sample using a chromatographic column, followed by detection with a UV or fluorescence detector.

       - **Procedure**:

         1. Sample preparation involves derivatization of MDA with a suitable reagent (e.g., 2,4-dinitrophenylhydrazine).
         2. The derivatized MDA is separated using an HPLC column.

3. Detection is carried out using UV or fluorescence detection.

2. **4-Hydroxynonenal (4-HNE)**:

- **Formation**: 4-HNE is a highly reactive α,β-unsaturated aldehyde formed during the peroxidation of omega-6 PUFAs, such as linoleic acid. It is considered a major bioactive marker of lipid peroxidation due to its ability to form adducts with proteins, DNA, and other biomolecules.
- **Detection Methods**:

  - **Enzyme-Linked Immunosorbent Assay (ELISA)**: ELISA kits specific for 4-HNE-protein adducts are available and widely used for quantifying 4-HNE in biological samples. These assays use antibodies that specifically recognize 4-HNE adducts, providing high sensitivity and specificity.

    - **Procedure**:

      1. Samples are incubated with a primary antibody specific to 4-HNE-protein adducts.
      2. A secondary antibody conjugated to an enzyme (e.g., horseradish peroxidase) is added.
      3. The enzymatic reaction produces a color change that is measured spectrophotometrically.

  - **Gas Chromatography-Mass Spectrometry (GC-MS)**: GC-MS is a highly sensitive and specific method for measuring 4-HNE. It involves derivatization of 4-HNE, followed by separation using gas chromatography and detection with mass spectrometry.

    - **Procedure**:

      1. Sample preparation involves derivatization of 4-HNE (e.g., using pentafluorobenzylhydroxylamine).
      2. The derivatized 4-HNE is separated using a gas chromatograph.

3. Detection is carried out using a mass spectrometer to identify and quantify 4-HNE.

3. **Isoprostanes**:

- **Formation**: Isoprostanes are a family of prostaglandin-like compounds formed non-enzymatically by the free radical-catalyzed peroxidation of arachidonic acid. They are considered reliable markers of oxidative stress and lipid peroxidation.
- **Detection Methods**:

  - **Liquid Chromatography-Tandem Mass Spectrometry (LC-MS/MS)**: LC-MS/MS is the gold standard for measuring isoprostanes due to its high sensitivity and specificity. This method allows for the precise quantification of isoprostanes in complex biological matrices.

    - **Procedure**:

      1. Biological samples are extracted and purified to isolate isoprostanes.
      2. The purified isoprostanes are separated using liquid chromatography.
      3. Detection is carried out using tandem mass spectrometry, providing accurate identification and quantification.

  - **Immunoassays**: Immunoassays, including ELISA, are also available for measuring isoprostanes. These assays use antibodies specific to isoprostanes and provide a convenient and relatively sensitive method for their quantification.

    - **Procedure**:

      1. Samples are incubated with a primary antibody specific to isoprostanes.
      2. A secondary antibody conjugated to an enzyme is added.
      3. The enzymatic reaction produces a color change that is measured spectrophotometrically.

Significance of Measuring Lipid Peroxidation Products:

1. **Biomarkers of Oxidative Stress:** Lipid peroxidation products, such as MDA, 4-HNE, and isoprostanes, serve as reliable biomarkers of oxidative stress in biological systems. Their measurement provides insight into the extent of oxidative damage and the effectiveness of antioxidant defenses.
2. **Disease Diagnosis and Monitoring:** Elevated levels of lipid peroxidation products are associated with various diseases, including cardiovascular diseases, neurodegenerative disorders, diabetes, and cancer. Measuring these products can aid in the diagnosis, monitoring, and prognosis of these conditions.
3. **Evaluation of Antioxidant Therapies:** Monitoring lipid peroxidation products is essential for evaluating the efficacy of antioxidant therapies and interventions. Reductions in these biomarkers indicate the effectiveness of treatments in mitigating oxidative stress.
4. **Research Applications:** The measurement of lipid peroxidation products is widely used in research to study the mechanisms of oxidative damage, the role of oxidative stress in disease pathogenesis, and the development of novel therapeutic strategies.

The measurement of lipid peroxidation products, including malondialdehyde (MDA), 4-hydroxynonenal (4-HNE), and isoprostanes, is crucial for assessing oxidative stress and free radical-mediated damage in biological systems. Various detection methods, such as the TBARS assay, HPLC, ELISA, GC-MS, and LC-MS/MS, provide reliable and specific quantification of these biomarkers. Understanding the formation, detection, and significance of lipid peroxidation products is essential for diagnosing diseases, monitoring therapeutic interventions, and conducting research on oxidative stress and its implications for health and disease.

4.3.2 Lipid Hydroperoxides

Introduction: Lipid hydroperoxides are primary products of lipid peroxidation, formed when reactive oxygen species (ROS) attack polyunsaturated fatty acids (PUFAs) in cell membranes. These hydroperoxides are relatively stable compared to free radicals and can propagate further oxidation, leading to extensive cellular damage. The measurement of lipid hydroperoxides provides valuable information on the early stages of lipid peroxidation and the oxidative status of biological systems.

Formation of Lipid Hydroperoxides:

1. **Initiation:**

   - Lipid peroxidation begins with the abstraction of a hydrogen atom from a PUFA by a hydroxyl radical ($\cdot$OH), resulting in the formation of a lipid radical (L$\cdot$).
   - **Reaction:** $RH + \cdot OH \rightarrow R\cdot + H_2O$

2. **Propagation:**

   - The lipid radical (L$\cdot$) reacts with molecular oxygen (O2) to form a lipid peroxyl radical (LOO$\cdot$).
   - **Reaction:** $R\cdot + O2 \rightarrow ROO\cdot$
   - The lipid peroxyl radical then abstracts a hydrogen atom from another PUFA, forming a lipid hydroperoxide (LOOH) and a new lipid radical, propagating the chain reaction.
   - **Reaction:** $ROO\cdot + RH \rightarrow ROOH + R\cdot$

Detection and Measurement of Lipid Hydroperoxides:

1. **Ferrous Oxidation-Xylenol Orange (FOX) Assay:**

   - The FOX assay is a colorimetric method that detects lipid hydroperoxides based on their ability to oxidize ferrous ions (Fe2+) to ferric ions (Fe3+). The ferric ions then form a complex with xylenol orange, producing a color change that can be measured spectrophotometrically.
   - **Procedure:**

     1. Biological samples (e.g., plasma, tissue homogenates) are mixed with the FOX reagent, which contains ferrous ions and xylenol orange.
     2. The mixture is incubated to allow the oxidation of ferrous ions by lipid hydroperoxides.
     3. The resulting ferric-xylenol orange complex is measured spectrophotometrically at 560 nm.

2. **Iodometric Assay**:

- The iodometric assay quantifies lipid hydroperoxides based on their ability to oxidize iodide ions (I-) to iodine (I2). The amount of iodine formed is proportional to the concentration of lipid hydroperoxides and can be measured spectrophotometrically.
- **Procedure**:

  1. Samples are mixed with potassium iodide (KI) in an acidic medium.
  2. Lipid hydroperoxides oxidize iodide ions to iodine.
  3. The iodine formed is measured spectrophotometrically at 352 nm.

3. **High-Performance Liquid Chromatography (HPLC)**:

- HPLC is a highly sensitive and specific method for measuring lipid hydroperoxides. It involves the separation of lipid hydroperoxides from other components in the sample using a chromatographic column, followed by detection with a UV or fluorescence detector.
- **Procedure**:

  1. Samples are prepared and injected into the HPLC system.
  2. Lipid hydroperoxides are separated using a chromatographic column.
  3. Detection is carried out using UV or fluorescence detection, allowing precise quantification.

4. **Chemiluminescence-Based Assays**:

- Chemiluminescence-based assays detect lipid hydroperoxides based on the light emitted during their reaction with specific reagents. These assays provide high sensitivity and can measure low levels of lipid hydroperoxides in biological samples.
- **Procedure**:

  1. Samples are mixed with chemiluminescent reagents that react with lipid hydroperoxides.
  2. The emitted light is measured using a luminometer.

3. The intensity of the light emitted is proportional to the concentration of lipid hydroperoxides in the sample.

Significance of Measuring Lipid Hydroperoxides:

1. **Early Indicators of Oxidative Stress**: Lipid hydroperoxides are primary products of lipid peroxidation and serve as early indicators of oxidative stress in biological systems. Their measurement can provide insights into the initial stages of oxidative damage before more extensive lipid degradation occurs.
2. **Biomarkers for Disease Diagnosis and Monitoring**: Elevated levels of lipid hydroperoxides are associated with various diseases, including cardiovascular diseases, neurodegenerative disorders, diabetes, and cancer. Measuring these products can aid in the diagnosis, monitoring, and prognosis of these conditions.
3. **Evaluation of Antioxidant Therapies**: Monitoring lipid hydroperoxides is essential for evaluating the efficacy of antioxidant therapies and interventions. Reductions in these biomarkers indicate the effectiveness of treatments in mitigating oxidative stress.
4. **Research Applications**: The measurement of lipid hydroperoxides is widely used in research to study the mechanisms of oxidative damage, the role of oxidative stress in disease pathogenesis, and the development of novel therapeutic strategies.

The measurement of lipid hydroperoxides is crucial for assessing oxidative stress and free radical-mediated damage in biological systems. Various detection methods, such as the FOX assay, iodometric assay, HPLC, and chemiluminescence-based assays, provide reliable and specific quantification of these primary lipid peroxidation products. Understanding the formation, detection, and significance of lipid hydroperoxides is essential for diagnosing diseases, monitoring therapeutic interventions, and conducting research on

4.3.3 Malondialdehyde

Introduction: Malondialdehyde (MDA) is a well-known biomarker of oxidative stress and lipid peroxidation. It is one of the most abundant and commonly measured products of polyunsaturated fatty acid (PUFA) oxidation. MDA is formed through the decomposition of lipid hydroperoxides and can cause further damage by forming adducts with

DNA and proteins. Measuring MDA levels in biological samples is a valuable method for assessing the extent of lipid peroxidation and oxidative stress.
Formation of Malondialdehyde (MDA):

1. **Lipid Peroxidation Initiation:**

   ○ Lipid peroxidation begins with the abstraction of a hydrogen atom from a PUFA by reactive oxygen species (ROS), such as hydroxyl radicals ($\cdot OH$), resulting in the formation of a lipid radical ($L\cdot$).
   ○ **Reaction:** $RH + \cdot OH \rightarrow R\cdot + H_2O$

2. **Propagation:**

   ○ The lipid radical ($L\cdot$) reacts with molecular oxygen (O_2) to form a lipid peroxyl radical ($LOO\cdot$).
   ○ **Reaction:** $R\cdot + O_2 \rightarrow ROO\cdot$
   ○ The lipid peroxyl radical abstracts a hydrogen atom from another PUFA, forming a lipid hydroperoxide (LOOH) and a new lipid radical, propagating the chain reaction.
   ○ **Reaction:** $ROO\cdot + RH \rightarrow ROOH + R\cdot$ $R\cdot ROO\cdot + RH \rightarrow ROOH + R\cdot$

3. **Decomposition:**

   ○ Lipid hydroperoxides (LOOH) decompose to form secondary products, including MDA. The breakdown of lipid hydroperoxides involves cleavage of the carbon-carbon bonds in the fatty acid chains.
   ○ **Reaction:** $LOOH \rightarrow MDA + OtherProducts$

Detection and Measurement of Malondialdehyde (MDA):

1. **Thiobarbituric Acid Reactive Substances (TBARS) Assay:**

   ○ The TBARS assay is the most commonly used method for measuring MDA. It is based on the reaction between MDA and thiobarbituric acid (TBA) to form a pink chromogen that can be quantified spectrophotometrically.
   ○ **Procedure:**

1. Biological samples (e.g., plasma, serum, tissue homogenates) are mixed with TBA reagent.
2. The mixture is heated to induce the reaction between MDA and TBA.
3. The resulting pink chromogen is measured spectrophotometrically at 532 nm.
4. The concentration of MDA is calculated using a standard curve generated with known concentrations of MDA.

- **Advantages**: The TBARS assay is simple, cost-effective, and widely used.
- **Limitations**: The TBARS assay is not entirely specific for MDA, as other aldehydes can also react with TBA, leading to potential overestimation.

2. **High-Performance Liquid Chromatography (HPLC)**:

- HPLC is a more specific and accurate method for measuring MDA. It involves the separation of MDA from other components in the sample using a chromatographic column, followed by detection with a UV or fluorescence detector.
- **Procedure**:

1. Sample preparation involves derivatization of MDA with a suitable reagent (e.g., 2,4-dinitrophenylhydrazine or DNPH).
2. The derivatized MDA is separated using an HPLC column.
3. Detection is carried out using UV or fluorescence detection.
4. The concentration of MDA is determined by comparing the sample peak area to that of a standard curve.

- **Advantages**: HPLC provides high specificity and sensitivity for MDA measurement.
- **Limitations**: HPLC requires specialized equipment and is more time-consuming and expensive than the TBARS assay.

3. **Gas Chromatography-Mass Spectrometry (GC-MS)**:

○ GC-MS is another highly sensitive and specific method for measuring MDA. It involves derivatization of MDA, followed by separation using gas chromatography and detection with mass spectrometry.

○ **Procedure**:

1. Sample preparation involves derivatization of MDA (e.g., using pentafluorobenzylhydroxylamine or PFBHA).
2. The derivatized MDA is separated using a gas chromatograph.
3. Detection is carried out using a mass spectrometer to identify and quantify MDA.
4. The concentration of MDA is determined by comparing the sample peak area to that of a standard curve.

○ **Advantages**: GC-MS provides excellent sensitivity and specificity for MDA measurement.

○ **Limitations**: GC-MS is expensive, requires specialized equipment, and is time-consuming.

Significance of Measuring Malondialdehyde (MDA):

1. **Biomarker of Oxidative Stress**: MDA is a widely recognized biomarker of oxidative stress and lipid peroxidation. Measuring MDA levels provides insight into the extent of oxidative damage in biological systems.
2. **Disease Diagnosis and Monitoring**: Elevated MDA levels are associated with various diseases, including cardiovascular diseases, neurodegenerative disorders, diabetes, and cancer. Measuring MDA can aid in the diagnosis, monitoring, and prognosis of these conditions.
3. **Evaluation of Antioxidant Therapies**: Monitoring MDA levels is essential for evaluating the efficacy of antioxidant therapies and interventions. Reductions in MDA levels indicate the effectiveness of treatments in mitigating oxidative stress.
4. **Research Applications**: The measurement of MDA is widely used in research to study the mechanisms of oxidative damage, the role of oxidative stress in disease pathogenesis, and the development of novel therapeutic strategies.

The measurement of malondialdehyde (MDA) is crucial for assessing oxidative stress and free radical-mediated damage in biological systems.

Various detection methods, such as the TBARS assay, HPLC, and GC-MS, provide reliable and specific quantification of MDA. Understanding the formation, detection, and significance of MDA is essential for diagnosing diseases, monitoring therapeutic interventions, and conducting research on oxidative stress and its implications for health and disease.

Table 1: Types of Free Radicals

Type	Description	Examples
Reactive Oxygen Species (ROS)	Highly reactive molecules derived from oxygen	Superoxide anion ($O_2^{\bullet-}$), Hydrogen peroxide (H_2O_2), Hydroxyl radical ($\bullet OH$), Singlet oxygen ($1O_2$)
Reactive Nitrogen Species (RNS)	Reactive molecules derived from nitrogen	Nitric oxide ($NO\bullet$), Peroxynitrite ($ONOO-$), Nitrogen dioxide ($NO_2\bullet$)

Table 2: Endogenous Sources of Free Radicals

Source	Description	Examples
Mitochondria	Electron transport chain generates superoxide anions	Superoxide anion ($O_2^{\bullet-}$)
Peroxisomes	Enzymes like xanthine oxidase generate hydrogen peroxide	Hydrogen peroxide (H_2O_2)
Endoplasmic Reticulum	Protein folding processes generate ROS	Hydrogen peroxide (H_2O_2)
Phagocytic Cells	Immune cells produce ROS to destroy pathogens	Superoxide anion ($O_2^{\bullet-}$), Hydrogen peroxide (H_2O_2)

Table 3: Exogenous Sources of Free Radicals

Source	Description
Ultraviolet (UV) Radiation	Generates ROS in skin cells
Ionizing Radiation	Generates ROS through water radiolysis
Pollutants	Air pollutants like ozone and nitrogen dioxide increase ROS production
Tobacco Smoke	Contains free radicals and chemicals that generate ROS
Chemicals and Drugs	Certain chemicals enhance ROS production

Table 4: Mechanisms of Free Radical Damage

Mechanism	Description
Lipid Peroxidation	Free radicals attack polyunsaturated fatty acids, leading to lipid peroxides and membrane damage
Protein Oxidation	Free radicals modify amino acid side chains, leading to protein structure and function changes
DNA Damage	Free radicals cause strand breaks, base modifications, and cross-linking

Table 7: Key Free Radicals and Their Reactions

Free Radical	Key Reactions
Superoxide Anion ($O_2^{\cdot-}$)	Can undergo dismutation to form hydrogen peroxide, precursor for other ROS
Hydrogen Peroxide (H_2O_2)	Generates hydroxyl radicals in presence of transition metals
Hydroxyl Radical ($\cdot OH$)	Highly reactive, can attack and damage all types of macromolecules
Nitric Oxide ($NO\cdot$)	Can react with superoxide anion to form peroxynitrite, a potent oxidant

Table 8: Consequences of Oxidative Damage

Target	Consequences
Lipids	Membrane damage, loss of integrity, increased permeability
Proteins	Altered structure and function, aggregation, enzymatic activity loss
DNA	Mutations, impaired gene expression, genomic instability, cancer development

FIVE

FREE RADICALS IN DISEASE

5.1 Role in Specific Diseases

5.1.1 Diabetes Mellitus

Introduction: **Diabetes mellitus** is a chronic metabolic disorder characterized by hyperglycemia due to defects in insulin secretion, insulin action, or both. Oxidative stress, resulting from an imbalance between the production of free radicals and the body's antioxidant defenses, plays a significant role in the pathogenesis and complications of diabetes. **Free radicals**, particularly **reactive oxygen species (ROS)**, contribute to the development and progression of diabetes and its associated complications through various mechanisms.

Mechanisms of Free Radical Involvement in Diabetes Mellitus:

1. **Hyperglycemia-Induced Oxidative Stress**:

   - **Glucose Autoxidation**: High levels of glucose in the blood can undergo autoxidation, producing superoxide anion ($O_2{\cdot}^-$), hydrogen peroxide (**H2O$_2$**), and hydroxyl radicals ($\cdot$OH). These ROS can damage cells and tissues.

     - **Reaction**: $Glucose + O_2 \rightarrow O_2{\cdot}^- + Other\ Products$

   - **Protein Glycation**: Chronic hyperglycemia leads to the non-enzymatic glycation of proteins, forming advanced glycation end-products (AGEs). AGEs can generate ROS and activate inflammatory pathways, exacerbating oxidative stress.

- **Reaction:** Glucose+Protein→Schiff Base→Amadori Product→AGEs

2. Mitochondrial Dysfunction:

- ○ **Increased ROS Production:** In diabetes, mitochondrial dysfunction is common, leading to increased production of ROS. Hyperglycemia enhances the flow of electrons through the mitochondrial electron transport chain, resulting in the excessive generation of superoxide anion.
- ○ **Impact:** Excessive ROS production damages mitochondrial DNA, proteins, and lipids, impairing mitochondrial function and further increasing ROS production, creating a vicious cycle.

3. NADPH Oxidase Activation:

- ○ **Enzyme Activation:** Hyperglycemia and insulin resistance activate NADPH oxidase, an enzyme that generates superoxide anion by transferring electrons from NADPH to oxygen.
- ○ **Impact:** NADPH oxidase-derived ROS contribute to endothelial dysfunction, inflammation, and the progression of diabetic complications.

4. Polyol Pathway:

- ○ **Sorbitol Accumulation:** Under hyperglycemic conditions, excess glucose is converted to sorbitol via the enzyme aldose reductase. Sorbitol is then converted to fructose by sorbitol dehydrogenase, consuming NADPH and reducing the availability of NADPH for antioxidant defenses.
- ○ **Impact:** Decreased NADPH levels impair the regeneration of glutathione (GSH), a crucial intracellular antioxidant, leading to increased oxidative stress.

Consequences of Oxidative Stress in Diabetes Mellitus:

1. **Beta-Cell Dysfunction**:

   - **Oxidative Damage**: Pancreatic beta-cells are particularly susceptible to oxidative damage due to their low antioxidant capacity. ROS can damage beta-cell DNA, proteins, and lipids, impairing insulin secretion and contributing to beta-cell apoptosis.
   - **Impact**: Beta-cell dysfunction and loss lead to decreased insulin production, exacerbating hyperglycemia and the progression of diabetes.

2. **Insulin Resistance**:

   - **Inflammatory Pathways**: Oxidative stress activates inflammatory signaling pathways, such as NF-κB, leading to the production of pro-inflammatory cytokines. These cytokines interfere with insulin signaling, promoting insulin resistance.
   - **Impact**: Insulin resistance impairs glucose uptake by tissues, further increasing blood glucose levels and perpetuating oxidative stress.

3. **Vascular Complications**:

   - **Endothelial Dysfunction**: ROS damage endothelial cells, leading to impaired vasodilation, increased vascular permeability, and the development of atherosclerosis.
   - **Microvascular Complications**: Oxidative stress contributes to the development of diabetic retinopathy, nephropathy, and neuropathy by damaging small blood vessels in the eyes, kidneys, and nerves.
   - **Macrovascular Complications**: Increased ROS levels promote the formation of atherosclerotic plaques, increasing the risk of cardiovascular diseases such as coronary artery disease, stroke, and peripheral artery disease.

Antioxidant Defense Mechanisms:

1. **Enzymatic Antioxidants**:

   - **Superoxide Dismutase (SOD)**: Converts superoxide anion to hydrogen peroxide, reducing the levels of superoxide radicals.

- **Catalase**: Decomposes hydrogen peroxide into water and oxygen, preventing the formation of hydroxyl radicals.
- **Glutathione Peroxidase (GPx)**: Reduces hydrogen peroxide and lipid hydroperoxides using glutathione as a substrate.

2. **Non-Enzymatic Antioxidants**:

- **Vitamin C (Ascorbic Acid)**: A water-soluble antioxidant that scavenges ROS and regenerates other antioxidants, such as vitamin E.
- **Vitamin E (Tocopherols)**: A lipid-soluble antioxidant that protects cell membranes from lipid peroxidation.
- **Glutathione (GSH)**: A tripeptide that acts as a major intracellular antioxidant, maintaining the redox state and detoxifying peroxides.

3. **Nutritional and Pharmacological Interventions**:

- **Dietary Antioxidants**: Consuming a diet rich in antioxidants, such as fruits, vegetables, nuts, and whole grains, can enhance the body's antioxidant defenses.
- **Pharmacological Antioxidants**: Supplementation with antioxidants, such as alpha-lipoic acid, N-acetylcysteine, and coenzyme Q10, can help reduce oxidative stress in diabetic patients.
- **Anti-Inflammatory Agents**: Medications that reduce inflammation, such as aspirin and statins, can also help mitigate oxidative stress and its complications.

Oxidative stress, driven by the overproduction of free radicals and inadequate antioxidant defenses, plays a critical role in the pathogenesis and complications of diabetes mellitus. Understanding the mechanisms by which free radicals contribute to beta-cell dysfunction, insulin resistance, and vascular complications is essential for developing effective therapeutic strategies. Enhancing antioxidant defenses through dietary, lifestyle, and pharmacological interventions can help mitigate oxidative stress, improve glycemic control, and reduce the risk of diabetic complications.

5.1.2 Inflammation

Introduction: Inflammation is a complex biological response to harmful stimuli such as pathogens, damaged cells, or irritants. It is a protective mechanism aimed at removing the injurious stimuli and initiating the healing process. However, chronic inflammation can lead to various diseases, including cardiovascular diseases, cancer, diabetes, and neurodegenerative disorders. **Free radicals**, particularly **reactive oxygen species (ROS)** and **reactive nitrogen species (RNS)**, play a significant role in the initiation and propagation of inflammatory responses.

Mechanisms of Free Radical Involvement in Inflammation:

1. **Activation of Immune Cells:**

   - **Phagocytic Cells**: Immune cells such as neutrophils, macrophages, and monocytes are activated in response to inflammatory signals. These cells generate large amounts of ROS and RNS during the respiratory burst to destroy invading pathogens and clear damaged tissue.
   - **NADPH Oxidase**: The enzyme NADPH oxidase is activated in phagocytic cells, producing superoxide anion ($O_2^{\cdot-}$) from oxygen.
   - **Myeloperoxidase (MPO)**: Neutrophils release MPO, which converts hydrogen peroxide (H_2O_2) into hypochlorous acid (HOCl), a potent antimicrobial agent.
   - **Inducible Nitric Oxide Synthase (iNOS)**: Macrophages and other immune cells express iNOS, producing nitric oxide ($NO^{\cdot}$) from L-arginine. Nitric oxide reacts with superoxide anion to form peroxynitrite ($ONOO^-$), a highly reactive RNS.

2. **Oxidative Damage and Inflammatory Signaling:**

   - **Lipid Peroxidation**: ROS can induce lipid peroxidation, generating lipid hydroperoxides and secondary products such as malondialdehyde (MDA) and 4-hydroxynonenal (4-HNE). These products can further damage cellular membranes and activate inflammatory pathways.
   - **Protein Oxidation**: Oxidative modification of proteins can alter their structure and function, leading to the activation of pro-inflammatory signaling pathways. For example, oxidized proteins can activate the nuclear factor kappa B (NF-κB) pathway, promoting the expression of pro-inflammatory cytokines.
   - **DNA Damage**: ROS-induced DNA damage can activate the p53 pathway and other stress response pathways, leading to the

production of inflammatory mediators.

3. **Activation of Inflammatory Pathways**:

   ○ **NF-κB Pathway**: ROS and RNS activate the NF-κB pathway, a key regulator of inflammation. NF-κB translocates to the nucleus and promotes the transcription of pro-inflammatory cytokines, chemokines, and adhesion molecules.
   ○ **Mitogen-Activated Protein Kinases (MAPKs)**: ROS activate MAPKs, including extracellular signal-regulated kinase (ERK), c-Jun N-terminal kinase (JNK), and p38 MAPK. These kinases regulate the production of pro-inflammatory cytokines and mediate inflammatory responses.
   ○ **Janus Kinase/Signal Transducer and Activator of Transcription (JAK/STAT) Pathway**: The JAK/STAT pathway is activated by cytokines and growth factors. ROS can enhance the activation of this pathway, promoting the expression of inflammatory genes.

Consequences of Chronic Inflammation Mediated by Free Radicals:

1. **Tissue Damage**:

   ○ **Oxidative Stress**: Persistent production of ROS and RNS leads to chronic oxidative stress, causing continuous damage to cellular components, including lipids, proteins, and DNA.
   ○ **Fibrosis**: Chronic inflammation can result in fibrosis, characterized by excessive deposition of extracellular matrix components, leading to tissue stiffness and impaired function.

2. **Autoimmune Diseases**:

   ○ **Immune Dysregulation**: Chronic oxidative stress can dysregulate the immune system, promoting autoimmunity. Oxidatively modified self-antigens can be recognized as foreign, triggering an autoimmune response.
   ○ **Examples**: Diseases such as rheumatoid arthritis, systemic lupus erythematosus, and multiple sclerosis involve oxidative stress and chronic inflammation.

3. **Cardiovascular Diseases**:

- **Atherosclerosis**: Chronic inflammation and oxidative stress contribute to the development of atherosclerosis. ROS induce endothelial dysfunction, promote the oxidation of low-density lipoprotein (LDL), and facilitate the formation of atherosclerotic plaques.
- **Hypertension**: Oxidative stress can impair nitric oxide bioavailability, leading to endothelial dysfunction and increased vascular resistance, contributing to hypertension.

4. **Cancer**:

- **DNA Mutations**: ROS-induced DNA damage can lead to mutations and genomic instability, promoting carcinogenesis. Inflammatory cytokines and growth factors can support tumor growth and metastasis.
- **Tumor Microenvironment**: Chronic inflammation creates a pro-tumorigenic microenvironment, characterized by increased angiogenesis, immune evasion, and tissue remodeling.

5. **Neurodegenerative Diseases**:

- **Oxidative Damage**: Chronic oxidative stress and inflammation in the brain can lead to neurodegenerative diseases such as Alzheimer's disease, Parkinson's disease, and amyotrophic lateral sclerosis (ALS).
- **Neuronal Death**: ROS and RNS can cause neuronal death through oxidative damage to lipids, proteins, and DNA, as well as the activation of apoptotic pathways.

Antioxidant and Anti-Inflammatory Defense Mechanisms:

1. **Endogenous Antioxidants**:

- **Superoxide Dismutase (SOD)**: Converts superoxide anion to hydrogen peroxide, reducing oxidative stress.
- **Catalase**: Decomposes hydrogen peroxide into water and oxygen.

- ◦ **Glutathione Peroxidase (GPx)**: Reduces hydrogen peroxide and lipid hydroperoxides.

2. **Dietary Antioxidants**:

   - ◦ **Vitamin C (Ascorbic Acid)**: Scavenges ROS and regenerates other antioxidants.
   - ◦ **Vitamin E (Tocopherols)**: Protects cell membranes from lipid peroxidation.
   - ◦ **Polyphenols**: Found in fruits, vegetables, tea, and wine, polyphenols have strong antioxidant and anti-inflammatory properties.

3. **Pharmacological Interventions**:

   - ◦ **Non-Steroidal Anti-Inflammatory Drugs (NSAIDs)**: Inhibit cyclooxygenase (COX) enzymes, reducing the production of pro-inflammatory prostaglandins.
   - ◦ **Corticosteroids**: Suppress inflammation by inhibiting multiple inflammatory pathways.
   - ◦ **Statins**: Reduce oxidative stress and inflammation by lowering cholesterol levels and modulating immune responses.

Free radicals, particularly ROS and RNS, play a critical role in the initiation and propagation of inflammation. Chronic inflammation mediated by oxidative stress contributes to the pathogenesis of various diseases, including cardiovascular diseases, cancer, autoimmune disorders, and neurodegenerative diseases. Understanding the mechanisms by which free radicals influence inflammation and the consequences of chronic oxidative stress is essential for developing effective therapeutic strategies. Enhancing antioxidant and anti-inflammatory defenses through dietary, lifestyle, and pharmacological interventions can help mitigate oxidative stress and reduce the risk of inflammation-related diseases.

5.1.3 Ischemic Reperfusion Injury

Introduction: Ischemic reperfusion (I/R) injury is a complex pathological process that occurs when blood supply to an organ or tissue is temporarily interrupted (ischemia) and then restored (reperfusion). While reperfusion is essential to prevent permanent tissue damage, it paradoxically results in additional injury due to the generation of free radicals, particularly reactive oxygen species (ROS). This condition is commonly associated with heart attacks, strokes, organ transplantation, and other clinical scenarios involving transient loss of blood flow.

Mechanisms of Free Radical Involvement in Ischemic Reperfusion Injury:

1. **Ischemia Phase:**

   - **Reduced Oxygen Supply:** During ischemia, the lack of oxygen impairs oxidative phosphorylation in mitochondria, leading to a depletion of ATP and accumulation of metabolic waste products such as lactate and hydrogen ions.
   - **Anaerobic Metabolism:** Cells switch to anaerobic metabolism, resulting in the production of lactic acid and a decrease in intracellular pH.
   - **Ion Imbalance:** The energy-dependent ion pumps (such as Na+/K+ ATPase) fail, causing an influx of sodium and calcium ions and efflux of potassium ions, leading to cellular edema and dysfunction.

2. **Reperfusion Phase:**

   - **Sudden Oxygen Supply:** Reintroduction of oxygen during reperfusion leads to a burst of ROS production through multiple pathways, including mitochondrial respiration, xanthine oxidase activation, and NADPH oxidase activity.
   - **Mitochondrial ROS Generation:** Mitochondria, upon reoxygenation, generate superoxide anion ($O_2^{\cdot-}$) due to the sudden influx of oxygen and the electron leakage from the electron transport chain.
   - **Xanthine Oxidase Activation:** During ischemia, ATP is degraded to hypoxanthine. Upon reperfusion, xanthine oxidase converts hypoxanthine to uric acid, producing superoxide anion and hydrogen peroxide.
   - **NADPH Oxidase Activation:** Reperfusion activates NADPH oxidase in neutrophils and endothelial cells, leading to the production of superoxide anion.
   - **Inflammatory Response:** Reperfusion triggers an inflammatory response, recruiting neutrophils and other immune cells to the affected area. These cells generate additional ROS and release pro-

inflammatory cytokines.

Consequences of Ischemic Reperfusion Injury:

1. **Oxidative Damage:**

   - **Lipid Peroxidation**: ROS attack polyunsaturated fatty acids in cell membranes, leading to the formation of lipid hydroperoxides and secondary products such as malondialdehyde (MDA) and 4-hydroxynonenal (4-HNE). This damages cellular membranes, resulting in increased permeability and loss of membrane integrity.
   - **Protein Oxidation**: ROS modify amino acid residues, leading to protein dysfunction, enzyme inactivation, and formation of protein aggregates.
   - **DNA Damage**: ROS cause single and double-strand breaks in DNA, as well as base modifications, leading to mutations and impaired cellular functions.

2. **Calcium Overload:**

   - **Intracellular Calcium Accumulation**: Ischemia and subsequent reperfusion lead to calcium overload in cells due to impaired calcium pumps and increased permeability of cellular membranes.
   - **Mitochondrial Dysfunction**: Excessive intracellular calcium disrupts mitochondrial function, further increasing ROS production and triggering the opening of the mitochondrial permeability transition pore (mPTP), leading to cell death.

3. **Inflammatory Response:**

   - **Neutrophil Infiltration**: Reperfusion attracts neutrophils to the affected tissue, where they release ROS, proteases, and pro-inflammatory cytokines, exacerbating tissue damage.
   - **Cytokine Release**: Pro-inflammatory cytokines such as TNF-α, IL-1β, and IL-6 are released, promoting further inflammation and injury.

4. **Cell Death:**

- **Apoptosis**: Oxidative stress and calcium overload activate apoptotic pathways, leading to programmed cell death. Key players include caspases, Bcl-2 family proteins, and cytochrome c release from mitochondria.
- **Necrosis**: Severe oxidative damage and loss of ATP lead to uncontrolled cell death (necrosis), characterized by cell swelling, membrane rupture, and inflammation.

Antioxidant and Therapeutic Interventions:

1. **Antioxidant Therapies**:

   - **Superoxide Dismutase (SOD)**: Converts superoxide anion to hydrogen peroxide, reducing oxidative stress.
   - **Catalase**: Decomposes hydrogen peroxide into water and oxygen.
   - **Glutathione Peroxidase (GPx)**: Reduces hydrogen peroxide and lipid hydroperoxides.
   - **Exogenous Antioxidants**: Administration of antioxidants such as vitamin C, vitamin E, and N-acetylcysteine (NAC) can help reduce oxidative stress during reperfusion.

2. **Pharmacological Interventions**:

   - **Calcium Channel Blockers**: These drugs can help reduce calcium overload and protect against mitochondrial dysfunction.
   - **Anti-Inflammatory Agents**: Medications such as corticosteroids and non-steroidal anti-inflammatory drugs (NSAIDs) can reduce the inflammatory response and limit tissue damage.
   - **Ischemic Preconditioning**: Brief periods of ischemia followed by reperfusion before a prolonged ischemic event can condition tissues to better withstand subsequent I/R injury. This process triggers protective signaling pathways that reduce oxidative stress and inflammation.

3. **Therapeutic Hypothermia**:

   - **Cooling Tissues**: Lowering the temperature of the affected tissues can reduce metabolic demand, ROS production, and inflammation, providing protection against I/R injury.

Ischemic reperfusion injury involves complex interactions between oxidative stress, calcium overload, and inflammation, leading to significant tissue damage. Understanding the mechanisms by which free radicals contribute to I/R injury is crucial for developing effective therapeutic strategies. Antioxidant therapies, pharmacological interventions, and ischemic preconditioning are among the approaches used to mitigate the effects of I/R injury and improve clinical outcomes. Reducing oxidative stress and inflammation during reperfusion can help preserve tissue function and prevent long-term complications associated with ischemic events.

5.1.4 Cancer

Introduction: **Cancer** is a multifaceted disease characterized by uncontrolled cell growth and proliferation. **Free radicals**, particularly **reactive oxygen species (ROS)** and **reactive nitrogen species (RNS)**, play a crucial role in the development and progression of cancer. While low levels of ROS/RNS are essential for normal cellular signaling, elevated levels can induce oxidative stress, leading to DNA damage, genomic instability, and alterations in cellular processes that promote carcinogenesis.

Mechanisms of Free Radical Involvement in Cancer:

1. **DNA Damage and Mutagenesis**:

   - **Oxidative DNA Damage**: ROS such as hydroxyl radicals ($\cdot$OH) can cause various types of DNA damage, including base modifications, single-strand breaks (SSBs), and double-strand breaks (DSBs). One of the most common oxidative DNA lesions is 8-oxo-7,8-dihydroguanine (8-oxoG), which can mispair with adenine during DNA replication, leading to G to T

   transversions.

   - **Mutagenesis**: The accumulation of oxidative DNA damage can result in mutations that activate oncogenes or inactivate tumor suppressor genes, promoting uncontrolled cell growth and tumor development.

2. **Genomic Instability**:

- ○ **Chromosomal Aberrations**: ROS-induced DNA damage can lead to chromosomal aberrations such as translocations, deletions, and amplifications, contributing to genomic instability.
- ○ **Microsatellite Instability**: Oxidative stress can impair the DNA mismatch repair (MMR) system, leading to microsatellite instability, a condition associated with various types of cancer.

3. **Activation of Oncogenic Pathways**:

- ○ **NF-κB Pathway**: ROS can activate the NF-κB pathway, which plays a pivotal role in cell survival, proliferation, and inflammation. Activated NF-κB translocates to the nucleus, where it promotes the expression of genes involved in tumorigenesis, such as anti-apoptotic proteins (e.g., Bcl-2), pro-inflammatory cytokines, and growth factors.
- ○ **MAPK Pathway**: ROS activate mitogen-activated protein kinases (MAPKs), including extracellular signal-regulated kinase (ERK), c-Jun N-terminal kinase (JNK), and p38 MAPK. These kinases regulate cellular responses to stress and promote cell proliferation and survival.
- ○ **PI3K/Akt Pathway**: ROS can stimulate the phosphoinositide 3-kinase (PI3K)/Akt pathway, leading to increased cell survival, growth, and metabolism.

4. **Evasion of Apoptosis**:

- ○ **Anti-Apoptotic Signals**: Cancer cells often evade apoptosis by upregulating anti-apoptotic proteins and downregulating pro-apoptotic proteins. ROS-mediated activation of NF-κB and PI3K/Akt pathways enhances the expression of anti-apoptotic proteins such as Bcl-2 and survivin.
- ○ **DNA Repair Pathways**: While ROS induce DNA damage, cancer cells can upregulate DNA repair pathways to survive oxidative stress. However, the error-prone repair mechanisms can lead to mutations and genomic instability.

5. **Tumor Microenvironment**:

- ○ **Inflammation**: Chronic inflammation driven by ROS and RNS creates a tumor-promoting microenvironment. Inflammatory cells such as macrophages and neutrophils infiltrate the tumor site and produce cytokines, chemokines, and additional ROS, further promoting tumor growth and progression.
- ○ **Angiogenesis**: ROS can stimulate the production of vascular endothelial growth factor (VEGF) and other angiogenic factors, promoting the formation of new blood vessels to supply the growing tumor with oxygen and nutrients.

6. **Metastasis**:

- ○ **Epithelial-Mesenchymal Transition (EMT)**: ROS can induce epithelial-mesenchymal transition, a process by which epithelial cells lose their polarity and adhesion properties, gaining migratory and invasive capabilities. EMT is a critical step in cancer metastasis.
- ○ **Matrix Metalloproteinases (MMPs)**: ROS upregulate the expression of MMPs, enzymes that degrade the extracellular matrix, facilitating tumor invasion and metastasis.

Antioxidant and Therapeutic Interventions:

1. **Antioxidant Therapies**:

- ○ **Vitamin C (Ascorbic Acid)**: A water-soluble antioxidant that scavenges ROS and regenerates other antioxidants. It has shown potential in reducing oxidative DNA damage and inhibiting tumor growth.
- ○ **Vitamin E (Tocopherols)**: A lipid-soluble antioxidant that protects cell membranes from lipid peroxidation. It has been studied for its role in cancer prevention and as an adjuvant therapy.
- ○ **Polyphenols**: Found in fruits, vegetables, tea, and wine, polyphenols such as quercetin, resveratrol, and catechins have strong antioxidant and anti-cancer properties.

2. **Pharmacological Interventions**:

- ○ **Chemotherapy**: Certain chemotherapeutic agents, such as doxorubicin and cisplatin, generate ROS to induce DNA damage and apoptosis in cancer cells. However, this can also cause oxidative damage to healthy cells, leading to side effects.
- ○ **Radiotherapy**: Ionizing radiation used in cancer treatment generates ROS to kill cancer cells. Combining radiotherapy with antioxidants can protect normal tissues from radiation-induced oxidative damage.
- ○ **Targeted Therapies**: Drugs targeting specific signaling pathways activated by ROS, such as PI3K/Akt inhibitors, MAPK inhibitors, and NF-κB inhibitors, are being developed to treat various cancers.

3. **Lifestyle and Dietary Interventions**:

- ○ **Dietary Antioxidants**: A diet rich in antioxidants from fruits, vegetables, nuts, and whole grains can help reduce oxidative stress and lower cancer risk.
- ○ **Regular Exercise**: Exercise enhances the body's antioxidant defenses and reduces oxidative stress, contributing to cancer prevention.
- ○ **Avoidance of Carcinogens**: Reducing exposure to environmental carcinogens, such as tobacco smoke, pollution, and UV radiation, can decrease the generation of ROS and the associated cancer risk.

Free radicals, particularly ROS and RNS, play a critical role in the initiation, promotion, and progression of cancer through mechanisms such as DNA damage, genomic instability, activation of oncogenic pathways, evasion of apoptosis, and modulation of the tumor microenvironment. Understanding these mechanisms is essential for developing effective cancer prevention and treatment strategies. Antioxidant therapies, pharmacological interventions, and lifestyle modifications can help mitigate oxidative stress, reduce cancer risk, and improve therapeutic outcomes.

5.1.5 Atherosclerosis

Introduction: **Atherosclerosis** is a chronic inflammatory disease characterized by the buildup of plaques within the arterial walls. This condition can lead to serious cardiovascular diseases, including coronary artery disease, stroke, and peripheral artery disease. **Free radicals**, particularly **reactive oxygen species (ROS)**, play a crucial role in the initiation and progression of atherosclerosis. The oxidative modification of low-density lipoprotein (LDL) and the resulting inflammatory response are key events in the pathogenesis of atherosclerosis.

Mechanisms of Free Radical Involvement in Atherosclerosis:

1. **Oxidation of LDL:**

   - **LDL Oxidation:** ROS such as superoxide anion ($O_2^{\cdot-}$), hydrogen peroxide (H_2O_2), and hydroxyl radicals ($\cdot OH$) can oxidize LDL particles in the arterial wall. This oxidative modification of LDL (oxLDL) is a critical early step in the development of atherosclerotic plaques.
   - **Impact:** OxLDL is more atherogenic than native LDL. It is readily taken up by macrophages via scavenger receptors, leading to the formation of foam cells and the development of fatty streaks in the arterial wall.

2. **Endothelial Dysfunction:**

   - **ROS Production:** Endothelial cells exposed to risk factors such as hypertension, hyperlipidemia, and smoking produce increased levels of ROS. This oxidative stress impairs endothelial function.
   - **Nitric Oxide (NO) Inactivation:** ROS react with nitric oxide (NO), reducing its bioavailability. NO is a crucial molecule for maintaining vascular homeostasis, promoting vasodilation, and inhibiting platelet aggregation and smooth muscle cell proliferation.
   - **Impact:** Reduced NO levels lead to endothelial dysfunction, characterized by impaired vasodilation, increased vascular permeability, and enhanced leukocyte adhesion.

3. **Inflammatory Response:**

   - **Monocyte Recruitment:** OxLDL and endothelial dysfunction promote the expression of adhesion molecules (e.g., VCAM-1, ICAM-1) on endothelial cells, facilitating the adhesion and migration of monocytes into the intima of the artery.
   - **Foam Cell Formation:** Monocytes differentiate into macrophages and engulf oxLDL via scavenger receptors, transforming into foam cells. Foam cells release pro-inflammatory cytokines and chemokines,

amplifying the inflammatory response.

- **Cytokine Production**: Inflammatory cytokines such as TNF-α, IL-1β, and IL-6 further recruit immune cells and stimulate the production of more ROS, creating a vicious cycle of oxidative stress and inflammation.

4. Plaque Formation and Progression:

- **Smooth Muscle Cell Proliferation and Migration**: Growth factors and cytokines released by foam cells and damaged endothelial cells stimulate smooth muscle cell proliferation and migration from the media to the intima, contributing to plaque growth.
- **Extracellular Matrix Remodeling**: Matrix metalloproteinases (MMPs) are upregulated by ROS and inflammatory cytokines, degrading the extracellular matrix and destabilizing the plaque.
- **Necrotic Core Formation**: Continuous oxidative stress and inflammation lead to apoptosis of foam cells and smooth muscle cells, resulting in the formation of a necrotic core within the plaque.

5. Plaque Rupture and Thrombosis:

- **Plaque Instability**: Oxidative stress and MMP activity weaken the fibrous cap of the plaque, making it prone to rupture.
- **Thrombosis**: Plaque rupture exposes pro-thrombotic substances such as tissue factor, leading to the formation of a thrombus (blood clot) that can obstruct blood flow and cause acute cardiovascular events like myocardial infarction or stroke.

Antioxidant and Therapeutic Interventions:

1. Antioxidant Therapies:

- **Vitamin C (Ascorbic Acid)**: A water-soluble antioxidant that scavenges ROS and regenerates other antioxidants.
- **Vitamin E (Tocopherols)**: A lipid-soluble antioxidant that protects cell membranes from lipid peroxidation.
- **Polyphenols**: Found in fruits, vegetables, tea, and wine, polyphenols such as quercetin, resveratrol, and catechins have strong antioxidant

and anti-inflammatory properties.

- **Statins**: Statins lower cholesterol levels and have antioxidant properties that reduce oxidative stress and inflammation.

2. **Pharmacological Interventions**:

- **Lipid-Lowering Agents**: Statins, fibrates, and PCSK9 inhibitors reduce LDL cholesterol levels, decreasing the substrate available for oxidation.
- **Anti-Inflammatory Drugs**: Non-steroidal anti-inflammatory drugs (NSAIDs) and corticosteroids can reduce inflammation and its contribution to atherosclerosis.
- **Angiotensin-Converting Enzyme (ACE) Inhibitors**: These drugs lower blood pressure and have antioxidant effects that reduce endothelial oxidative stress.

3. **Lifestyle and Dietary Interventions**:

- **Healthy Diet**: A diet rich in antioxidants from fruits, vegetables, nuts, and whole grains can help reduce oxidative stress. Limiting the intake of saturated fats, trans fats, and cholesterol is crucial for lowering LDL levels.
- **Regular Exercise**: Physical activity enhances antioxidant defenses and improves endothelial function.
- **Smoking Cessation**: Smoking is a major source of oxidative stress. Quitting smoking can significantly reduce the risk of atherosclerosis.

Free radicals, particularly ROS, play a crucial role in the pathogenesis of atherosclerosis through mechanisms such as LDL oxidation, endothelial dysfunction, inflammatory response, and plaque instability. Understanding these mechanisms is essential for developing effective prevention and treatment strategies. Antioxidant therapies, pharmacological interventions, and lifestyle modifications can help mitigate oxidative stress, reduce inflammation, and lower the risk of atherosclerosis and its associated cardiovascular diseases.

5.1.6 Neurodegenerative Diseases (e.g., Alzheimer's, Parkinson's)

Introduction: Neurodegenerative diseases, such as **Alzheimer's disease (AD)** and **Parkinson's disease (PD)**, are characterized by the progressive loss of structure and function of neurons. These diseases have multifactorial etiologies, involving genetic, environmental, and lifestyle factors. **Free radicals**, particularly **reactive oxygen species (ROS)** and **reactive nitrogen species (RNS)**, play a significant role in the pathogenesis of neurodegenerative diseases through oxidative stress and damage to neuronal cells.

Mechanisms of Free Radical Involvement in Neurodegenerative Diseases:

1. **Oxidative Damage to Neurons:**

   - **Lipid Peroxidation:** Neuronal membranes are rich in polyunsaturated fatty acids (PUFAs), making them highly susceptible to ROS-induced lipid peroxidation. This leads to the formation of lipid hydroperoxides and secondary products like malondialdehyde (MDA) and 4-hydroxynonenal (4-HNE), which can disrupt membrane integrity and function.
   - **Protein Oxidation:** ROS can oxidize amino acid residues in proteins, leading to protein dysfunction, aggregation, and formation of inclusion bodies. In AD, oxidative modification of amyloid-beta (Aβ) peptides promotes their aggregation into toxic oligomers and plaques.
   - **DNA Damage:** ROS and RNS can cause oxidative damage to nuclear and mitochondrial DNA, leading to mutations, impaired mitochondrial function, and neuronal death.

2. **Mitochondrial Dysfunction:**

   - **Mitochondrial ROS Production:** Mitochondria are a major source of ROS in neurons. Dysfunctional mitochondria produce excessive ROS, which further impairs mitochondrial function and promotes oxidative stress.
   - **Impact:** Mitochondrial dysfunction leads to energy deficits, increased ROS production, and activation of apoptotic pathways, contributing to neuronal loss in neurodegenerative diseases.

3. **Impaired Antioxidant Defense:**

- ○ **Decreased Antioxidant Levels**: Neurodegenerative diseases are often associated with reduced levels of endogenous antioxidants, such as glutathione (GSH), superoxide dismutase (SOD), and catalase, making neurons more vulnerable to oxidative damage.
- ○ **Glutathione Depletion**: GSH is a critical antioxidant in the brain. Its depletion exacerbates oxidative stress and contributes to neuronal degeneration.

4. **Neuroinflammation**:

- ○ **Microglial Activation**: Microglia, the resident immune cells in the brain, become activated in response to neuronal injury and release pro-inflammatory cytokines, ROS, and RNS. Chronic microglial activation contributes to sustained neuroinflammation and neuronal damage.
- ○ **Cytokine Production**: Pro-inflammatory cytokines, such as TNF-α, IL-1β, and IL-6, amplify the inflammatory response and promote ROS production, creating a vicious cycle of oxidative stress and inflammation.

5. **Specific Mechanisms in Alzheimer's Disease (AD)**:

- ○ **Amyloid-Beta (Aβ) Aggregation**: Aβ peptides aggregate to form oligomers and plaques, which induce oxidative stress and mitochondrial dysfunction. Aβ can also bind to metal ions like copper and iron, catalyzing the production of ROS.
- ○ **Tau Protein Hyperphosphorylation**: Hyperphosphorylated tau proteins form neurofibrillary tangles, disrupting neuronal function and promoting oxidative damage.

6. **Specific Mechanisms in Parkinson's Disease (PD)**:

- ○ **Dopaminergic Neuron Loss**: PD is characterized by the selective loss of dopaminergic neurons in the substantia nigra. Dopamine metabolism generates ROS, and the accumulation of oxidized dopamine and its metabolites contributes to neuronal damage.
- ○ **Alpha-Synuclein Aggregation**: Misfolded alpha-synuclein proteins aggregate to form Lewy bodies, which impair cellular function and

promote oxidative stress.

Antioxidant and Therapeutic Interventions:

1. **Antioxidant Therapies**:

   - **Vitamin E (Tocopherols)**: A lipid-soluble antioxidant that protects cell membranes from lipid peroxidation. Vitamin E supplementation has shown potential in slowing the progression of AD.
   - **Vitamin C (Ascorbic Acid)**: A water-soluble antioxidant that scavenges ROS and regenerates other antioxidants. It may help reduce oxidative stress in neurodegenerative diseases.
   - **Coenzyme Q10 (Ubiquinone)**: An essential component of the mitochondrial electron transport chain with antioxidant properties. CoQ10 supplementation has been studied for its potential to improve mitochondrial function and reduce oxidative stress in PD.
   - **Polyphenols**: Found in fruits, vegetables, tea, and wine, polyphenols such as resveratrol, quercetin, and curcumin have strong antioxidant and anti-inflammatory properties and may provide neuroprotection.

2. **Pharmacological Interventions**:

   - **MAO-B Inhibitors**: Drugs such as selegiline and rasagiline inhibit monoamine oxidase B (MAO-B), an enzyme that metabolizes dopamine and generates ROS. These inhibitors help reduce oxidative stress and neurodegeneration in PD.
   - **Anti-Inflammatory Drugs**: Non-steroidal anti-inflammatory drugs (NSAIDs) and corticosteroids can reduce neuroinflammation and oxidative damage in neurodegenerative diseases.
   - **Chelation Therapy**: Metal chelators such as clioquinol and deferoxamine bind to metal ions, reducing metal-catalyzed ROS production and oxidative stress.

3. **Lifestyle and Dietary Interventions**:

   - **Healthy Diet**: A diet rich in antioxidants from fruits, vegetables, nuts, and whole grains can help reduce oxidative stress and lower the risk of neurodegenerative diseases.

- ◦ **Regular Exercise**: Physical activity enhances antioxidant defenses, improves mitochondrial function, and reduces neuroinflammation, contributing to neuroprotection.
- ◦ **Cognitive Stimulation**: Engaging in mentally stimulating activities can help maintain cognitive function and delay the onset of neurodegenerative diseases.

Free radicals, particularly ROS and RNS, play a crucial role in the pathogenesis of neurodegenerative diseases such as Alzheimer's and Parkinson's through mechanisms involving oxidative damage to neurons, mitochondrial dysfunction, impaired antioxidant defenses, and chronic neuroinflammation. Understanding these mechanisms is essential for developing effective prevention and treatment strategies. Antioxidant therapies, pharmacological interventions, and lifestyle modifications can help mitigate oxidative stress, reduce neuroinflammation, and protect against neuronal degeneration, potentially slowing the progression of neurodegenerative diseases.

5.1.7 Kidney Damage

Introduction: **Kidney damage**, also known as nephropathy, can result from various conditions, including diabetes, hypertension, infections, and exposure to toxins. **Free radicals**, particularly **reactive oxygen species (ROS)** and **reactive nitrogen species (RNS)**, play a significant role in the pathogenesis of kidney damage. Oxidative stress caused by an imbalance between free radical production and antioxidant defenses leads to cellular injury, inflammation, and fibrosis in kidney tissues.

Mechanisms of Free Radical Involvement in Kidney Damage:

1. **Oxidative Stress and Renal Cells**:

   - ◦ **Endothelial Cells**: ROS can damage the endothelial cells lining the blood vessels in the kidneys, leading to endothelial dysfunction and impaired blood flow. This can result in reduced glomerular filtration rate (GFR) and contribute to the development of chronic kidney disease (CKD).
   - ◦ **Glomerular Cells**: ROS can injure glomerular cells, including podocytes and mesangial cells, leading to glomerulosclerosis (scarring of the glomeruli) and proteinuria (protein in the urine).

- **Tubular Cells**: Tubular epithelial cells are susceptible to oxidative damage, which can cause tubular necrosis and impair renal reabsorption and secretion functions.

2. **ROS Production in Kidney Diseases**:

- **Diabetic Nephropathy**: High glucose levels in diabetes lead to increased ROS production through several mechanisms, including glucose autoxidation, activation of the polyol pathway, and advanced glycation end-product (AGE) formation. These ROS contribute to renal inflammation, fibrosis, and apoptosis.
- **Hypertensive Nephropathy**: Hypertension induces oxidative stress by activating the renin-angiotensin-aldosterone system (RAAS), which increases angiotensin II levels. Angiotensin II stimulates ROS production via NADPH oxidase, leading to endothelial dysfunction and renal damage.
- **Ischemia-Reperfusion Injury**: In conditions such as acute kidney injury (AKI), the restoration of blood flow (reperfusion) after a period of ischemia generates a burst of ROS, causing oxidative damage to renal tissues.

3. **Inflammatory Response**:

- **Cytokine Production**: ROS activate transcription factors such as NF-κB, leading to the production of pro-inflammatory cytokines (e.g., TNF-α, IL-1β, IL-6). These cytokines recruit immune cells to the kidneys, exacerbating inflammation and oxidative stress.
- **Macrophage Infiltration**: Infiltrating macrophages produce additional ROS and RNS, amplifying the inflammatory response and contributing to tissue injury.

4. **Fibrosis**:

- **Myofibroblast Activation**: ROS stimulate the activation of fibroblasts to myofibroblasts, which produce extracellular matrix components, leading to renal fibrosis. Transforming growth factor-beta (TGF-β) is a key mediator in this process, and its expression is upregulated by ROS.

- ○ **Extracellular Matrix Deposition**: Excessive deposition of extracellular matrix proteins, such as collagen, leads to scarring and loss of renal function.

5. **Mitochondrial Dysfunction**:

- ○ **Mitochondrial ROS Production**: Mitochondrial dysfunction in renal cells results in increased production of ROS, which further damages mitochondrial DNA, proteins, and lipids. This creates a vicious cycle of oxidative stress and cellular injury.
- ○ **Apoptosis**: Mitochondrial ROS can trigger apoptotic pathways by releasing cytochrome c and activating caspases, leading to programmed cell death and loss of renal cells.

Antioxidant and Therapeutic Interventions:

1. **Antioxidant Therapies**:

- ○ **N-Acetylcysteine (NAC)**: NAC is a precursor to glutathione (GSH), a major intracellular antioxidant. It helps replenish GSH levels and scavenge ROS, reducing oxidative stress in the kidneys.
- ○ **Vitamin C (Ascorbic Acid)**: A water-soluble antioxidant that scavenges ROS and regenerates other antioxidants. Vitamin C supplementation can reduce oxidative stress and improve renal function.
- ○ **Vitamin E (Tocopherols)**: A lipid-soluble antioxidant that protects cell membranes from lipid peroxidation. Vitamin E has shown potential in reducing oxidative damage in diabetic nephropathy.
- ○ **Coenzyme Q10 (Ubiquinone)**: An essential component of the mitochondrial electron transport chain with antioxidant properties. CoQ10 supplementation can improve mitochondrial function and reduce oxidative stress in renal cells.

2. **Pharmacological Interventions**:

- ○ **Angiotensin-Converting Enzyme (ACE) Inhibitors**: ACE inhibitors lower blood pressure and reduce oxidative stress by inhibiting the production of angiotensin II. They are commonly used to treat hypertensive nephropathy and diabetic nephropathy.

- **Angiotensin II Receptor Blockers (ARBs)**: ARBs block the effects of angiotensin II, reducing ROS production and inflammation in the kidneys. They are effective in managing hypertension and protecting renal function.
- **Statins**: Statins have antioxidant and anti-inflammatory properties in addition to their lipid-lowering effects. They can reduce oxidative stress and improve endothelial function in the kidneys.

3. **Lifestyle and Dietary Interventions**:

- **Healthy Diet**: A diet rich in antioxidants from fruits, vegetables, nuts, and whole grains can help reduce oxidative stress and lower the risk of kidney damage. Limiting the intake of sodium, saturated fats, and processed foods is also important for maintaining kidney health.
- **Regular Exercise**: Physical activity enhances antioxidant defenses, improves cardiovascular health, and helps control blood pressure, reducing the risk of kidney damage.
- **Smoking Cessation**: Smoking is a major source of oxidative stress. Quitting smoking can significantly reduce the risk of kidney damage and slow the progression of CKD.

Free radicals, particularly ROS and RNS, play a critical role in the pathogenesis of kidney damage through mechanisms involving oxidative stress, inflammation, fibrosis, and mitochondrial dysfunction. Understanding these mechanisms is essential for developing effective prevention and treatment strategies. Antioxidant therapies, pharmacological interventions, and lifestyle modifications can help mitigate oxidative stress, reduce inflammation, and protect against renal damage, potentially slowing the progression of kidney diseases.

5.1.8 Muscle Damage

Introduction: Muscle damage can occur due to a variety of causes, including strenuous exercise, trauma, ischemia, infections, and chronic conditions such as muscular dystrophies. **Free radicals**, particularly **reactive oxygen species (ROS)** and **reactive nitrogen species (RNS)**, play a significant role in the pathophysiology of muscle damage. Oxidative stress caused by an imbalance between free radical production and antioxidant defenses leads to structural and functional alterations in muscle cells.

Mechanisms of Free Radical Involvement in Muscle Damage:

1. **Exercise-Induced Muscle Damage:**

   - **ROS Production During Exercise**: Intense physical activity increases oxygen consumption in muscles, leading to enhanced mitochondrial ROS production. Additional sources of ROS include NADPH oxidase, xanthine oxidase, and the inflammatory response.
   - **Impact**: Excessive ROS can damage muscle cell membranes, proteins, and DNA, contributing to muscle fatigue, soreness, and weakness.

2. **Oxidative Damage to Muscle Cells:**

   - **Lipid Peroxidation**: ROS attack polyunsaturated fatty acids in muscle cell membranes, leading to lipid peroxidation. This results in the formation of lipid hydroperoxides and secondary products like malondialdehyde (MDA) and 4-hydroxynonenal (4-HNE), which compromise membrane integrity and function.
   - **Protein Oxidation**: ROS oxidize amino acid residues in muscle proteins, leading to structural modifications, loss of enzyme activity, and protein aggregation.
   - **DNA Damage**: ROS cause oxidative damage to nuclear and mitochondrial DNA, leading to mutations, impaired mitochondrial function, and apoptosis.

3. **Inflammatory Response:**

   - **Cytokine Production**: ROS activate transcription factors such as NF-κB, leading to the production of pro-inflammatory cytokines (e.g., TNF-α, IL-1β, IL-6). These cytokines recruit immune cells to the site of muscle injury, exacerbating inflammation and oxidative stress.
   - **Macrophage Infiltration**: Infiltrating macrophages produce additional ROS and RNS, amplifying the inflammatory response and contributing to muscle tissue injury and repair processes.

4. **Ischemia-Reperfusion Injury:**

- **ROS Burst**: Reperfusion of ischemic muscle tissue generates a burst of ROS, causing oxidative damage to muscle cells. This is a common mechanism of injury in conditions such as compartment syndrome and vascular occlusion.
- **Impact**: Reperfusion injury leads to muscle cell necrosis, increased membrane permeability, and leakage of muscle enzymes (e.g., creatine kinase) into the bloodstream.

5. **Chronic Muscle Conditions**:

- **Muscular Dystrophies**: Genetic disorders like Duchenne muscular dystrophy (DMD) are characterized by chronic muscle degeneration and inflammation. In DMD, the absence of dystrophin makes muscle cells more susceptible to mechanical stress and oxidative damage.
- **Mitochondrial Myopathies**: Disorders of mitochondrial function lead to excessive ROS production and oxidative damage, contributing to muscle weakness and exercise intolerance.

Antioxidant and Therapeutic Interventions:

1. **Antioxidant Therapies**:

- **Vitamin C (Ascorbic Acid)**: A water-soluble antioxidant that scavenges ROS and regenerates other antioxidants. Vitamin C supplementation can reduce oxidative stress and muscle damage.
- **Vitamin E (Tocopherols)**: A lipid-soluble antioxidant that protects muscle cell membranes from lipid peroxidation. Vitamin E has shown potential in reducing exercise-induced muscle damage.
- **Coenzyme Q10 (Ubiquinone)**: An essential component of the mitochondrial electron transport chain with antioxidant properties. CoQ10 supplementation can improve mitochondrial function and reduce oxidative stress in muscle cells.
- **Polyphenols**: Found in fruits, vegetables, tea, and wine, polyphenols such as quercetin, resveratrol, and catechins have strong antioxidant and anti-inflammatory properties and may provide protection against muscle damage.

2. **Pharmacological Interventions**:

- ◦ **NSAIDs**: Non-steroidal anti-inflammatory drugs (NSAIDs) can reduce inflammation and pain associated with muscle damage. However, prolonged use can impair muscle repair and regeneration.
- ◦ **Corticosteroids**: These drugs reduce inflammation and immune response. They are used in the treatment of chronic inflammatory muscle conditions but must be used cautiously due to potential side effects.
- ◦ **Creatine Supplementation**: Creatine enhances muscle energy metabolism and has antioxidant properties. It is commonly used to improve muscle performance and reduce exercise-induced muscle damage.

3. **Lifestyle and Dietary Interventions**:

- ◦ **Balanced Diet**: A diet rich in antioxidants from fruits, vegetables, nuts, and whole grains can help reduce oxidative stress and promote muscle health. Adequate protein intake is essential for muscle repair and growth.
- ◦ **Regular Exercise**: Moderate, regular exercise enhances the body's antioxidant defenses and improves muscle function. Overtraining should be avoided to prevent excessive oxidative stress and muscle damage.
- ◦ **Hydration**: Proper hydration is crucial for muscle function and recovery. Dehydration can exacerbate oxidative stress and muscle injury.

Free radicals, particularly ROS and RNS, play a critical role in the pathogenesis of muscle damage through mechanisms involving oxidative stress, inflammation, ischemia-reperfusion injury, and chronic muscle conditions. Understanding these mechanisms is essential for developing effective prevention and treatment strategies. Antioxidant therapies, pharmacological interventions, and lifestyle modifications can help mitigate oxidative stress, reduce inflammation, and protect against muscle damage, potentially improving muscle health and performance.

5.2 Free Radical Theory of Aging

5.2.1 Historical Perspective

Introduction: The **Free Radical Theory of Aging** is a widely discussed and researched hypothesis that suggests aging is primarily the result of accumulated damage caused by free radicals, particularly **reactive oxygen species (ROS)** and **reactive nitrogen species (RNS)**. This theory posits that oxidative stress, resulting from an imbalance between the production of free radicals and the body's antioxidant defenses, leads to cellular and molecular damage that manifests as aging and age-related diseases.

Historical Perspective:

1. **Early Observations**:

   - The concept that oxidative damage could contribute to aging dates back to the mid-20th century. Early researchers observed that organisms with higher metabolic rates tended to have shorter lifespans, suggesting a link between oxygen consumption, free radical production, and aging.
   - **Denham Harman**: In 1956, Denham Harman, an American gerontologist and biochemist, formally proposed the Free Radical Theory of Aging. Harman suggested that free radicals generated during normal metabolic processes could cause cumulative damage to cells and tissues, leading to the functional decline associated with aging.

     - **Harman's Hypothesis**: Harman's original hypothesis was based on the observation that ionizing radiation, which produces free radicals, could cause cellular damage similar to that seen in aging. He extended this idea to suggest that endogenous free radicals, produced during cellular respiration and other metabolic processes, could similarly cause aging.

2. **Development of the Theory**:

   - **1960s-1970s**: During the 1960s and 1970s, research in the field of biogerontology expanded, and the Free Radical Theory of Aging gained traction. Scientists began to investigate the sources and effects of free radicals in biological systems. Studies on the role of antioxidants, such as superoxide dismutase (SOD), catalase, and glutathione, in protecting cells from oxidative damage further supported the theory.

- **Mitochondrial Free Radical Theory of Aging**: In 1972, Harman refined his theory to focus on mitochondria, the primary sites of ROS production in cells. He proposed that mitochondrial DNA (mtDNA) is particularly susceptible to oxidative damage due to its proximity to the electron transport chain and lack of protective histones. Damage to mtDNA impairs mitochondrial function, leading to increased ROS production and a cycle of oxidative stress and cellular aging.

3. **Empirical Evidence**:

- **Lifespan Studies**: Numerous studies have investigated the relationship between oxidative stress and lifespan. Research on various organisms, including yeast, worms (C. elegans), flies (Drosophila melanogaster), and rodents, has shown that enhancing antioxidant defenses or reducing oxidative damage can extend lifespan. For example, overexpression of SOD and catalase in transgenic mice has been associated with increased lifespan and delayed onset of age-related diseases.
- **Caloric Restriction**: Caloric restriction (CR), a dietary intervention that reduces caloric intake without malnutrition, has been shown to extend lifespan and delay aging in multiple species. CR is believed to reduce metabolic rate and ROS production, thereby decreasing oxidative damage and supporting the Free Radical Theory of Aging.

4. **Challenges and Refinements**:

- **Contradictory Findings**: Despite substantial evidence supporting the Free Radical Theory of Aging, some studies have produced contradictory findings. For instance, certain antioxidant interventions have failed to extend lifespan in animal models or have produced inconsistent results. Additionally, some long-lived species exhibit higher levels of oxidative damage compared to shorter-lived species, challenging the theory's universality.
- **Network Theory of Aging**: In response to these challenges, researchers have proposed refinements to the Free Radical Theory of Aging. The Network Theory of Aging, for example, suggests that aging results from the interplay of multiple interconnected factors, including oxidative stress, genomic instability, inflammation, and

metabolic dysregulation. This broader perspective acknowledges that free radicals are a significant but not sole contributor to aging.

5. **Current Research and Perspectives**:

- **Modern Techniques**: Advances in molecular biology, genomics, and bioinformatics have provided new tools to study the role of free radicals in aging. Techniques such as high-throughput sequencing, proteomics, and metabolomics allow researchers to investigate the complex interactions between oxidative stress and other aging-related processes at a systems level.
- **Intervention Studies**: Ongoing research aims to develop targeted interventions to modulate oxidative stress and improve healthspan. These include pharmacological agents that enhance endogenous antioxidant defenses, mitochondrial-targeted antioxidants, and lifestyle interventions such as exercise and dietary modifications.

The Free Radical Theory of Aging, first proposed by Denham Harman in the 1950s, has significantly influenced our understanding of the biological mechanisms underlying aging. While substantial evidence supports the role of oxidative stress in aging and age-related diseases, the theory has been refined and expanded to accommodate contradictory findings and integrate other contributing factors. Current research continues to explore the complex interplay between free radicals and aging, with the goal of developing effective strategies to promote healthy aging and extend lifespan.

5.2.2 Mechanisms

Introduction: The **Free Radical Theory of Aging** posits that aging and age-related diseases are primarily caused by the accumulation of damage induced by free radicals, particularly **reactive oxygen species (ROS)** and **reactive nitrogen species (RNS)**. These reactive species can damage cellular components, including lipids, proteins, and nucleic acids, leading to the functional decline of cells and tissues. Understanding the mechanisms by which free radicals contribute to aging is crucial for developing interventions to mitigate their effects and promote healthy aging.

Mechanisms of Free Radical-Induced Aging:

1. **Oxidative Damage to Lipids**:

- **Lipid Peroxidation**: ROS such as hydroxyl radicals ($\cdot$OH) can initiate the peroxidation of polyunsaturated fatty acids in cell membranes. This process generates lipid peroxides and secondary products like malondialdehyde (MDA) and 4-hydroxynonenal (4-HNE), which compromise membrane integrity and function.

Impact: Lipid peroxidation disrupts membrane fluidity and permeability, impairs membrane-bound proteins, and can trigger cell death. Accumulation of lipid peroxidation products is associated with various age-related diseases, including cardiovascular diseases and neurodegenerative disorders.

1. **Oxidative Damage to Proteins**:

   - **Protein Oxidation**: ROS can modify amino acid residues in proteins, leading to the formation of carbonyl groups, disulfide bonds, and other oxidative modifications. These changes can alter protein structure and function, resulting in the loss of enzyme activity, receptor function, and protein-protein interactions.

Impact: Oxidatively damaged proteins are prone to aggregation and can form insoluble inclusion bodies. This accumulation of damaged proteins is a hallmark of aging and is implicated in age-related diseases such as Alzheimer's disease (e.g., amyloid plaques) and Parkinson's disease (e.g., Lewy bodies).

3. **Oxidative Damage to DNA:**

   - **DNA Oxidation**: ROS can induce various forms of DNA damage, including base modifications, single-strand breaks (SSBs), and double-strand breaks (DSBs). One of the most common oxidative DNA lesions is 8-oxo-7,8-dihydroguanine (8-oxoG), which can mispair with adenine during DNA replication, leading to mutations.

Impact: Accumulation of DNA damage can lead to genomic instability, impaired cell function, and apoptosis. Mutations resulting from oxidative DNA damage contribute to the development of cancer and other age-related diseases.

4. **Mitochondrial Dysfunction**:

   - **Mitochondrial ROS Production**: Mitochondria are a major source of ROS due to their role in oxidative phosphorylation. Dysfunctional mitochondria produce excessive ROS, which can further damage mitochondrial DNA (mtDNA), proteins, and lipids.

   Impact: Mitochondrial dysfunction leads to decreased ATP production, increased ROS generation, and activation of cell death pathways. This vicious cycle of oxidative stress and mitochondrial damage is a key driver of cellular aging and contributes to age-related declines in energy metabolism and cellular function.

5. **Telomere Shortening**:

   - **Oxidative Stress and Telomeres**: Telomeres, the protective caps at the ends of chromosomes, shorten with each cell division. ROS accelerate telomere shortening by inducing DNA damage at telomeric regions, which are particularly sensitive to oxidative stress.

     - **Impact**: Telomere shortening leads to cellular senescence, a state of permanent cell cycle arrest. Senescent cells accumulate with age and secrete pro-inflammatory cytokines and other factors that contribute to tissue dysfunction and aging.

6. **Inflammatory Response**:

   - **Chronic Inflammation**: Oxidative stress activates inflammatory signaling pathways, such as NF-κB and MAPKs, leading to the production of pro-inflammatory cytokines (e.g., TNF-α, IL-1β, IL-6). Chronic inflammation, or "inflammaging," is a characteristic of aging and contributes to the progression of age-related diseases.

7. **Autophagy and Proteostasis**:

   - **Impaired Autophagy**: Autophagy is a cellular process that degrades and recycles damaged organelles and proteins. Oxidative stress can impair autophagy, leading to the accumulation of damaged cellular components.

- **Impact**: Reduced autophagic activity contributes to the buildup of dysfunctional mitochondria and protein aggregates, promoting cellular senescence and aging. Enhancing autophagy has been shown to extend lifespan in various model organisms.

8. **Cellular Senescence**:

- **Senescence Induction**: Oxidative stress induces cellular senescence through DNA damage, telomere shortening, and activation of p53 and p16^INK4a pathways. Senescent cells adopt a senescence-associated secretory phenotype (SASP), releasing inflammatory cytokines, growth factors, and proteases.

  - **Impact**: Senescent cells accumulate in tissues over time, contributing to chronic inflammation, tissue remodeling, and functional decline. The SASP factors promote tumorigenesis and other age-related pathologies.

The Free Radical Theory of Aging highlights the central role of oxidative stress in the aging process and age-related diseases. Through mechanisms such as lipid peroxidation, protein oxidation, DNA damage, mitochondrial dysfunction, telomere shortening, chronic inflammation, impaired autophagy, and cellular senescence, free radicals contribute to the functional decline of cells and tissues. Understanding these mechanisms is crucial for developing strategies to mitigate oxidative damage, enhance antioxidant defenses, and promote healthy aging.

5.2.3 Evidence and Debates

Introduction: The **Free Radical Theory of Aging** suggests that oxidative damage caused by free radicals, particularly **reactive oxygen species (ROS)** and **reactive nitrogen species (RNS)**, is a primary driver of aging and age-related diseases. While substantial evidence supports this theory, it remains a topic of active debate within the scientific community. Here, we discuss the key pieces of evidence that support the theory and the ongoing debates that challenge its universality.

Evidence Supporting the Free Radical Theory of Aging:

1. **Correlation Between Oxidative Stress and Aging**:

   - **Increased Oxidative Damage with Age**: Numerous studies have shown that levels of oxidative damage to DNA, proteins, and lipids increase with age in various organisms, including humans. For example, higher levels of 8-oxo-7,8-dihydroguanine (8-oxoG) in DNA and protein carbonyls in tissues are commonly observed in older individuals.
   - **Antioxidant Defense Decline**: Aging is often accompanied by a decline in endogenous antioxidant defenses. Enzymes such as superoxide dismutase (SOD), catalase, and glutathione peroxidase (GPx) show reduced activity in aged tissues, leading to increased susceptibility to oxidative stress.

2. **Intervention Studies**:

   - **Antioxidant Supplementation**: Experiments with antioxidant supplementation in various model organisms have shown mixed but often positive results. For instance, overexpression of antioxidant enzymes like SOD and catalase in transgenic mice has been associated with increased lifespan and delayed onset of age-related diseases.
   - **Caloric Restriction (CR)**: CR is one of the most robust interventions known to extend lifespan in a wide range of species. CR reduces metabolic rate and ROS production, thereby decreasing oxidative damage. Studies have shown that CR can increase lifespan and improve healthspan, partially by enhancing antioxidant defenses and reducing oxidative stress.

3. **Genetic Evidence**:

   - **Long-Lived Mutants**: Genetic mutations that enhance oxidative stress resistance often correlate with increased lifespan. For example, mutations that upregulate the insulin/IGF-1 signaling pathway, which is known to increase oxidative stress resistance, have been shown to extend lifespan in C. elegans, Drosophila, and mice.
   - **Mitochondrial DNA Mutations**: Mitochondrial DNA (mtDNA) mutations that reduce ROS production or enhance mitochondrial

function have been linked to increased lifespan and delayed aging in various model organisms.

Debates and Challenges to the Free Radical Theory of Aging:

1. **Contradictory Findings:**

   - **Mixed Results with Antioxidants:** While some studies have shown that antioxidant supplementation can extend lifespan, others have found no significant effects or even negative outcomes. For example, large-scale human clinical trials with antioxidants like vitamin E and beta-carotene have not consistently shown benefits in extending lifespan or preventing age-related diseases.
   - **Paradoxical Effects:** Some long-lived species and individuals exhibit higher levels of oxidative damage compared to their shorter-lived counterparts, challenging the straightforward correlation between oxidative damage and lifespan.

2. **Complexity of Aging:**

   - **Multifactorial Nature of Aging:** Aging is a highly complex and multifactorial process involving genetic, environmental, and stochastic factors. While oxidative stress is a significant contributor, it is not the sole driver of aging. Other factors, such as genomic instability, telomere attrition, epigenetic alterations, loss of proteostasis, and altered intercellular communication, also play crucial roles.
   - **Network Theory of Aging:** The Network Theory of Aging posits that aging results from the interplay of multiple interconnected processes, including oxidative stress, inflammation, and metabolic dysregulation. This broader perspective acknowledges that free radicals are a significant but not exclusive factor in aging.

3. **Adaptive Responses:**

   - **Hormesis:** The concept of hormesis suggests that low levels of stress, including oxidative stress, can stimulate adaptive responses that enhance resilience and promote longevity. For example, exercise-induced ROS production activates stress response pathways that improve mitochondrial function and antioxidant defenses.

- **Signaling Roles of ROS**: ROS are not merely damaging agents; they also serve as important signaling molecules that regulate various physiological processes. Low levels of ROS can activate pathways that promote cellular adaptation, repair, and survival. This dual role complicates the simplistic view of ROS as purely detrimental.

4. **Role of Mitochondria**:

- **Mitochondrial Uncoupling**: Mitochondrial uncoupling reduces the production of ROS by dissipating the proton gradient across the mitochondrial membrane. Studies have shown that mitochondrial uncoupling can extend lifespan and improve healthspan in model organisms, highlighting the importance of mitochondrial function in aging.
- **Mitochondrial Quality Control**: Mechanisms such as mitophagy (selective autophagy of damaged mitochondria) and biogenesis (generation of new mitochondria) are crucial for maintaining mitochondrial health. Enhancing these quality control processes can mitigate oxidative damage and support healthy aging.

The Free Radical Theory of Aging provides a valuable framework for understanding the role of oxidative stress in aging and age-related diseases. While substantial evidence supports the involvement of free radicals in the aging process, the theory is not without its challenges and debates. Contradictory findings, the multifactorial nature of aging, adaptive responses to oxidative stress, and the complex roles of ROS in cellular signaling all contribute to a nuanced understanding of aging. Future research will continue to explore these complexities, aiming to develop targeted interventions that mitigate oxidative damage and promote healthy aging.

Table 1: Mechanisms of Free Radical Involvement in Diabetes Mellitus

Mechanism	Description
Hyperglycemia-Induced Oxidative Stress	High glucose levels lead to glucose autoxidation and protein glycation, producing ROS.
Mitochondrial Dysfunction	Increased ROS production due to hyperglycemia damages mitochondrial DNA, proteins, and lipids.
NADPH Oxidase Activation	Hyperglycemia and insulin resistance activate NADPH oxidase, generating superoxide anion.
Polyol Pathway	Excess glucose is converted to sorbitol, consuming NADPH and reducing antioxidant defenses.

Table 2: Consequences of Oxidative Stress in Diabetes Mellitus

Consequence	Impact
Beta-Cell Dysfunction	ROS damage beta-cell DNA, proteins, and lipids, impairing insulin secretion and causing apoptosis.
Insulin Resistance	Oxidative stress activates inflammatory pathways, interfering with insulin signaling.
Vascular Complications	ROS damage endothelial cells, leading to diabetic retinopathy, nephropathy, neuropathy, and atherosclerosis.

Table 3: Antioxidant Defense Mechanisms

Type	Examples	Function
Enzymatic Antioxidants	Superoxide dismutase (SOD), Catalase, Glutathione peroxidase (GPx)	Detoxify ROS and prevent oxidative damage
Non-Enzymatic Antioxidants	Vitamin C, Vitamin E, Glutathione	Scavenge ROS and regenerate other antioxidants

Table 4: Mechanisms of Free Radical Involvement in Inflammation

Mechanism	Description
Activation of Immune Cells	Immune cells generate large amounts of ROS and RNS during respiratory burst.
Oxidative Damage and Inflammatory Signaling	ROS induce lipid peroxidation, protein oxidation, and DNA damage, activating inflammatory pathways.
Activation of Inflammatory Pathways	ROS activate NF-κB, MAPKs, and JAK/STAT pathways, promoting inflammation.

Table 5: Consequences of Chronic Inflammation Mediated by Free Radicals

Consequence	Impact
Tissue Damage	Persistent ROS production causes chronic oxidative stress and fibrosis.
Autoimmune Diseases	Chronic oxidative stress dysregulates the immune system, promoting autoimmunity.
Cardiovascular Diseases	ROS contribute to atherosclerosis and hypertension.
Cancer	ROS-induced DNA mutations promote carcinogenesis and tumor microenvironment.
Neurodegenerative Diseases	Chronic oxidative stress leads to neurodegenerative diseases such as Alzheimer's and Parkinson's.

Table 6: Mechanisms of Free Radical Involvement in Ischemic Reperfusion Injury

Phase	Mechanism
Ischemia Phase	Reduced oxygen supply, anaerobic metabolism, ion imbalance.
Reperfusion Phase	Sudden oxygen supply leads to ROS burst, mitochondrial ROS generation, xanthine oxidase activation.
Inflammatory Response	Reperfusion triggers neutrophil infiltration and cytokine release, exacerbating oxidative damage.

Table 7: Consequences of Ischemic Reperfusion Injury

Consequence	Description
Oxidative Damage	ROS cause lipid peroxidation, protein oxidation, and DNA damage.
Calcium Overload	Intracellular calcium accumulation disrupts mitochondrial function and triggers cell death.
Inflammatory Response	Neutrophil infiltration and cytokine release promote further injury.
Cell Death	Oxidative stress and calcium overload lead to apoptosis and necrosis.

Table 8: Antioxidant and Therapeutic Interventions

Intervention	Examples	Function
Antioxidant Therapies	Superoxide dismutase (SOD), Catalase, Glutathione peroxidase (GPx), Vitamin C, Vitamin E, Coenzyme Q10	Reduce oxidative stress and improve mitochondrial function
Pharmacological Interventions	NSAIDs, Corticosteroids, Statins	Reduce inflammation and oxidative damage
Lifestyle and Dietary Interventions	Healthy diet, Regular exercise, Smoking cessation	Enhance antioxidant defenses and reduce oxidative stress

SIX
ANTIOXIDANTS

6.1 Endogenous Antioxidants

6.1.1 Enzymatic Antioxidant Defense

Introduction: **Antioxidants** are molecules that inhibit the oxidation of other molecules, thereby protecting cells from the damage caused by free radicals, particularly **reactive oxygen species (ROS)** and **reactive nitrogen species (RNS)**. **Endogenous antioxidants** are produced within the body and form a critical part of the cellular defense system against oxidative stress. Among them, **enzymatic antioxidants** play a key role in neutralizing free radicals and maintaining cellular homeostasis.

Key Enzymatic Antioxidants:

1. **Superoxide Dismutase (SOD)**:

   - **Function**: SOD catalyzes the dismutation of superoxide anion ($O_2^{\cdot-}$) into oxygen (O_2) and hydrogen peroxide (H_2O_2). This reaction is essential for mitigating the harmful effects of superoxide, one of the primary ROS produced in cells.
   - **Isoforms**: There are three isoforms of SOD, each localized in different cellular compartments:

     - **SOD1 (Cu/Zn-SOD)**: Found in the cytoplasm and mitochondrial intermembrane space. It contains copper and zinc as cofactors.
     - **SOD2 (Mn-SOD)**: Located in the mitochondrial matrix and contains manganese as a cofactor. SOD2 is crucial for protecting mitochondria from oxidative damage.

- **SOD3 (EC-SOD)**: Present in the extracellular space and also contains copper and zinc as cofactors.

- **Significance**: Deficiencies or mutations in SOD enzymes are linked to various diseases, including amyotrophic lateral sclerosis (ALS), indicating their critical role in protecting against oxidative damage.

2. **Catalase**:

- **Function**: Catalase catalyzes the decomposition of hydrogen peroxide (H_2O_2) into water (H_2O) and oxygen (O_2). Hydrogen peroxide, while less reactive than superoxide, can be converted into more harmful ROS, such as hydroxyl radicals, if not efficiently removed.
- **Localization**: Catalase is predominantly found in peroxisomes, organelles that play a vital role in detoxifying hydrogen peroxide generated during various metabolic processes.
- **Significance**: Catalase activity is crucial for preventing oxidative damage in cells, particularly in organs with high metabolic activity, such as the liver and kidneys. Impaired catalase function is associated with diseases like acatalasemia.

3. **Glutathione Peroxidase (GPx)**:

- **Function**: GPx reduces hydrogen peroxide (H_2O_2) and organic hydroperoxides to water and corresponding alcohols, using glutathione (GSH) as a substrate. This process helps protect cells from oxidative damage.
- **Isoforms**: There are several isoforms of GPx, each with specific functions and localizations:

  - **GPx1**: Ubiquitously expressed and located in the cytoplasm and mitochondria. It is essential for general cellular protection against oxidative stress.
  - **GPx2**: Primarily found in the gastrointestinal tract, playing a role in protecting the gut lining from oxidative damage.
  - **GPx3**: Present in plasma and extracellular fluids, providing systemic antioxidant protection.

- **GPx4**: Known as phospholipid hydroperoxide glutathione peroxidase, it can reduce lipid hydroperoxides and is crucial for maintaining membrane integrity.

- **Significance**: GPx enzymes are essential for detoxifying peroxides and maintaining the redox balance in cells. Deficiencies in GPx activity are associated with increased susceptibility to oxidative stress and related pathologies, including cancer and cardiovascular diseases.

Mechanisms and Regulation:

1. **Gene Expression**:

- **Nrf2 Pathway**: The transcription factor nuclear factor erythroid 2–related factor 2 (Nrf2) regulates the expression of various antioxidant enzymes, including SOD, catalase, and GPx. Under oxidative stress, Nrf2 translocates to the nucleus and binds to antioxidant response elements (AREs) in the promoters of target genes, enhancing their transcription.

  - **Impact**: Activation of the Nrf2 pathway boosts cellular antioxidant defenses, reducing oxidative damage and promoting cell survival.

2. **Post-Translational Modifications**:

- **Phosphorylation and Acetylation**: Enzymatic antioxidants can be regulated by post-translational modifications, such as phosphorylation and acetylation, which can alter their activity, stability, and subcellular localization.

  - **Example**: Phosphorylation of SOD2 enhances its activity and mitochondrial localization, improving mitochondrial protection against ROS.

3. **Cofactor Availability**:

- ○ **Metal Ions**: The activity of SOD and catalase depends on the availability of metal ion cofactors (e.g., copper, zinc, manganese, iron). Deficiencies in these essential metals can impair antioxidant enzyme function and increase oxidative stress.

  - ▪ **Impact**: Ensuring adequate intake of essential micronutrients is crucial for maintaining optimal antioxidant enzyme activity.

Enzymatic antioxidants, including superoxide dismutase (SOD), catalase, and glutathione peroxidase (GPx), play critical roles in defending cells against oxidative stress. These enzymes work synergistically to neutralize reactive oxygen species (ROS) and maintain cellular redox balance. Understanding the mechanisms of their regulation and function is essential for developing strategies to enhance antioxidant defenses and mitigate oxidative damage, thereby promoting health and longevity.

6.1.2 Non-Enzymatic Antioxidant Defense

6.1.2.1 Glutathione

Introduction: Glutathione (GSH) is a tripeptide composed of glutamine, cysteine, and glycine. It is one of the most important non-enzymatic antioxidants in the body, playing a crucial role in protecting cells from oxidative damage by neutralizing reactive oxygen species (ROS) and reactive nitrogen species (RNS). Glutathione exists in two forms: reduced glutathione (GSH) and oxidized glutathione (GSSG), with the GSH/GSSG ratio serving as an important indicator of cellular redox status.

Biosynthesis of Glutathione:

1. **Synthesis Pathway**:

   - ○ **Step 1**: Glutamate and cysteine are combined by the enzyme **gamma-glutamylcysteine synthetase (GCS)** to form gamma-glutamylcysteine.
   - ○ **Step 2**: Gamma-glutamylcysteine is then combined with glycine by the enzyme **glutathione synthetase (GS)** to produce glutathione.

2. **Regulation**:

   - ○ **Nrf2 Pathway**: The expression of enzymes involved in glutathione synthesis is regulated by the Nrf2 pathway. Under oxidative stress,

Nrf2 activates the transcription of genes encoding gamma-glutamylcysteine synthetase and glutathione synthetase, increasing glutathione production.

- **Feedback Inhibition**: Glutathione itself can inhibit gamma-glutamylcysteine synthetase, providing a feedback mechanism to regulate its own synthesis based on cellular needs.

Functions of Glutathione:

1. **Detoxification**:

   - **Direct Scavenging of ROS**: Glutathione can directly scavenge ROS such as hydroxyl radicals ($\cdot OH$), superoxide anion ($O_2 \cdot^-$), and hydrogen peroxide (H_2O_2), neutralizing them and preventing oxidative damage.
   - **Reduction of Peroxides**: Glutathione peroxidase (GPx) uses glutathione as a substrate to reduce hydrogen peroxide and lipid hydroperoxides to water and corresponding alcohols.
   - **Conjugation Reactions**: Glutathione-S-transferases (GSTs) catalyze the conjugation of glutathione to electrophilic compounds, facilitating their detoxification and excretion.

2. **Redox Homeostasis**:

   - **Maintaining Redox Balance**: The ratio of reduced glutathione (GSH) to oxidized glutathione (GSSG) is a critical indicator of cellular oxidative stress. Under normal conditions, GSH is predominant, maintaining a reducing environment. During oxidative stress, GSH is oxidized to GSSG, and the GSH/GSSG ratio decreases.
   - **Glutathione Reductase**: This enzyme regenerates GSH from GSSG using NADPH as a reducing agent, helping to maintain redox balance.

3. **Cellular Functions**:

   - **Protein Synthesis and Repair**: Glutathione is involved in the synthesis and repair of proteins by maintaining the reduced state of cysteine residues in proteins, which is essential for their proper folding and function.

- ◦ **Regulation of Cell Signaling**: Glutathione modulates various signaling pathways, including those involved in cell proliferation, apoptosis, and immune responses. For example, it can influence the activity of transcription factors such as NF-κB and AP-1.
- ◦ **Immune Function**: Glutathione plays a vital role in immune function by enhancing the proliferation of lymphocytes and the activity of natural killer (NK) cells and macrophages.

Clinical Implications:

1. **Glutathione Deficiency**:

   - ◦ **Causes**: Glutathione deficiency can result from genetic defects, poor diet, chronic diseases, and excessive oxidative stress. Conditions such as HIV/AIDS, liver disease, and neurodegenerative disorders are associated with low glutathione levels.
   - ◦ **Consequences**: Deficiency in glutathione impairs detoxification processes, increases susceptibility to oxidative damage, and compromises immune function, contributing to the progression of various diseases.

2. **Therapeutic Interventions**:

   - ◦ **Glutathione Supplementation**: Oral, intravenous, and inhaled forms of glutathione are used to boost glutathione levels in patients with deficiency. However, the effectiveness of oral supplementation is limited due to poor bioavailability.
   - ◦ **NAC (N-Acetylcysteine)**: NAC is a precursor to cysteine, which is a rate-limiting substrate for glutathione synthesis. NAC supplementation can increase glutathione levels and is used to treat conditions such as acetaminophen overdose, chronic obstructive pulmonary disease (COPD), and liver diseases.
   - ◦ **Dietary Interventions**: Consuming foods rich in glutathione precursors, such as sulfur-containing amino acids (found in garlic, onions, and cruciferous vegetables) and selenium (found in Brazil nuts and seafood), can support glutathione synthesis.

Glutathione is a crucial non-enzymatic antioxidant that protects cells from oxidative damage, maintains redox homeostasis, and supports various cellular functions. Its role in detoxification, redox regulation, and immune function underscores its importance in maintaining health and preventing disease. Understanding the mechanisms of glutathione synthesis and function is essential for developing therapeutic strategies to enhance its levels and combat oxidative stress-related conditions.

6.1.2.2 Vitamin C

Introduction: Vitamin C, also known as **ascorbic acid**, is a water-soluble vitamin that plays a vital role in various biological processes, including acting as a potent antioxidant. It is essential for the maintenance of connective tissue, wound healing, and the proper functioning of the immune system. Due to its antioxidant properties, vitamin C helps protect cells from oxidative damage caused by free radicals, particularly **reactive oxygen species (ROS)** and **reactive nitrogen species (RNS)**.

Functions of Vitamin C:

1. **Antioxidant Defense**:

   - **Scavenging ROS**: Vitamin C directly scavenges ROS, such as superoxide anion ($O_2^{\cdot-}$), hydroxyl radical ($\cdot OH$), and singlet oxygen ($^1O_2$), neutralizing them and preventing oxidative damage to cellular components.
   - **Regeneration of Other Antioxidants**: Vitamin C regenerates other antioxidants, such as vitamin E (tocopherol) and glutathione, back to their active forms. This recycling amplifies the overall antioxidant capacity of the cell.

2. **Collagen Synthesis**:

   - **Cofactor for Hydroxylation**: Vitamin C is a crucial cofactor for the enzymes prolyl hydroxylase and lysyl hydroxylase, which hydroxylate proline and lysine residues in collagen precursors. This hydroxylation is necessary for the proper folding, stability, and function of collagen.

3. **Immune Function**:

- ◦ **Enhancement of Immune Response**: Vitamin C enhances the proliferation and function of immune cells, including T cells, B cells, phagocytes, and natural killer (NK) cells. It also promotes chemotaxis and phagocytosis, aiding in the clearance of pathogens.
- ◦ **Regulation of Cytokine Production**: Vitamin C modulates the production of cytokines, such as interferons and interleukins, which are critical for coordinating the immune response.

4. **Neurotransmitter Synthesis**:

- ◦ **Cofactor for Enzymes**: Vitamin C acts as a cofactor for enzymes involved in the synthesis of neurotransmitters, including dopamine, norepinephrine, and serotonin. This role is crucial for maintaining proper neurological function and mental health.

Sources and Bioavailability:

1. **Dietary Sources**:

- ◦ **Fruits and Vegetables**: Vitamin C is abundant in citrus fruits (oranges, lemons, grapefruits), berries (strawberries, blueberries), kiwi, bell peppers, broccoli, Brussels sprouts, and spinach.
- ◦ **Fortified Foods**: Some foods and beverages are fortified with vitamin C to enhance their nutritional value.

2. **Bioavailability**:

- ◦ **Absorption**: Vitamin C is absorbed in the small intestine through active transport mechanisms. The efficiency of absorption decreases with increasing doses, with a plateau at higher intake levels.
- ◦ **Transport and Storage**: Once absorbed, vitamin C is transported in the blood and distributed to tissues. It is stored in relatively high concentrations in the adrenal glands, pituitary gland, liver, spleen, and leukocytes.

Clinical Implications:

1. **Deficiency**:

- ○ **Scurvy**: Vitamin C deficiency leads to scurvy, characterized by symptoms such as fatigue, weakness, bleeding gums, joint pain, and impaired wound healing. Scurvy results from the impaired synthesis of collagen.
- ○ **Increased Susceptibility to Infections**: Deficiency in vitamin C can weaken the immune system, making individuals more susceptible to infections.

2. Therapeutic Uses:

- ○ **Cold and Flu**: While vitamin C is commonly used to prevent and treat the common cold, evidence on its effectiveness is mixed. Regular supplementation may reduce the duration and severity of colds, particularly in individuals under physical stress.
- ○ **Cancer Treatment**: High-dose intravenous vitamin C is being explored as an adjunct therapy in cancer treatment. It may enhance the effectiveness of chemotherapy and reduce treatment-related side effects, although more research is needed to confirm its efficacy.
- ○ **Cardiovascular Health**: Vitamin C's antioxidant properties may protect against oxidative damage to blood vessels, reducing the risk of cardiovascular diseases. It also helps maintain endothelial function and lower blood pressure.

3. Antioxidant Supplementation:

- ○ **General Health**: Regular intake of vitamin C through diet or supplements can support overall health by enhancing antioxidant defenses, supporting immune function, and promoting collagen synthesis.
- ○ **Oxidative Stress-Related Conditions**: Vitamin C supplementation may benefit conditions associated with increased oxidative stress, such as chronic inflammation, neurodegenerative diseases, and metabolic disorders.

Vitamin C is a vital non-enzymatic antioxidant with a broad range of biological functions, including antioxidant defense, collagen synthesis, immune support, and neurotransmitter synthesis. Its role in neutralizing free radicals and regenerating other antioxidants underscores its importance in maintaining cellular health and preventing oxidative damage. Adequate intake of vitamin C through diet or supplements is essential for preventing deficiency and supporting overall health, particularly in conditions characterized by increased oxidative stress.

6.1.2.3 Vitamin E

Introduction: **Vitamin E** is a group of fat-soluble compounds with distinctive antioxidant properties. The most biologically active form of vitamin E is **alpha-tocopherol**, but other forms, including beta-, gamma-, and delta-tocopherol, as well as tocotrienols, also contribute to its antioxidant activity. Vitamin E plays a crucial role in protecting cell membranes from oxidative damage caused by free radicals, particularly **reactive oxygen species (ROS)** and **reactive nitrogen species (RNS)**.

Functions of Vitamin E:

1. **Antioxidant Defense**:

   - **Lipid Peroxidation Inhibition**: Vitamin E is a potent chain-breaking antioxidant that prevents the propagation of lipid peroxidation in cell membranes. It reacts with lipid peroxyl radicals, converting them into non-radical products and thus terminating the lipid peroxidation chain reaction.
   - **Regeneration by Vitamin C**: The tocopherol radical formed during the antioxidant action of vitamin E can be regenerated back to its active form by vitamin C, enhancing the overall antioxidant network.

2. **Membrane Stabilization**:

   - **Protection of Cell Membranes**: By preventing lipid peroxidation, vitamin E helps maintain the integrity and fluidity of cell membranes, which is essential for proper cellular function and communication.
   - **Interaction with Phospholipids**: Vitamin E interacts with phospholipids in the cell membrane, contributing to the stabilization of membrane structure.

3. **Anti-Inflammatory Properties**:

   - **Inhibition of Pro-Inflammatory Enzymes**: Vitamin E modulates the activity of enzymes involved in inflammation, such as cyclooxygenase (COX) and lipoxygenase (LOX), reducing the production of pro-inflammatory mediators like prostaglandins and leukotrienes.

- **Reduction of Cytokine Production**: Vitamin E also influences the expression of inflammatory cytokines (e.g., TNF-α, IL-1β, IL-6), further contributing to its anti-inflammatory effects.

4. **Immune Function**:

- **Enhancement of Immune Response**: Vitamin E enhances the function of immune cells, including T cells, B cells, and macrophages. It promotes phagocytic activity, cytokine production, and the proliferation of lymphocytes.
- **Protection Against Oxidative Stress**: By reducing oxidative stress, vitamin E helps maintain the function and viability of immune cells, supporting overall immune health.

Sources and Bioavailability:

1. **Dietary Sources**:

- **Plant Oils**: Vitamin E is abundant in plant oils, such as wheat germ oil, sunflower oil, safflower oil, and olive oil.
- **Nuts and Seeds**: Almonds, hazelnuts, and sunflower seeds are excellent sources of vitamin E.
- **Green Leafy Vegetables**: Spinach, kale, and broccoli also provide significant amounts of vitamin E.
- **Fortified Foods**: Some cereals, juices, and margarines are fortified with vitamin E to enhance their nutritional value.

2. **Bioavailability**:

- **Absorption**: Vitamin E is absorbed in the small intestine along with dietary fats. Its absorption is enhanced by the presence of dietary fat and bile acids.
- **Transport and Storage**: Once absorbed, vitamin E is incorporated into chylomicrons and transported to the liver. The liver then redistributes vitamin E to various tissues via very low-density lipoproteins (VLDL).

Vitamin E is stored primarily in adipose tissue, liver, and muscle.

Clinical Implications:

1. **Deficiency**:

   - **Causes**: Vitamin E deficiency can result from malabsorption disorders, genetic abnormalities affecting lipoprotein metabolism (e.g., abetalipoproteinemia), or insufficient dietary intake.
   - **Symptoms**: Deficiency symptoms include peripheral neuropathy, muscle weakness, impaired immune function, and hemolytic anemia due to increased oxidative damage to red blood cells.

2. **Therapeutic Uses**:

   - **Cardiovascular Health**: Vitamin E's antioxidant properties may protect against the oxidative modification of low-density lipoprotein (LDL) cholesterol, a key step in the development of atherosclerosis. Some studies suggest that vitamin E supplementation may reduce the risk of cardiovascular diseases, though results are mixed.
   - **Neuroprotection**: Vitamin E has been studied for its potential to protect against neurodegenerative diseases such as Alzheimer's disease and Parkinson's disease. Its ability to reduce oxidative stress and inflammation in the brain may contribute to its neuroprotective effects.
   - **Skin Health**: Topical and oral vitamin E are used to protect the skin from oxidative damage caused by UV radiation and environmental pollutants. It is commonly included in skincare products for its moisturizing and anti-aging benefits.

3. **Antioxidant Supplementation**:

   - **General Health**: Regular intake of vitamin E through diet or supplements can support overall health by enhancing antioxidant defenses, reducing inflammation, and supporting immune function.
   - **Oxidative Stress-Related Conditions**: Vitamin E supplementation may benefit conditions associated with increased oxidative stress, such as diabetes, chronic inflammation, and certain cancers.

Vitamin E is a crucial non-enzymatic antioxidant that protects cell membranes from oxidative damage, supports immune function, and has anti-inflammatory properties. Its role in neutralizing free radicals and maintaining membrane integrity underscores its importance in cellular health and the prevention of oxidative stress-related diseases. Adequate intake of vitamin E through diet or supplements is essential for preventing deficiency and supporting overall health, particularly in conditions characterized by increased oxidative stress.

6.1.2.4 α-Lipoic Acid

Introduction: α-**Lipoic Acid (ALA)**, also known as thioctic acid, is a naturally occurring compound that acts as a potent antioxidant. It is unique due to its ability to function in both water-soluble and fat-soluble environments, providing broad-spectrum antioxidant protection. ALA plays a critical role in mitochondrial energy metabolism and has been studied extensively for its therapeutic potential in various oxidative stress-related conditions.

Functions of α-Lipoic Acid:

1. **Antioxidant Defense**:

   - **Direct Scavenging of Free Radicals**: ALA can directly neutralize a variety of free radicals, including reactive oxygen species (ROS) and reactive nitrogen species (RNS). This helps prevent oxidative damage to lipids, proteins, and DNA.
   - **Regeneration of Other Antioxidants**: ALA has the unique ability to regenerate other antioxidants, such as vitamin C, vitamin E, and glutathione, thereby enhancing the overall antioxidant defense system.

2. **Mitochondrial Function and Energy Metabolism**:

   - **Cofactor in Mitochondrial Enzymes**: ALA serves as a cofactor for mitochondrial enzyme complexes involved in the oxidative decarboxylation of pyruvate and alpha-ketoglutarate, which are critical steps in the Krebs cycle and energy production.

     - **Enzymes**: Pyruvate dehydrogenase and alpha-ketoglutarate dehydrogenase

- **Enhancement of ATP Production**: By supporting these enzyme functions, ALA helps optimize mitochondrial energy metabolism and ATP production, which is crucial for cellular energy balance.

3. **Metal Chelation**:

- **Binding and Neutralizing Metals**: ALA can chelate metal ions such as iron and copper, which can catalyze the formation of harmful free radicals through Fenton and Haber-Weiss reactions. By binding these metals, ALA helps reduce metal-induced oxidative stress.

4. **Anti-Inflammatory Properties**:

- **Inhibition of NF-κB Pathway**: ALA can inhibit the activation of nuclear factor kappa B (NF-κB), a key regulator of inflammation. This results in reduced production of pro-inflammatory cytokines and mediators.
- **Reduction of Inflammatory Cytokines**: ALA modulates the levels of inflammatory cytokines such as TNF-α, IL-1β, and IL-6, contributing to its anti-inflammatory effects.

Sources and Bioavailability:

1. **Dietary Sources**:

- **Animal Products**: ALA is found in small amounts in red meat, particularly in organ meats like liver and heart.
- **Plant Sources**: Spinach, broccoli, and tomatoes contain modest amounts of ALA.

2. **Bioavailability**:

- **Absorption**: ALA is absorbed in the small intestine through active transport mechanisms. Its bioavailability can vary based on the form of ALA (free acid form vs. salt form) and the presence of dietary fats.
- **Transport and Distribution**: After absorption, ALA is transported in the blood and distributed to various tissues, where it exerts its antioxidant effects. It crosses the blood-brain barrier, providing

neuroprotective benefits.

Clinical Implications:

1. **Diabetes and Diabetic Complications:**

   - **Blood Glucose Regulation**: ALA improves insulin sensitivity and glucose uptake in cells, helping to regulate blood glucose levels in patients with diabetes.
   - **Neuropathy**: ALA has been shown to alleviate symptoms of diabetic neuropathy, such as pain, burning, and numbness, by reducing oxidative stress and improving nerve function.

2. **Neuroprotection:**

   - **Cognitive Function**: ALA supports cognitive function and protects against neurodegenerative diseases by reducing oxidative damage and inflammation in the brain.
   - **Neurodegenerative Diseases**: Studies suggest that ALA may benefit conditions such as Alzheimer's disease, Parkinson's disease, and multiple sclerosis by enhancing mitochondrial function and reducing oxidative stress.

3. **Cardiovascular Health:**

   - **Endothelial Function**: ALA improves endothelial function and reduces oxidative damage to blood vessels, thereby lowering the risk of cardiovascular diseases.
   - **Lipid Profile**: ALA can positively affect lipid profiles by reducing levels of LDL cholesterol and increasing HDL cholesterol.

4. **Skin Health:**

   - **Anti-Aging**: ALA's antioxidant properties help protect the skin from oxidative damage caused by UV radiation and environmental pollutants, promoting skin health and reducing signs of aging.

Supplementation and Dosage:

1. **Forms of Supplementation**:

   ◦ **Oral Supplements**: ALA is available in various oral formulations, including capsules and tablets. It is often used as a dietary supplement to boost antioxidant defenses and support metabolic health.
   ◦ **Intravenous Administration**: In clinical settings, ALA can be administered intravenously for more rapid and potent effects, particularly in the management of acute conditions such as diabetic neuropathy.

2. **Dosage**:

   ◦ **General Health**: Typical doses range from 300 to 600 mg per day for general antioxidant support and health benefits.
   ◦ **Therapeutic Use**: Higher doses, up to 1,200 mg per day, may be used under medical supervision for specific therapeutic purposes, such as treating diabetic neuropathy or neurodegenerative diseases.

α-Lipoic acid (ALA) is a versatile and potent non-enzymatic antioxidant with broad-spectrum benefits. Its ability to function in both water- and fat-soluble environments, regenerate other antioxidants, support mitochondrial function, and chelate metals makes it a valuable compound in the fight against oxidative stress. ALA's therapeutic potential in managing diabetes, neurodegenerative diseases, cardiovascular health, and skin aging highlights its importance in promoting overall health and combating oxidative damage. Adequate intake through diet or supplementation can help harness its protective effects and support optimal health.

6.1.2.5 Melatonin

Introduction: Melatonin is a hormone primarily produced by the pineal gland in the brain. It is well-known for regulating sleep-wake cycles but also possesses significant antioxidant properties. Melatonin's ability to scavenge free radicals and enhance the body's antioxidant defense system makes it an important non-enzymatic antioxidant, particularly in protecting cells from oxidative stress and associated damage.

Functions of Melatonin:

1. **Regulation of Sleep-Wake Cycles**:

- **Circadian Rhythm**: Melatonin is crucial for maintaining circadian rhythms. Its secretion is influenced by light exposure, with levels peaking at night to promote sleep and declining during the day to help wakefulness.
- **Sleep Induction**: By binding to melatonin receptors in the brain, melatonin helps regulate sleep onset and quality, making it an essential component of healthy sleep patterns.

2. **Antioxidant Defense**:

- **Direct Free Radical Scavenging**: Melatonin can directly neutralize a wide range of free radicals, including hydroxyl radicals ($\cdot$OH), superoxide anions ($O2\cdot$-), and peroxynitrite (ONOO-). This helps protect cellular components from oxidative damage.
- **Stimulation of Antioxidant Enzymes**: Melatonin enhances the activity of antioxidant enzymes such as superoxide dismutase (SOD), glutathione peroxidase (GPx), and catalase, further bolstering the body's ability to combat oxidative stress.

3. **Mitochondrial Protection**:

- **Mitochondrial Antioxidant**: Melatonin is particularly effective in protecting mitochondria from oxidative damage. It helps maintain mitochondrial function and integrity by reducing mitochondrial ROS production and enhancing mitochondrial antioxidant defenses.
- **Energy Production**: By preserving mitochondrial function, melatonin supports efficient ATP production and overall cellular energy metabolism.

4. **Anti-Inflammatory Properties**:

- **Inhibition of Pro-Inflammatory Cytokines**: Melatonin modulates the immune response by reducing the production of pro-inflammatory cytokines such as TNF-α, IL-1β, and IL-6. This anti-inflammatory effect helps mitigate chronic inflammation and associated tissue damage.
- **Suppression of NF-κB Pathway**: Melatonin inhibits the activation of the nuclear factor kappa B (NF-κB) pathway, a key regulator of

inflammation, thereby reducing the expression of inflammatory mediators.

Sources and Bioavailability:

1. **Endogenous Production:**

   - **Pineal Gland**: The primary source of melatonin is the pineal gland in the brain. Its production is stimulated by darkness and inhibited by light, aligning melatonin secretion with the sleep-wake cycle.
   - **Other Tissues**: Melatonin is also produced in smaller amounts in other tissues, including the gastrointestinal tract, retina, and immune cells.

2. **Dietary Sources:**

   - **Foods**: While dietary sources of melatonin are limited, certain foods contain small amounts of melatonin, including tart cherries, grapes, tomatoes, and some grains.
   - **Supplements**: Melatonin is widely available as an over-the-counter supplement in various forms, including tablets, capsules, and liquid formulations.

3. **Bioavailability:**

   - **Absorption**: Melatonin is rapidly absorbed from the gastrointestinal tract when taken orally. Its bioavailability can be influenced by factors such as age, time of day, and individual metabolic differences.
   - **Transport and Distribution**: Once absorbed, melatonin is distributed throughout the body, crossing the blood-brain barrier to exert its effects on the central nervous system. It is also transported to other tissues to provide systemic antioxidant protection.

Clinical Implications:

1. **Sleep Disorders:**

- **Insomnia**: Melatonin supplements are commonly used to treat insomnia and other sleep disorders by helping to regulate sleep-wake cycles and improve sleep quality.
- **Jet Lag**: Melatonin is effective in reducing symptoms of jet lag by synchronizing the body's internal clock with the new time zone, facilitating better adaptation to travel across time zones.
- **Shift Work**: Individuals who work night shifts or rotating shifts can benefit from melatonin supplementation to help adjust their sleep patterns and improve daytime sleep.

2. **Neuroprotection**:

- **Cognitive Function**: Melatonin supports cognitive function and protects against neurodegenerative diseases by reducing oxidative stress and inflammation in the brain.
- **Neurodegenerative Diseases**: Studies suggest that melatonin may benefit conditions such as Alzheimer's disease, Parkinson's disease, and multiple sclerosis by enhancing mitochondrial function and reducing neuronal damage.

3. **Cardiovascular Health**:

- **Blood Pressure Regulation**: Melatonin helps regulate blood pressure by promoting vasodilation and reducing oxidative stress in blood vessels, thereby lowering the risk of cardiovascular diseases.
- **Cardioprotection**: Melatonin's antioxidant and anti-inflammatory properties contribute to its cardioprotective effects, reducing the risk of atherosclerosis and other heart-related conditions.

4. **Cancer Treatment**:

- **Adjunct Therapy**: Melatonin has been studied as an adjunct therapy in cancer treatment due to its ability to enhance the efficacy of chemotherapy and radiation therapy while reducing their side effects.
- **Anti-Cancer Properties**: Melatonin exhibits anti-cancer properties by inhibiting tumor growth, promoting apoptosis of cancer cells, and modulating the immune response.

Supplementation and Dosage:

1. **Forms of Supplementation:**

   - **Oral Supplements:** Melatonin is available in various oral formulations, including immediate-release and extended-release tablets and capsules. These supplements are used to regulate sleep patterns and provide antioxidant protection.
   - **Topical and Intravenous Forms:** In clinical settings, melatonin may be administered topically or intravenously for specific therapeutic purposes, such as reducing inflammation and oxidative stress in localized tissues.

2. **Dosage:**

   - **Sleep Regulation:** Typical doses for sleep-related issues range from 0.5 to 5 mg taken 30 to 60 minutes before bedtime. The appropriate dose can vary based on individual needs and response.
   - **Therapeutic Use:** Higher doses, up to 20 mg per day, may be used under medical supervision for specific therapeutic purposes, such as neuroprotection or cancer adjunct therapy.

Melatonin is a versatile non-enzymatic antioxidant with broad-spectrum benefits, including regulation of sleep-wake cycles, protection against oxidative stress, anti-inflammatory effects, and support for mitochondrial function. Its therapeutic potential in managing sleep disorders, neurodegenerative diseases, cardiovascular health, and cancer highlights its importance in promoting overall health and mitigating oxidative damage. Adequate intake through endogenous production, dietary sources, or supplementation can help harness its protective effects and support optimal health.

6.2 Synthetic Antioxidants

6.2.1 Butylated Hydroxy Toluene (BHT)

Introduction: Butylated Hydroxy Toluene (BHT) is a synthetic antioxidant widely used to prevent oxidative rancidity in foods, cosmetics, pharmaceuticals, and other products containing fats and oils. Its primary function is to stabilize free radicals and inhibit the oxidation process, thereby extending the shelf life and preserving the quality of products. BHT is structurally similar to vitamin E and is effective in protecting against oxidative stress.

Chemical Properties and Mechanism of Action:

1. **Chemical Structure:**

   - **Structure:** BHT is a lipophilic organic compound with the chemical formula $C_{15}H_{24}O$. It consists of a hydroxyl group (-OH) attached to a benzene ring, which is substituted with two tert-butyl groups.

2. **Antioxidant Mechanism:**

   - **Free Radical Scavenging:** BHT donates a hydrogen atom from its hydroxyl group to free radicals, neutralizing them and forming a stable BHT radical. This action interrupts the free radical chain reaction that leads to lipid peroxidation.
   - **Stabilization of BHT Radical:** The BHT radical formed after donating a hydrogen atom is stabilized by the resonance of the benzene ring and the steric hindrance provided by the tert-butyl groups, making it less reactive and preventing further oxidative damage.

Applications of BHT:

1. **Food Industry:**

   - **Preservative:** BHT is commonly used as a preservative in a variety of food products, including fats, oils, margarine, cereals, and snack foods. It helps prevent the oxidation of lipids, which can lead to rancidity and off-flavors.
   - **Synergistic Effects:** BHT is often used in combination with other antioxidants, such as butylated hydroxyanisole (BHA) and propyl gallate, to enhance its antioxidant efficacy and provide broader protection against oxidation.

2. **Cosmetics and Pharmaceuticals:**

   - **Stabilizing Agent:** BHT is used in cosmetics and personal care products, such as moisturizers, lipsticks, and sunscreens, to prevent the oxidation of active ingredients and extend the shelf life of the products.

- **Pharmaceuticals**: In the pharmaceutical industry, BHT is used to stabilize formulations containing lipophilic ingredients, ensuring their potency and effectiveness over time.

3. **Industrial Applications**:

- **Lubricants and Fuels**: BHT is used as an additive in lubricants and fuels to prevent oxidation and maintain performance characteristics.
- **Plastics and Rubber**: BHT is incorporated into plastics and rubber to inhibit oxidative degradation, improving their durability and longevity.

Safety and Toxicity:

1. **Regulatory Status**:

- **Food Additive**: BHT is approved for use as a food additive by regulatory agencies such as the U.S. Food and Drug Administration (FDA) and the European Food Safety Authority (EFSA). It is generally recognized as safe (GRAS) when used within specified limits.
- **Cosmetic Ingredient**: BHT is also approved for use in cosmetics and personal care products by regulatory authorities, with guidelines on safe concentration levels.

2. **Toxicological Studies**:

- **Acute Toxicity**: BHT has low acute toxicity, with high doses required to produce adverse effects in animal studies.
- **Chronic Toxicity and Carcinogenicity**: Long-term studies in animals have produced mixed results regarding the carcinogenic potential of BHT. While some studies suggest no significant carcinogenic effects, others indicate a possible risk at high doses. The relevance of these findings to humans is still under investigation.
- **Safety Evaluation**: Regulatory agencies have established acceptable daily intake (ADI) levels for BHT based on comprehensive safety evaluations. These levels are intended to ensure that BHT

consumption through food and other products remains within safe limits.

Health Implications and Controversies:

1. **Potential Health Benefits**:

   - **Antioxidant Protection**: As an antioxidant, BHT may provide protection against oxidative stress-related conditions when consumed within safe limits. Its role in preserving the stability of food and other products contributes to overall product safety and quality.
   - **Possible Therapeutic Uses**: Some research suggests that BHT may have potential therapeutic applications, such as antiviral and anti-inflammatory effects. However, more studies are needed to confirm these potential benefits.

2. **Health Concerns**:

   - **Allergic Reactions**: In rare cases, individuals may experience allergic reactions or sensitivities to BHT, particularly when used in cosmetics or personal care products.
   - **Controversial Studies**: Some studies have raised concerns about the potential for BHT to disrupt endocrine function or contribute to hyperactivity in children. These findings are not conclusive, and further research is needed to clarify these potential risks.

Butylated Hydroxy Toluene (BHT) is a widely used synthetic antioxidant with applications in the food industry, cosmetics, pharmaceuticals, and various industrial sectors. Its ability to stabilize free radicals and prevent oxidative damage makes it valuable in preserving the quality and extending the shelf life of products. While BHT is generally recognized as safe when used within regulatory limits, ongoing research and safety evaluations are essential to ensure its continued safe use. Understanding the balance between its antioxidant benefits and potential health risks is crucial for making informed decisions about its application and consumption.

6.2.2 Butylated Hydroxy Anisole (BHA)

Introduction: **Butylated Hydroxy Anisole (BHA)** is a synthetic antioxidant widely used to preserve fats and oils in food, cosmetics, pharmaceuticals, and various industrial products. Like Butylated Hydroxy Toluene (BHT), BHA prevents oxidative rancidity, thereby extending the shelf life and maintaining the quality of products. BHA is often used in combination with other antioxidants to enhance its efficacy.

Chemical Properties and Mechanism of Action:

1. **Chemical Structure**:

   ◦ **Structure**: BHA is a mixture of two isomers: 2-tert-butyl-4-hydroxyanisole and 3-tert-butyl-4-hydroxyanisole. It is a lipophilic compound with the chemical formula $C_{11}H_{16}O_2$.

2. **Antioxidant Mechanism**:

   ◦ **Free Radical Scavenging**: BHA donates a hydrogen atom from its hydroxyl group to free radicals, neutralizing them and forming a stable BHA radical. This action stops the free radical chain reaction that leads to lipid peroxidation.
   ◦ **Stabilization of BHA Radical**: The BHA radical formed after donating a hydrogen atom is stabilized by the resonance of the aromatic ring and the presence of the tert-butyl group, making it less reactive and preventing further oxidative damage.

Applications of BHA:

1. **Food Industry**:

   ◦ **Preservative**: BHA is commonly used as a preservative in food products, including fats, oils, baked goods, snacks, and cereals. It helps prevent the oxidation of lipids, which can lead to rancidity and off-flavors.
   ◦ **Synergistic Effects**: BHA is often used in combination with other antioxidants, such as BHT and propyl gallate, to provide synergistic effects and broader protection against oxidation.

2. **Cosmetics and Pharmaceuticals**:

- ◦ **Stabilizing Agent**: BHA is used in cosmetics and personal care products, such as moisturizers, lipsticks, and sunscreens, to prevent the oxidation of active ingredients and extend the shelf life of the products.
- ◦ **Pharmaceuticals**: In the pharmaceutical industry, BHA is used to stabilize formulations containing lipophilic ingredients, ensuring their potency and effectiveness over time.

3. **Industrial Applications**:

- ◦ **Plastics and Rubber**: BHA is incorporated into plastics and rubber to inhibit oxidative degradation, improving their durability and longevity.
- ◦ **Lubricants and Fuels**: BHA is used as an additive in lubricants and fuels to prevent oxidation and maintain performance characteristics.

Safety and Toxicity:

1. **Regulatory Status**:

- ◦ **Food Additive**: BHA is approved for use as a food additive by regulatory agencies such as the U.S. Food and Drug Administration (FDA) and the European Food Safety Authority (EFSA). It is generally recognized as safe (GRAS) when used within specified limits.
- ◦ **Cosmetic Ingredient**: BHA is also approved for use in cosmetics and personal care products by regulatory authorities, with guidelines on safe concentration levels.

2. **Toxicological Studies**:

- ◦ **Acute Toxicity**: BHA has low acute toxicity, with high doses required to produce adverse effects in animal studies.
- ◦ **Chronic Toxicity and Carcinogenicity**: Long-term studies in animals have produced mixed results regarding the carcinogenic potential of BHA. While some studies suggest no significant carcinogenic effects, others indicate a possible risk at high doses. The relevance of these findings to humans is still under investigation.

- ○ **Safety Evaluation**: Regulatory agencies have established acceptable daily intake (ADI) levels for BHA based on comprehensive safety evaluations. These levels are intended to ensure that BHA consumption through food and other products remains within safe limits.

Health Implications and Controversies:

1. **Potential Health Benefits**:

   - ○ **Antioxidant Protection**: As an antioxidant, BHA may provide protection against oxidative stress-related conditions when consumed within safe limits. Its role in preserving the stability of food and other products contributes to overall product safety and quality.
   - ○ **Possible Therapeutic Uses**: Some research suggests that BHA may have potential therapeutic applications, such as antiviral and anti-inflammatory effects. However, more studies are needed to confirm these potential benefits.

2. **Health Concerns**:

   - ○ **Allergic Reactions**: In rare cases, individuals may experience allergic reactions or sensitivities to BHA, particularly when used in cosmetics or personal care products.
   - ○ **Controversial Studies**: Some studies have raised concerns about the potential for BHA to disrupt endocrine function or contribute to hyperactivity in children. These findings are not conclusive, and further research is needed to clarify these potential risks.

Butylated Hydroxy Anisole (BHA) is a widely used synthetic antioxidant with applications in the food industry, cosmetics, pharmaceuticals, and various industrial sectors. Its ability to stabilize free radicals and prevent oxidative damage makes it valuable in preserving the quality and extending the shelf life of products. While BHA is generally recognized as safe when used within regulatory limits, ongoing research and safety evaluations are essential to ensure its continued safe use. Understanding the balance between its antioxidant benefits and potential health risks is crucial for making informed decisions about its application and consumption.

SEVEN

FOOD LAWS AND REGULATIONS

7.1 Food Safety Regulations

7.1.1 FDA (Food and Drug Administration)

Introduction: The **Food and Drug Administration (FDA)** is a federal agency of the United States Department of Health and Human Services. It is responsible for protecting public health by ensuring the safety, efficacy, and security of human and veterinary drugs, biological products, medical devices, food supplies, cosmetics, and products that emit radiation. The FDA plays a critical role in food safety regulations, aiming to ensure that food products are safe, sanitary, and properly labeled.

History and Mission:

1. **Establishment and Evolution:**

   - **Origins**: The FDA traces its origins to the 1906 Pure Food and Drug Act, which was enacted to address issues of adulteration and mislabeling of food and drugs. The agency has since evolved to encompass a broader range of responsibilities.
   - **Modern Era**: The FDA's role in food safety was significantly expanded by the Food Safety Modernization Act (FSMA) of 2011, which shifted the focus from responding to food safety issues to preventing them.

2. **Mission and Goals:**

- **Protect Public Health**: The FDA's primary mission is to protect public health by ensuring that food products are safe to eat and free from contaminants.
- **Promote Public Health**: In addition to safety, the FDA aims to promote public health by ensuring that foods are wholesome and properly labeled to provide consumers with accurate information.
- **Regulate Food Supply**: The FDA regulates approximately 80% of the U.S. food supply, including domestic and imported food products, ensuring that they meet established safety standards.

Regulatory Framework:

1. **Food Safety Modernization Act (FSMA)**:

   - **Overview**: The FSMA, signed into law in 2011, represents the most significant overhaul of food safety regulations in over 70 years. It aims to shift the focus from reacting to foodborne illnesses to preventing them.
   - **Key Provisions**: The FSMA includes several key provisions, such as mandatory preventive controls for food facilities, enhanced oversight of imported foods, and the establishment of science-based standards for the safe production and harvesting of fruits and vegetables.
   - **Preventive Controls**: Food facilities are required to develop and implement a written food safety plan that identifies potential hazards and outlines preventive measures to control these hazards.

2. **Hazard Analysis and Critical Control Points (HACCP)**:

   - **Principles**: HACCP is a systematic approach to food safety that identifies, evaluates, and controls hazards throughout the food production process. It is based on seven principles: conducting a hazard analysis, identifying critical control points (CCPs), establishing critical limits, monitoring CCPs, taking corrective actions, verifying the system, and keeping records.
   - **Implementation**: HACCP is mandatory for certain food industries, including seafood and juice processing. The FDA provides guidance and oversight to ensure proper implementation.

3. **Good Manufacturing Practices (GMPs):**

   - **Standards**: GMPs are a set of regulations that outline the minimum sanitary and processing requirements for producing safe and wholesome food. These standards cover various aspects of food production, including personnel, facilities, equipment, and record-keeping.
   - **Compliance**: Food manufacturers must comply with GMPs to ensure that their products are not adulterated or misbranded. The FDA conducts inspections and enforces compliance with GMP standards.

Inspection and Enforcement:

1. **Food Facility Inspections:**

   - **Routine Inspections**: The FDA conducts routine inspections of food facilities to ensure compliance with food safety regulations. These inspections are based on risk assessment, with higher-risk facilities receiving more frequent inspections.
   - **Focused Inspections**: In response to specific concerns, the FDA may conduct focused inspections, such as investigating outbreaks of foodborne illness or following up on consumer complaints.

2. **Enforcement Actions:**

   - **Warning Letters**: When the FDA identifies violations of food safety regulations, it may issue warning letters to food facilities, outlining the violations and requiring corrective actions.
   - **Recalls**: The FDA has the authority to request or mandate recalls of food products that pose a risk to public health. Recalls can be voluntary or mandatory, depending on the severity of the risk.
   - **Seizures and Injunctions**: In cases of serious or repeated violations, the FDA may take legal action, including seizing adulterated or misbranded products or seeking injunctions to halt production until compliance is achieved.

Labeling and Consumer Information:

1. **Nutrition Labeling**:

   - **Nutrition Facts Label**: The FDA requires most packaged foods to carry a Nutrition Facts label that provides information on serving size, calories, and key nutrients. This labeling helps consumers make informed dietary choices.
   - **Ingredient Lists**: Food products must also include a list of ingredients, presented in descending order of predominance by weight. This transparency allows consumers to identify potential allergens and understand the composition of the product.

2. **Health Claims and Nutrient Content Claims**:

   - **Health Claims**: The FDA regulates health claims on food labels to ensure that they are supported by scientific evidence and are not misleading. Health claims describe a relationship between a food or food component and reduced risk of a disease or health-related condition.
   - **Nutrient Content Claims**: These claims characterize the level of a nutrient in a food product, such as "low fat" or "high in fiber." The FDA sets specific criteria for these claims to ensure consistency and accuracy.

The Food and Drug Administration (FDA) plays a vital role in ensuring the safety and quality of the U.S. food supply. Through regulations such as the Food Safety Modernization Act (FSMA), Hazard Analysis and Critical Control Points (HACCP), and Good Manufacturing Practices (GMPs), the FDA aims to prevent foodborne illnesses and protect public health. The FDA's rigorous inspection and enforcement activities, combined with comprehensive labeling requirements, help maintain consumer confidence in the safety and integrity of food products. Understanding the FDA's regulatory framework and its impact on food safety is essential for industry stakeholders and consumers alike.

7.1.2 FPO (Fruit Products Order)

Introduction: The **Fruit Products Order (FPO)** is a regulatory framework established in India to ensure the quality and safety of processed fruit and vegetable products. Originally issued under the Essential Commodities Act of 1955, the FPO is administered by the Ministry of Food

Processing Industries (MFPI). It sets standards for the production, processing, and marketing of fruit and vegetable products to protect consumers and promote fair trade practices.

Historical Background and Objectives:

1. **Establishment and Evolution**:

   - **Historical Context**: The FPO was first introduced in 1955 to regulate the production and distribution of fruit and vegetable products, ensuring that they met specific safety and quality standards.
   - **Revisions and Updates**: Over the years, the FPO has undergone several revisions to adapt to changing industry practices and advancements in food processing technology. These updates aim to maintain the relevance and effectiveness of the regulations.

2. **Objectives**:

   - **Consumer Protection**: The primary objective of the FPO is to protect consumers by ensuring that fruit and vegetable products are safe, hygienic, and of high quality.
   - **Standardization**: The FPO promotes standardization in the processing and marketing of fruit and vegetable products, facilitating fair trade and preventing adulteration and misbranding.
   - **Industry Regulation**: By setting clear guidelines and standards, the FPO regulates the fruit and vegetable processing industry, encouraging best practices and improving overall product quality.

Key Provisions of the FPO:

1. **Licensing and Registration**:

   - **Mandatory Licensing**: Under the FPO, all manufacturers of fruit and vegetable products must obtain a license from the Ministry of Food Processing Industries (MFPI). The license ensures that the manufacturer complies with the standards and regulations set forth in the FPO.
   - **Renewal and Inspection**: Licenses must be renewed periodically, and the renewal process includes inspections to verify ongoing

compliance with FPO standards.

2. **Standards for Processing and Hygiene**:

   - **Quality Standards**: The FPO specifies detailed quality standards for various fruit and vegetable products, including fruit juices, jams, jellies, squashes, pickles, and canned fruits and vegetables. These standards cover aspects such as minimum fruit content, permissible additives, and sensory characteristics.
   - **Hygiene and Sanitation**: The FPO mandates stringent hygiene and sanitation practices in processing facilities. These include guidelines for the cleanliness of equipment and facilities, personal hygiene of workers, and control of pests and contaminants.

3. **Labeling Requirements**:

   - **Product Labeling**: The FPO requires that all fruit and vegetable products be accurately labeled with essential information, including the name of the product, list of ingredients, net weight, date of manufacture, and best-before date.
   - **Nutritional Information**: Labels must also provide nutritional information, including details on caloric content, carbohydrates, proteins, fats, vitamins, and minerals.
   - **Batch Identification**: Each batch of product must have a unique identification code to facilitate traceability and recall if necessary.

4. **Additives and Preservatives**:

   - **Permissible Additives**: The FPO defines a list of permissible food additives and preservatives that can be used in fruit and vegetable products. These additives must be used within the specified limits to ensure safety.
   - **Prohibited Substances**: Certain substances are prohibited under the FPO due to their potential health risks. The use of these substances in fruit and vegetable products is strictly forbidden.

Inspection and Enforcement:

1. **Regular Inspections**:

   - **Facility Inspections**: The FPO mandates regular inspections of processing facilities by authorized officers to ensure compliance with the prescribed standards. Inspections cover all aspects of production, from raw material handling to final product packaging.
   - **Sampling and Testing**: During inspections, samples of products may be taken for laboratory testing to verify compliance with quality and safety standards.

2. **Enforcement Actions**:

   - **Non-Compliance**: If a facility is found to be non-compliant with FPO standards, enforcement actions can be taken. These may include warnings, fines, suspension of licenses, or closure of the facility until compliance is achieved.
   - **Recalls and Seizures**: In cases where products are found to be unsafe or adulterated, the FPO authorities can mandate recalls or seizures of the affected products to protect public health.

Impact and Importance:

1. **Consumer Confidence**:

   - **Safety Assurance**: The FPO provides consumers with assurance that the fruit and vegetable products they purchase are safe, hygienic, and of high quality.
   - **Informed Choices**: Clear labeling requirements enable consumers to make informed choices about the products they buy, including understanding their nutritional content and ingredient composition.

2. **Industry Benefits**:

   - **Standardization**: By establishing clear standards and guidelines, the FPO promotes standardization within the industry, facilitating fair competition and improving product quality.
   - **Market Access**: Compliance with FPO standards can enhance the marketability of Indian fruit and vegetable products, both

domestically and internationally, by meeting recognized safety and quality benchmarks.

The Fruit Products Order (FPO) is a crucial regulatory framework that ensures the safety, quality, and standardization of processed fruit and vegetable products in India. By setting stringent standards for processing, hygiene, labeling, and additives, the FPO protects consumers and promotes best practices within the industry. Regular inspections and enforcement actions help maintain compliance and uphold the integrity of the food supply. Understanding the FPO's provisions and their impact is essential for manufacturers, regulators, and consumers to ensure the continued safety and quality of fruit and vegetable products.

7.1.3 MPO (Meat Products Order)

Introduction: The **Meat Products Order (MPO)** is a regulatory framework established in India to ensure the safety, hygiene, and quality of meat and meat products. The MPO was introduced under the Essential Commodities Act of 1955 and is administered by the Ministry of Food Processing Industries (MFPI). It sets standards for the production, processing, and marketing of meat and meat products to protect consumers and promote best practices within the meat industry.

Historical Background and Objectives:

1. **Establishment and Evolution:**

   - **Historical Context**: The MPO was introduced to regulate the meat industry in India, addressing concerns about the safety and quality of meat products. It aims to prevent adulteration, contamination, and misbranding.
   - **Revisions and Updates**: The MPO has undergone revisions to keep pace with advancements in meat processing technology and changes in industry practices. These updates ensure that the regulations remain relevant and effective.

2. **Objectives:**

   - **Consumer Protection**: The primary objective of the MPO is to protect consumers by ensuring that meat and meat products are safe, hygienic, and of high quality.

- **Standardization**: The MPO promotes standardization in the processing and marketing of meat products, preventing adulteration and ensuring consistency in product quality.
- **Industry Regulation**: By setting clear guidelines and standards, the MPO regulates the meat processing industry, encouraging best practices and improving overall product quality.

Key Provisions of the MPO:

1. **Licensing and Registration**:

   - **Mandatory Licensing**: Under the MPO, all manufacturers of meat and meat products must obtain a license from the Ministry of Food Processing Industries (MFPI). This license ensures that the manufacturer complies with the standards and regulations set forth in the MPO.
   - **Renewal and Inspection**: Licenses must be renewed periodically, and the renewal process includes inspections to verify ongoing compliance with MPO standards.

2. **Standards for Processing and Hygiene**:

   - **Quality Standards**: The MPO specifies detailed quality standards for various meat products, including fresh meat, processed meat, sausages, and canned meat. These standards cover aspects such as permissible additives, microbiological safety, and sensory characteristics.
   - **Hygiene and Sanitation**: The MPO mandates stringent hygiene and sanitation practices in meat processing facilities. These guidelines address the cleanliness of equipment and facilities, personal hygiene of workers, and control of pests and contaminants.

3. **Labeling Requirements**:

   - **Product Labeling**: The MPO requires that all meat and meat products be accurately labeled with essential information, including the name of the product, list of ingredients, net weight, date of manufacture, and best-before date.

- **Nutritional Information**: Labels must provide nutritional information, including details on caloric content, proteins, fats, vitamins, and minerals.
- **Batch Identification**: Each batch of product must have a unique identification code to facilitate traceability and recall if necessary.

4. **Additives and Preservatives**:

- **Permissible Additives**: The MPO defines a list of permissible food additives and preservatives that can be used in meat products. These additives must be used within the specified limits to ensure safety.
- **Prohibited Substances**: Certain substances are prohibited under the MPO due to their potential health risks. The use of these substances in meat products is strictly forbidden.

Inspection and Enforcement:

1. **Regular Inspections**:

- **Facility Inspections**: The MPO mandates regular inspections of meat processing facilities by authorized officers to ensure compliance with the prescribed standards. Inspections cover all aspects of production, from raw material handling to final product packaging.
- **Sampling and Testing**: During inspections, samples of products may be taken for laboratory testing to verify compliance with quality and safety standards.

2. **Enforcement Actions**:

- **Non-Compliance**: If a facility is found to be non-compliant with MPO standards, enforcement actions can be taken. These may include warnings, fines, suspension of licenses, or closure of the facility until compliance is achieved.
- **Recalls and Seizures**: In cases where products are found to be unsafe or adulterated, the MPO authorities can mandate recalls or seizures of the affected products to protect public health.

Impact and Importance:

1. **Consumer Confidence**:

   - **Safety Assurance**: The MPO provides consumers with assurance that the meat products they purchase are safe, hygienic, and of high quality.
   - **Informed Choices**: Clear labeling requirements enable consumers to make informed choices about the products they buy, including understanding their nutritional content and ingredient composition.

2. **Industry Benefits**:

   - **Standardization**: By establishing clear standards and guidelines, the MPO promotes standardization within the industry, facilitating fair competition and improving product quality.
   - **Market Access**: Compliance with MPO standards can enhance the marketability of Indian meat products, both domestically and internationally, by meeting recognized safety and quality benchmarks.

The Meat Products Order (MPO) is a crucial regulatory framework that ensures the safety, hygiene, and quality of meat and meat products in India. By setting stringent standards for processing, hygiene, labeling, and additives, the MPO protects consumers and promotes best practices within the industry. Regular inspections and enforcement actions help maintain compliance and uphold the integrity of the food supply. Understanding the MPO's provisions and their impact is essential for manufacturers, regulators, and consumers to ensure the continued safety and quality of meat products.

7.1.4 AGMARK

Introduction: AGMARK is a certification mark employed by the Indian government to ensure the quality and standardization of agricultural products. The term AGMARK is derived from the words 'Agri' (agriculture) and 'mark' (certification mark). This certification is regulated by the Directorate of Marketing and Inspection, an agency of the Ministry of Agriculture and Farmers Welfare, under the Agricultural Produce (Grading and Marking) Act of 1937.

Historical Background and Objectives:

1. **Establishment and Evolution:**

   - **Origins:** The AGMARK certification was introduced in 1937 to provide a standardized grading system for agricultural products in India. The goal was to protect consumers from substandard products and promote fair trade practices.
   - **Evolution:** Over the decades, the AGMARK system has expanded and evolved to cover a wide range of agricultural commodities, adapting to new agricultural practices and technological advancements.

2. **Objectives:**

   - **Consumer Protection:** AGMARK aims to protect consumers by ensuring the availability of high-quality agricultural products that meet defined standards of purity and quality.
   - **Standardization:** The certification promotes the standardization of agricultural products, facilitating domestic and international trade by providing reliable quality benchmarks.
   - **Quality Assurance:** By setting strict quality criteria and standards, AGMARK ensures that agricultural products are processed, packed, and marketed under hygienic and controlled conditions.

Key Provisions of AGMARK:

1. **Standards and Grading:**

   - **Quality Standards:** AGMARK defines specific quality standards for a wide range of agricultural products, including cereals, pulses, fruits, vegetables, vegetable oils, ghee, spices, honey, and other commodities. These standards cover aspects such as size, color, weight, moisture content, purity, and freedom from adulterants.
   - **Grading System:** Products are graded based on their quality, and each grade reflects a different level of quality. For example, wheat may be graded as Grade A, Grade B, etc., with Grade A representing the highest quality.

2. **Certification and Licensing:**

- **Mandatory Certification**: To use the AGMARK certification, producers and processors must obtain a license from the Directorate of Marketing and Inspection. This ensures that only certified facilities that meet the required standards can use the AGMARK mark.
- **Inspection and Testing**: Licensed facilities are subject to regular inspections and testing by AGMARK authorities to verify compliance with the established standards. Samples of products are tested in AGMARK-certified laboratories to ensure they meet quality criteria.

3. **Labeling Requirements**:

- **Product Labeling**: Products certified under AGMARK must be accurately labeled with essential information, including the name of the product, grade, net weight, date of packing, and certification details.
- **AGMARK Seal**: The AGMARK seal is a recognizable symbol of quality that is displayed on certified products. This seal provides consumers with assurance that the product has been inspected and meets high-quality standards.

Inspection and Enforcement:

1. **Regular Inspections**:

- **Facility Inspections**: AGMARK authorities conduct regular inspections of certified facilities to ensure ongoing compliance with quality standards. These inspections cover all aspects of production, processing, and packaging.
- **Sampling and Testing**: During inspections, samples of products are collected and tested in AGMARK-certified laboratories to verify that they meet the required quality standards.

2. **Enforcement Actions**:

- **Non-Compliance**: If a facility is found to be non-compliant with AGMARK standards, enforcement actions can be taken. These may include warnings, fines, suspension of licenses, or revocation of certification.

- ○ **Product Recalls**: In cases where products are found to be substandard or adulterated, AGMARK authorities can mandate recalls of the affected products to protect consumer health.

Impact and Importance:

1. **Consumer Confidence**:

   - ○ **Quality Assurance**: The AGMARK certification provides consumers with assurance that the agricultural products they purchase are of high quality and free from adulteration.
   - ○ **Informed Choices**: Clear labeling and the presence of the AGMARK seal enable consumers to make informed choices about the products they buy, ensuring they get value for their money.

2. **Industry Benefits**:

   - ○ **Market Access**: Compliance with AGMARK standards can enhance the marketability of agricultural products, both domestically and internationally, by meeting recognized quality benchmarks.
   - ○ **Fair Trade**: AGMARK promotes fair trade practices by providing a standardized grading system that facilitates transparent and equitable transactions between producers, processors, and consumers.

AGMARK is a vital certification mark that ensures the quality and standardization of agricultural products in India. By setting stringent quality standards and grading criteria, AGMARK protects consumers, promotes fair trade, and enhances the marketability of Indian agricultural products. Regular inspections and enforcement actions help maintain compliance and uphold the integrity of the AGMARK certification. Understanding the provisions and impact of AGMARK is essential for producers, processors, regulators, and consumers to ensure the continued availability of high-quality agricultural products.

7.1.5 HACCP (Hazard Analysis Critical Control Point)

Introduction: Hazard Analysis Critical Control Point (HACCP) is a systematic, preventive approach to food safety that addresses physical, chemical, and biological hazards as a means of prevention rather than end-product inspection. HACCP is used in the food industry to identify potential food safety hazards, so key actions, known as Critical Control Points (CCPs), can be taken to reduce or eliminate these risks.

Historical Background and Objectives:

1. **Establishment and Evolution:**

   - **Origins:** The HACCP system was initially developed in the 1960s by the Pillsbury Company, NASA, and the U.S. Army Laboratories to ensure the safety of food for astronauts. Its success led to broader adoption in the food industry.
   - **Global Adoption:** HACCP has since been recognized and recommended by various international organizations, including the World Health Organization (WHO) and the Food and Agriculture Organization (FAO), and is mandated in many countries as part of food safety regulations.

2. **Objectives:**

   - **Preventive Approach:** HACCP aims to prevent food safety hazards rather than relying solely on end-product testing. It emphasizes identifying and controlling potential hazards throughout the food production process.
   - **Consumer Protection:** The primary objective is to ensure the safety of food products, thereby protecting public health and reducing the incidence of foodborne illnesses.
   - **Regulatory Compliance:** HACCP helps food businesses comply with national and international food safety regulations, facilitating trade and consumer trust.

Principles of HACCP:

1. **Conduct a Hazard Analysis:**

   - **Identify Hazards:** Determine potential physical, chemical, and biological hazards that could affect food safety at each stage of the production process.

- **Evaluate Hazards**: Assess the likelihood and severity of these hazards to prioritize which ones need control measures.

2. **Determine the Critical Control Points (CCPs)**:

- **Identify CCPs**: Identify points in the process where control measures can be applied to prevent, eliminate, or reduce hazards to acceptable levels. CCPs are critical to ensuring food safety.
- **Examples**: Examples of CCPs include cooking, cooling, packaging, and metal detection steps.

3. **Establish Critical Limits**:

- **Define Critical Limits**: Set maximum or minimum values for parameters that must be controlled at CCPs to ensure food safety. These limits could include temperature, time, pH, and other measurable criteria.
- **Monitoring Requirements**: Establish procedures for monitoring these critical limits to ensure they are consistently met.

4. **Establish Monitoring Procedures**:

- **Monitoring Methods**: Develop methods and procedures to monitor CCPs and ensure that critical limits are being met. This may include visual inspections, measurements, and testing.
- **Frequency**: Determine the frequency of monitoring and assign responsibility to specific personnel.

5. **Establish Corrective Actions**:

- **Define Corrective Actions**: Develop specific actions to be taken when monitoring indicates that a CCP is not within the established critical limits. These actions should ensure that the CCP is brought back under control and prevent potentially unsafe food from reaching consumers.
- **Documentation**: Record corrective actions taken to provide a traceable history of the issue and its resolution.

6. **Establish Verification Procedures**:

   - **Verification Methods**: Implement procedures to verify that the HACCP system is working effectively. This may include audits, reviews of records, and testing of end products.
   - **Validation**: Validate that the control measures and critical limits are capable of controlling the identified hazards.

7. **Establish Record-Keeping and Documentation Procedures**:

   - **Documentation**: Maintain comprehensive records of all HACCP activities, including hazard analyses, CCP determinations, critical limits, monitoring activities, corrective actions, and verification procedures.
   - **Compliance**: Ensure that records are readily accessible and demonstrate compliance with HACCP principles and regulatory requirements.

Applications and Benefits of HACCP:

1. **Food Industry Applications**:

   - **Broad Scope**: HACCP is applicable to all segments of the food industry, including primary production, processing, manufacturing, distribution, and retail.
   - **Adaptability**: The HACCP system is adaptable to various types of food operations and products, from small-scale food producers to large multinational companies.

2. **Benefits**:

   - **Enhanced Food Safety**: By focusing on prevention, HACCP significantly enhances the safety of food products, reducing the risk of foodborne illnesses.
   - **Improved Compliance**: HACCP helps businesses comply with national and international food safety regulations, facilitating market access and consumer trust.

- **Cost-Effective**: Implementing HACCP can be cost-effective in the long run by reducing the need for extensive end-product testing and minimizing the costs associated with food recalls and foodborne illness outbreaks.
- **Continuous Improvement**: The systematic approach of HACCP promotes continuous improvement in food safety management practices.

Challenges and Implementation:

1. **Challenges**:

- **Resource Intensive**: Implementing HACCP can be resource-intensive, requiring significant time, expertise, and financial investment, particularly for small and medium-sized enterprises (SMEs).
- **Training and Expertise**: Effective HACCP implementation requires well-trained personnel with expertise in food safety and hazard analysis. Ongoing training and education are essential to maintain the system's effectiveness.
- **Documentation**: Maintaining comprehensive and accurate documentation can be challenging but is critical for demonstrating compliance and traceability.

2. **Implementation Steps**:

- **Commitment from Management**: Successful HACCP implementation requires strong commitment and support from top management.
- **Form a HACCP Team**: Assemble a multidisciplinary team with the necessary expertise to develop and implement the HACCP plan.
- **Conduct a Preliminary Hazard Analysis**: Identify and evaluate potential hazards associated with the product and process.
- **Develop and Implement the HACCP Plan**: Follow the HACCP principles to develop a detailed plan, including CCPs, critical limits, monitoring procedures, corrective actions, verification, and documentation.
- **Training and Education**: Provide comprehensive training for all personnel involved in the HACCP system to ensure they understand

their roles and responsibilities.

The Hazard Analysis Critical Control Point (HACCP) system is a proactive, systematic approach to food safety that focuses on preventing hazards rather than relying solely on end-product testing. By identifying and controlling potential hazards throughout the food production process, HACCP enhances food safety, protects public health, and helps businesses comply with regulatory requirements. Despite the challenges associated with its implementation, the benefits of HACCP, including improved food safety, regulatory compliance, and cost-effectiveness, make it an essential component of modern food safety management systems. Understanding and applying HACCP principles is crucial for all stakeholders in the food industry to ensure the production of safe, high-quality food products.

7.1.6 GMP (Good Manufacturing Practices)

Introduction: Good Manufacturing Practices (GMP) are a set of guidelines and regulations aimed at ensuring that food products are consistently produced and controlled according to quality standards. GMP covers all aspects of production, from raw material sourcing to final product distribution, to minimize risks associated with production and processing. Adherence to GMP is essential for maintaining food safety, quality, and consumer confidence.

Historical Background and Objectives:

1. **Establishment and Evolution:**

   - **Origins:** GMP regulations were first developed in the mid-20th century to address increasing concerns about food safety and product quality. They have since evolved to encompass a wide range of industries, including pharmaceuticals, cosmetics, and medical devices.
   - **Global Standards:** GMP guidelines have been adopted and adapted by various countries and international organizations, such as the World Health Organization (WHO) and the Food and Agriculture Organization (FAO), to ensure global consistency in food safety standards.

2. **Objectives:**

- **Consumer Protection**: The primary objective of GMP is to ensure that food products are safe for consumption and free from contamination.
- **Quality Assurance**: GMP aims to maintain high quality standards throughout the production process, ensuring that products meet specified quality attributes.
- **Regulatory Compliance**: GMP helps food businesses comply with national and international food safety regulations, facilitating trade and consumer trust.

Key Provisions of GMP:

1. **Personnel and Training:**

   - **Qualified Personnel**: GMP requires that all personnel involved in production are adequately qualified, trained, and supervised to ensure they understand and follow the necessary procedures.
   - **Ongoing Training**: Regular training programs should be implemented to keep staff updated on GMP requirements, safety protocols, and quality control measures.

2. **Facilities and Equipment:**

   - **Design and Maintenance**: Production facilities and equipment must be designed, constructed, and maintained to prevent contamination and ensure smooth operations. This includes proper sanitation, pest control, and maintenance of equipment.
   - **Equipment Calibration**: All equipment used in the production process must be regularly calibrated and validated to ensure accurate and consistent performance.

3. **Production and Process Controls:**

   - **Standard Operating Procedures (SOPs)**: GMP requires the development and implementation of SOPs for all aspects of production, including raw material handling, processing, packaging, and storage.
   - **Process Validation**: Critical processes must be validated to demonstrate that they consistently produce products meeting

predetermined specifications and quality attributes.

- **Batch Records**: Detailed batch records should be maintained to document each step of the production process, ensuring traceability and accountability.

4. **Sanitation and Hygiene**:

- **Hygiene Standards**: High standards of personal hygiene must be maintained by all personnel to prevent contamination. This includes the use of protective clothing, handwashing protocols, and restrictions on eating and drinking in production areas.
- **Sanitation Procedures**: Regular cleaning and sanitation procedures must be established and followed for facilities, equipment, and utensils to prevent microbial contamination.

5. **Quality Control**:

- **Raw Material Testing**: Raw materials must be tested and verified to meet quality standards before use in production.
- **In-Process Controls**: Regular in-process checks should be conducted to ensure that production parameters are within specified limits and that the process is under control.
- **Finished Product Testing**: Final products must undergo rigorous testing to verify that they meet all quality and safety standards before release to the market.

6. **Documentation and Record-Keeping**:

- **Comprehensive Records**: GMP requires comprehensive documentation of all aspects of production, including SOPs, batch records, testing results, and deviation reports. These records must be accurate, complete, and readily accessible for review.
- **Traceability**: Documentation should enable full traceability of products from raw materials to finished goods, facilitating recalls if necessary.

Inspection and Enforcement:

1. **Regular Inspections**:

   - **Facility Inspections**: Regulatory authorities conduct regular inspections of production facilities to ensure compliance with GMP standards. These inspections cover all aspects of production, from raw material handling to final product packaging.
   - **Audits**: In addition to regulatory inspections, internal and third-party audits should be conducted to assess GMP compliance and identify areas for improvement.

2. **Enforcement Actions**:

   - **Non-Compliance**: If a facility is found to be non-compliant with GMP standards, enforcement actions can be taken. These may include warnings, fines, suspension of production, or closure of the facility until compliance is achieved.
   - **Recalls**: In cases where products are found to be unsafe or do not meet quality standards, regulatory authorities can mandate recalls to protect consumer health.

Impact and Importance:

1. **Consumer Confidence**:

   - **Quality Assurance**: GMP provides consumers with assurance that the food products they purchase are produced under stringent quality control measures, ensuring safety and consistency.
   - **Informed Choices**: Clear labeling and adherence to GMP standards enable consumers to make informed choices about the products they buy.

2. **Industry Benefits**:

   - **Market Access**: Compliance with GMP standards enhances the marketability of food products, both domestically and internationally, by meeting recognized quality and safety benchmarks.

- **Operational Efficiency**: Implementing GMP can improve operational efficiency by standardizing processes, reducing waste, and minimizing the risk of product recalls.

Good Manufacturing Practices (GMP) are essential guidelines and regulations that ensure the safety, quality, and consistency of food products. By covering all aspects of production, from raw material sourcing to final product distribution, GMP helps protect consumers and maintain high standards within the food industry. Regular inspections, thorough documentation, and strict enforcement actions help ensure compliance with GMP standards, fostering consumer trust and facilitating market access. Understanding and implementing GMP principles is crucial for all stakeholders in the food production process to ensure the production of safe, high-quality food products.

7.2 Adulteration of Foods

7.2.1 Definition and Types

Introduction: **Adulteration of foods** refers to the practice of adding, substituting, or removing substances in food products in a way that compromises their quality, safety, or nutritional value. This unethical practice can pose significant health risks to consumers and undermine trust in the food supply chain. Understanding the various types of food adulteration and their implications is essential for developing effective strategies to combat this issue.

Definition of Food Adulteration:

1. **Legal Definition**:

   - **General Definition**: Food adulteration is defined as the deliberate addition or substitution of substances in food products that can degrade their quality, safety, or nutritional value. This can include adding harmful substances, removing valuable ingredients, or using substandard raw materials.
   - **Regulatory Definition**: According to various food safety regulations, adulteration involves the presence of any foreign substance or impurity in food that makes it unfit for consumption, either due to safety concerns or quality degradation.

Types of Food Adulteration:

1. **Intentional Adulteration:**

   - **Economic Adulteration**: Adding cheaper substances to increase the quantity or weight of a product to gain economic profit. Examples include adding water to milk, starch to spices, or artificial sweeteners to honey.

     - **Example**: Adding chalk powder to flour to increase weight.

   - **Toxic Adulteration**: Introducing harmful substances that can pose serious health risks. These substances may include toxic chemicals, non-edible colors, and other hazardous materials.

     - **Example**: Adding lead chromate to turmeric to enhance its yellow color.

2. **Incidental Adulteration:**

   - **Contamination**: Accidental introduction of impurities or contaminants during production, processing, or packaging. This can include physical contaminants (e.g., dirt, hair), chemical contaminants (e.g., pesticides, heavy metals), and biological contaminants (e.g., bacteria, viruses).

     - **Example**: Contamination of grains with aflatoxins produced by molds.

   - **Improper Handling**: Adulteration due to poor handling practices, such as inadequate storage conditions, improper transportation, or lack of hygiene during processing.

     - **Example**: Spoilage of food due to improper refrigeration.

3. **Misbranding and Misrepresentation:**

   - **False Labeling**: Providing false or misleading information on food labels regarding ingredients, origin, nutritional content, or quality. This can mislead consumers and result in the consumption of adulterated products.

- **Example**: Labeling a product as "organic" when it does not meet organic standards.

- **Substitution**: Replacing a high-quality ingredient with a lower-quality or different ingredient without informing consumers. This can degrade the quality and authenticity of the product.

- **Example**: Using synthetic vanilla flavor instead of natural vanilla extract.

4. **Additive Adulteration**:

- **Unauthorized Additives**: Using additives that are not approved for use in food products or exceeding the permissible limits of approved additives. These additives can affect the safety and quality of the food.

- **Example**: Using non-permitted artificial colors in confectionery items.

- **Excessive Use of Preservatives**: Overuse of preservatives to extend shelf life can pose health risks and affect the sensory qualities of food.

- **Example**: Excessive use of sulfites in dried fruits to maintain color.

Impact of Food Adulteration:

1. **Health Risks**:

- **Short-Term Effects**: Consumption of adulterated food can lead to immediate health issues such as food poisoning, gastrointestinal disorders, and allergic reactions.
- **Long-Term Effects**: Prolonged consumption of adulterated food can result in chronic health problems, including organ damage, developmental issues in children, and increased risk of cancer and other serious illnesses.

2. **Economic Consequences**:

  - **Consumer Loss**: Adulteration leads to financial losses for consumers who pay for substandard or unsafe products.
  - **Industry Impact**: Adulteration can damage the reputation of food manufacturers and brands, leading to loss of consumer trust and market share. It can also result in costly recalls and legal penalties.

3. **Regulatory and Legal Issues**:

  - **Regulatory Actions**: Governments and regulatory bodies impose strict regulations and monitoring to prevent food adulteration. Non-compliance can result in severe penalties, including fines, product recalls, and suspension of licenses.
  - **Legal Liability**: Food manufacturers and sellers can be held legally liable for harm caused by adulterated products, leading to lawsuits and compensation claims.

Preventive Measures and Strategies:

1. **Regulatory Frameworks**:

  - **Legislation**: Implementation of stringent food safety laws and regulations to define and penalize food adulteration.
  - **Surveillance and Monitoring**: Regular inspections, sampling, and testing of food products by regulatory authorities to detect and prevent adulteration.

2. **Industry Practices**:

  - **Quality Control Systems**: Adoption of robust quality control and assurance systems, such as Good Manufacturing Practices (GMP) and Hazard Analysis Critical Control Point (HACCP), to maintain high standards of food safety.
  - **Traceability Systems**: Implementation of traceability systems to track the origin and movement of food products throughout the supply chain, ensuring accountability and transparency.

3. **Consumer Awareness**:

   - **Education and Awareness Campaigns**: Educating consumers about the risks of food adulteration and how to identify and avoid adulterated products.
   - **Advocacy and Reporting**: Encouraging consumers to report suspected cases of food adulteration to regulatory authorities for investigation and action.

Food adulteration is a significant challenge that poses serious health risks to consumers and undermines the integrity of the food supply chain. Understanding the various types of adulteration and their impacts is crucial for developing effective preventive measures. Regulatory frameworks, industry practices, and consumer awareness all play vital roles in combating food adulteration and ensuring the availability of safe, high-quality food products. Collaborative efforts among stakeholders are essential to maintain food safety and protect public health.

7.2.2 Detection Methods

Introduction: Detecting food adulteration is crucial for ensuring the safety, quality, and authenticity of food products. Various methods are employed to identify adulterants, contaminants, and substandard practices in the food supply chain. These methods range from simple, traditional techniques to advanced, sophisticated analytical technologies.

Detection Methods:

1. **Physical Examination**:

   - **Visual Inspection**: This is the simplest method and involves examining the appearance, color, texture, and consistency of food products. Visual anomalies such as unusual colors, particles, or separation can indicate adulteration.

     - **Example**: Visual inspection of spices like turmeric for artificial coloring.

   - **Microscopic Examination**: Using a microscope to identify foreign particles, contaminants, or the presence of substandard ingredients in food products.

- **Example**: Microscopic examination of flour to detect starch adulteration.

2. **Chemical Tests**:

   - **Spot Tests**: Simple, rapid tests that involve applying a chemical reagent to a small sample of food to observe color changes or reactions that indicate the presence of adulterants.

     - **Example**: Testing milk for the presence of water by adding a drop on a polished surface and observing its flow pattern.

   - **Titration Methods**: Quantitative chemical analysis techniques that involve the addition of a titrant to a food sample until a reaction is complete, allowing the measurement of specific adulterants.

     - **Example**: Determining the acidity level in vinegar to check for dilution.

3. **Spectroscopic Methods**:

   - **Infrared Spectroscopy (IR)**: This method measures the absorption of infrared light by food components, providing information about their molecular composition. It is used to detect adulterants based on characteristic absorption patterns.

     - **Example**: Identifying adulteration in edible oils by analyzing their IR spectra.

   - **Ultraviolet-Visible Spectroscopy (UV-Vis)**: This technique involves measuring the absorbance of UV or visible light by food samples. It helps detect the presence of specific adulterants that absorb light at characteristic wavelengths.

     - **Example**: Detecting synthetic dyes in fruit juices using UV-Vis spectroscopy.

4. **Chromatographic Methods**:

- **High-Performance Liquid Chromatography (HPLC)**: HPLC separates, identifies, and quantifies components in a food sample based on their interactions with a stationary phase and a mobile phase. It is highly effective in detecting a wide range of adulterants.

  - **Example**: Analyzing honey for added sugars using HPLC.

- **Gas Chromatography (GC)**: GC separates volatile compounds in a food sample, allowing for the detection of adulterants based on their retention times and mass spectra.

  - **Example**: Detecting adulteration in essential oils by analyzing their volatile profiles.

5. **Mass Spectrometry (MS)**:

- **Coupled Techniques (GC-MS, LC-MS)**: Combining chromatography (GC or HPLC) with mass spectrometry enhances the detection capabilities by providing detailed molecular information. These methods are highly sensitive and specific.

  - **Example**: Identifying pesticide residues in fruits and vegetables using GC-MS.

- **Direct MS Techniques**: Methods like Matrix-Assisted Laser Desorption/Ionization (MALDI-MS) allow for the rapid identification of adulterants in complex food matrices.

  - **Example**: Detecting protein adulteration in milk powder using MALDI-MS.

6. **Nuclear Magnetic Resonance (NMR) Spectroscopy**:

- **NMR Analysis**: NMR provides detailed information about the molecular structure of food components. It is used to authenticate food products and detect adulteration based on characteristic NMR spectra.

- **Example**: Analyzing the authenticity of olive oil by comparing its NMR profile to that of pure olive oil.

7. **DNA-Based Methods**:

   - **Polymerase Chain Reaction (PCR)**: PCR amplifies specific DNA sequences, allowing for the identification of species or specific adulterants. It is widely used for detecting meat and fish adulteration.

     - **Example**: Identifying the species of meat in processed products to detect substitution.

   - **DNA Barcoding**: This method uses a short genetic sequence from a standardized region of the genome to identify and differentiate species, ensuring the authenticity of food products.

     - **Example**: Verifying the botanical origin of honey using DNA barcoding.

8. **Immunoassays**:

   - **Enzyme-Linked Immunosorbent Assay (ELISA)**: ELISA uses antibodies to detect specific proteins or antigens in food samples. It is highly sensitive and specific, making it suitable for detecting various adulterants and contaminants.

     - **Example**: Detecting aflatoxin contamination in grains using ELISA.

   - **Lateral Flow Immunoassay**: Similar to pregnancy tests, these assays use antibodies to detect specific adulterants in food samples, providing rapid and easy-to-interpret results.

     - **Example**: Rapid detection of gluten contamination in food products for people with celiac disease.

Detecting food adulteration is essential for ensuring food safety, quality, and consumer trust. A wide range of methods, from simple visual inspections to advanced analytical techniques, are employed to identify adulterants and contaminants in food products. Each method has its advantages and limitations, and the choice of method depends on the specific adulterant, the food matrix, and the required sensitivity and specificity. Implementing effective detection methods, along with robust regulatory frameworks and industry practices, is crucial for combating food adulteration and protecting public health.

7.2.3 Prevention and Control Measures

Introduction: Preventing and controlling food adulteration is essential to ensure the safety, quality, and integrity of food products. Effective measures require a multifaceted approach involving regulatory frameworks, industry practices, and consumer awareness. This section outlines key strategies and practices to prevent and control food adulteration.

Prevention and Control Measures:

1. **Regulatory Frameworks**:

   - **Legislation and Standards**: Implementing stringent food safety laws and standards is crucial. These regulations should clearly define what constitutes adulteration, set permissible limits for additives and contaminants, and outline penalties for non-compliance.

     - **Example**: The Food Safety and Standards Authority of India (FSSAI) sets regulations for food safety standards and enforces compliance to prevent adulteration.

   - **Regular Inspections and Audits**: Conducting regular inspections and audits of food production facilities ensures adherence to safety standards. Inspections should be carried out by trained professionals who can identify potential sources of adulteration.

     - **Example**: Routine inspections by regulatory authorities to verify compliance with Good Manufacturing Practices (GMP).

2. **Industry Practices**:

- **Good Manufacturing Practices (GMP)**: Implementing GMP ensures that food products are consistently produced and controlled according to quality standards. GMP covers all aspects of production, including raw material sourcing, processing, packaging, and storage.

  - **Example**: Maintaining hygienic conditions in processing facilities to prevent contamination.

- **Hazard Analysis Critical Control Point (HACCP)**: Adopting HACCP helps identify critical points in the production process where hazards, including adulteration, can be controlled. This preventive approach minimizes the risk of adulteration.

  - **Example**: Monitoring critical control points in the production of dairy products to prevent contamination.

- **Traceability Systems**: Implementing traceability systems allows tracking the movement of food products through the supply chain. This helps in identifying and addressing sources of adulteration.

  - **Example**: Using barcodes and RFID tags to trace the origin and journey of food products.

3. **Technological Innovations**:

- **Advanced Detection Methods**: Utilizing advanced detection methods, such as spectroscopy, chromatography, and DNA-based techniques, can identify adulterants with high precision and accuracy.

  - **Example**: Using high-performance liquid chromatography (HPLC) to detect synthetic dyes in food products.

- **Blockchain Technology**: Blockchain provides a secure and transparent way to record transactions and track food products through the supply chain, enhancing traceability and reducing the risk of adulteration.

- **Example**: Implementing blockchain to ensure the authenticity of organic food products.

4. **Quality Control and Assurance**:

   - **Supplier Verification**: Ensuring that raw materials are sourced from reputable suppliers who comply with food safety standards reduces the risk of adulteration at the source.

     - **Example**: Conducting audits and evaluations of suppliers to verify their adherence to quality standards.

   - **Testing and Certification**: Regular testing of raw materials and finished products for adulterants helps in early detection and prevention. Certification from recognized bodies provides assurance of product quality.

     - **Example**: Obtaining AGMARK certification for agricultural products to ensure quality and safety.

5. **Consumer Awareness and Education**:

   - **Awareness Campaigns**: Educating consumers about the risks of food adulteration and how to identify adulterated products empowers them to make informed choices.

     - **Example**: Public awareness campaigns by food safety authorities to highlight common adulterants and safe purchasing practices.

   - **Encouraging Reporting**: Establishing mechanisms for consumers to report suspected cases of food adulteration encourages vigilance and accountability in the food industry.

     - **Example**: Setting up consumer helplines and online portals for reporting food safety concerns.

6. **International Collaboration**:

- **Harmonization of Standards**: Collaborating with international food safety organizations to harmonize standards and regulations ensures consistency and safety in the global food supply chain.

  - **Example**: Participating in Codex Alimentarius Commission meetings to align national food safety standards with international guidelines.

- **Information Sharing**: Sharing information and best practices on food adulteration detection and prevention with other countries helps build a collective defense against adulteration.

  - **Example**: Collaborating with international food safety networks to exchange data on food adulteration incidents.

Preventing and controlling food adulteration requires a comprehensive approach that includes robust regulatory frameworks, stringent industry practices, technological innovations, and consumer awareness. By implementing these measures, stakeholders can work together to ensure the safety, quality, and integrity of food products, protecting public health and fostering consumer trust. Continuous improvement and collaboration among regulatory authorities, industry players, and consumers are essential to effectively combat food adulteration and maintain a safe food supply chain.

7.3 Regulations and Claims

7.3.1 Label Claims

Introduction: Label claims on food products provide consumers with important information about the nutritional content, health benefits, and overall quality of the food. Proper labeling is crucial for ensuring that consumers can make informed choices and for maintaining transparency in the food industry. Label claims must comply with regulatory standards to avoid misleading or deceiving consumers.

Types of Label Claims:

1. **Nutrient Content Claims**:

  - **Definition**: These claims describe the level of a nutrient or dietary substance in a product, using terms such as "free," "low," "reduced," "high," "good source of," etc.

- **Examples**:

  - **"Low Fat"**: Indicates that the product contains a small amount of fat, usually defined as less than 3 grams of fat per serving.
  - **"High in Fiber"**: Suggests that the product contains a significant amount of dietary fiber, typically more than 5 grams per serving.

- **Regulatory Standards**: Nutrient content claims must meet specific criteria established by food safety authorities. For example, in the United States, the Food and Drug Administration (FDA) sets guidelines for what constitutes a "low," "high," or "reduced" nutrient level.

2. **Health Claims**:

- **Definition**: Health claims describe a relationship between a food, food component, or dietary supplement ingredient and the reduction of risk of a disease or health-related condition.
- **Examples**:

  - **"Calcium and Osteoporosis"**: Indicates that adequate calcium intake, as part of a well-balanced diet, may reduce the risk of osteoporosis.
  - **"Soluble Fiber and Heart Disease"**: Suggests that diets low in saturated fat and cholesterol that include soluble fiber may reduce the risk of heart disease.

- **Regulatory Standards**: Health claims must be substantiated by scientific evidence and approved by regulatory authorities. They are often categorized into authorized health claims, qualified health claims, and structure/function claims, each with different levels of evidence requirements.

3. **Structure/Function Claims**:

- **Definition**: These claims describe the role of a nutrient or dietary ingredient in affecting or maintaining normal structure or function in humans.

- **Examples**:

  - **"Calcium Builds Strong Bones"**: Indicates that calcium contributes to the development and maintenance of strong bones.
  - **"Antioxidants Support Immune Health"**: Suggests that antioxidants help maintain a healthy immune system.

- **Regulatory Standards**: Structure/function claims do not require pre-approval by regulatory authorities but must be truthful and not misleading. They should also be supported by evidence demonstrating the claimed effect.

Regulatory Requirements and Compliance:

1. **Accuracy and Truthfulness**:

   - **Substantiation**: All label claims must be substantiated by credible scientific evidence. Manufacturers are responsible for ensuring that the claims are accurate and can be supported by research.
   - **Misleading Claims**: It is prohibited to make false or misleading claims about the nutritional content or health benefits of a product. Regulatory authorities monitor and enforce compliance to protect consumers.

2. **Labeling Standards**:

   - **Content and Format**: Regulatory guidelines dictate how information should be presented on food labels, including font size, placement, and wording of claims. This ensures that labels are clear and easy to understand.
   - **Ingredient List**: All ingredients must be listed on the label in descending order of predominance by weight. This transparency helps consumers identify potential allergens and make informed choices.

3. **Compliance and Enforcement**:

- **Inspections and Audits**: Regulatory authorities conduct regular inspections and audits of food products and labels to ensure compliance with labeling standards.
- **Penalties for Non-Compliance**: Non-compliance with labeling regulations can result in enforcement actions, including fines, product recalls, and legal penalties.

Consumer Education and Awareness:

1. **Understanding Label Claims**:

   - **Educational Campaigns**: Regulatory authorities and health organizations often conduct educational campaigns to help consumers understand food labels and make informed choices.
   - **Reading Labels**: Consumers should be encouraged to read and understand the nutritional content and claims on food labels to select products that meet their dietary needs and preferences.

2. **Identifying Misleading Claims**:

   - **Critical Evaluation**: Consumers should be aware of common marketing tactics and critically evaluate claims that seem too good to be true. Awareness of regulatory standards can help in identifying misleading or exaggerated claims.
   - **Reporting Concerns**: Consumers should report any suspicious or misleading label claims to regulatory authorities for investigation and action.

Label claims play a vital role in providing consumers with important information about the nutritional content and health benefits of food products. Ensuring the accuracy, truthfulness, and compliance of these claims with regulatory standards is essential for maintaining transparency and consumer trust in the food industry. Consumer education and awareness are also crucial for empowering individuals to make informed choices and identify misleading claims. By adhering to regulatory requirements and promoting accurate labeling, the food industry can contribute to a safer and more informed food supply.

7.3.2 Nutrient Content Claims

Introduction: **Nutrient content claims** on food labels provide information about the amount of a specific nutrient contained in a food product. These claims help consumers make informed dietary choices by highlighting products that meet their nutritional needs. Nutrient content claims must comply with regulatory standards to ensure accuracy and prevent misleading information.

Types of Nutrient Content Claims:

1. **"Free" Claims**:

   - **Definition**: Indicates that a food contains an insignificant amount of a specified nutrient.
   - **Examples**:

     - **"Fat-Free"**: Contains less than 0.5 grams of fat per serving.
     - **"Sugar-Free"**: Contains less than 0.5 grams of sugars per serving.

   - **Regulatory Standards**: These claims must meet specific criteria set by food safety authorities to ensure the amounts are negligible.

2. **"Low" Claims**:

   - **Definition**: Indicates that a food contains a low amount of a specified nutrient.
   - **Examples**:

     - **"Low Fat"**: Contains 3 grams of fat or less per serving.
     - **"Low Sodium"**: Contains 140 milligrams of sodium or less per serving.

   - **Regulatory Standards**: Defined by regulatory authorities, such as the FDA, to ensure that the nutrient levels are beneficial for health-conscious consumers.

3. **"Reduced" or "Less" Claims**:

   - **Definition**: Indicates that a food contains at least 25% less of a specified nutrient compared to a reference food.

- **Examples**:

  - **"Reduced Fat"**: Contains at least 25% less fat than the regular product.
  - **"Less Sugar"**: Contains at least 25% less sugar than the regular product.

- **Regulatory Standards**: These claims require a comparison to a standard product and must meet defined criteria.

4. **"High" or "Rich In" Claims**:

- **Definition**: Indicates that a food contains 20% or more of the Daily Value (DV) of a specified nutrient per serving.
- **Examples**:

  - **"High in Vitamin C"**: Contains 20% or more of the DV for vitamin C per serving.
  - **"Rich in Fiber"**: Contains 20% or more of the DV for dietary fiber per serving.

- **Regulatory Standards**: These claims must meet the percentage criteria established by food safety authorities.

5. **"Good Source" Claims**:

- **Definition**: Indicates that a food contains 10-19% of the Daily Value (DV) of a specified nutrient per serving.
- **Examples**:

  - **"Good Source of Calcium"**: Contains 10-19% of the DV for calcium per serving.
  - **"Good Source of Iron"**: Contains 10-19% of the DV for iron per serving.

- **Regulatory Standards**: These claims help consumers identify foods that contribute a moderate amount of essential nutrients to their diet.

6. **"More" or "Fortified" Claims**:

   - **Definition**: Indicates that a food contains at least 10% more of the Daily Value (DV) of a specified nutrient compared to a reference food.
   - **Examples**:

     - **"More Fiber"**: Contains at least 10% more fiber than the regular product.
     - **"Fortified with Vitamins"**: Contains added vitamins, providing at least 10% more of the DV compared to the regular product.

   - **Regulatory Standards**: These claims must involve a comparison to a standard product and meet defined criteria.

Regulatory Requirements and Compliance:

1. **Accuracy and Truthfulness**:

   - **Substantiation**: Nutrient content claims must be based on scientifically valid methods of nutrient analysis. Manufacturers must ensure that the claims are accurate and supported by reliable data.
   - **Misleading Claims**: It is prohibited to make false or misleading nutrient content claims. Regulatory authorities monitor and enforce compliance to protect consumers from deceptive practices.

2. **Labeling Standards**:

   - **Content and Format**: Regulatory guidelines specify how nutrient content claims should be presented on labels, including font size, placement, and wording. This ensures clarity and consistency, making it easier for consumers to understand the claims.
   - **Nutrient Analysis**: Foods making nutrient content claims must undergo laboratory analysis to verify the nutrient levels. These analyses must be conducted using approved methods.

3. **Compliance and Enforcement**:

- ○ **Inspections and Audits**: Regulatory authorities conduct regular inspections and audits of food labels to ensure compliance with nutrient content claim standards.
- ○ **Penalties for Non-Compliance**: Non-compliance with nutrient content claim regulations can result in enforcement actions, including fines, product recalls, and legal penalties.

Consumer Education and Awareness:

1. **Understanding Nutrient Content Claims**:

   - ○ **Educational Campaigns**: Regulatory authorities and health organizations often conduct educational campaigns to help consumers understand nutrient content claims and make informed dietary choices.
   - ○ **Reading Labels**: Consumers should be encouraged to read and understand the nutrient content claims on food labels to select products that meet their dietary needs and preferences.

2. **Identifying Misleading Claims**:

   - ○ **Critical Evaluation**: Consumers should be aware of marketing tactics and critically evaluate nutrient content claims that seem too good to be true. Awareness of regulatory standards can help in identifying misleading or exaggerated claims.
   - ○ **Reporting Concerns**: Consumers should report any suspicious or misleading nutrient content claims to regulatory authorities for investigation and action.

Nutrient content claims on food labels provide essential information about the nutritional value of food products. Ensuring the accuracy, truthfulness, and compliance of these claims with regulatory standards is crucial for maintaining transparency and consumer trust in the food industry. Consumer education and awareness are also vital for empowering individuals to make informed dietary choices and identify misleading claims. By adhering to regulatory requirements and promoting accurate labeling, the food industry can contribute to a healthier and more informed consumer base.

7.3.3 Health Claims

Introduction: **Health claims** on food labels provide information about the relationship between a food, food component, or dietary supplement ingredient and the reduction of risk of a disease or health-related condition. These claims help consumers make informed choices about foods that may contribute to their health and well-being. Health claims must be substantiated by scientific evidence and comply with regulatory standards to ensure they are truthful and not misleading.

Types of Health Claims:

1. **Authorized Health Claims**:

   - **Definition**: These claims are based on a significant agreement among qualified experts that the scientific evidence supports the relationship between a food component and a health benefit. They are authorized by regulatory authorities such as the FDA in the United States.
   - **Examples**:

     - **"Calcium and Osteoporosis"**: "Adequate calcium throughout life, as part of a well-balanced diet, may reduce the risk of osteoporosis."
     - **"Sodium and Hypertension"**: "Diets low in sodium may reduce the risk of high blood pressure, a disease associated with many factors."

   - **Regulatory Standards**: Authorized health claims must meet stringent evidence requirements and are subject to rigorous review and approval by regulatory bodies.

2. **Qualified Health Claims**:

   - **Definition**: These claims are based on emerging evidence that suggests a relationship between a food component and a health benefit. The evidence is not as strong as for authorized health claims, so these claims must include a qualifying statement to indicate the level of scientific support.
   - **Examples**:

- **"Omega-3 Fatty Acids and Heart Disease"**: "Supportive but not conclusive research shows that consumption of EPA and DHA omega-3 fatty acids may reduce the risk of coronary heart disease."

- **Regulatory Standards**: Qualified health claims must be accompanied by a disclaimer or qualifying statement to ensure consumers understand the level of scientific evidence supporting the claim.

3. **Structure/Function Claims**:

   - **Definition**: These claims describe the role of a nutrient or dietary ingredient in affecting or maintaining normal structure or function in the body. Unlike health claims, they do not link the nutrient to a reduction in disease risk.
   - **Examples**:

     - **"Calcium Builds Strong Bones"**: Indicates that calcium contributes to the development and maintenance of strong bones.
     - **"Fiber Supports Digestive Health"**: Suggests that dietary fiber helps maintain a healthy digestive system.

   - **Regulatory Standards**: Structure/function claims do not require pre-approval by regulatory authorities but must be truthful and not misleading. Manufacturers must notify regulatory authorities about the use of these claims and have substantiation on file.

Regulatory Requirements and Compliance:

1. **Scientific Substantiation**:

   - **Evidence Requirements**: Health claims must be substantiated by credible scientific evidence. Authorized health claims require significant scientific agreement (SSA) among experts, while qualified health claims need emerging evidence with appropriate disclaimers.
   - **Review Process**: Regulatory authorities, such as the FDA, review the scientific evidence supporting health claims to ensure they are valid and not misleading.

2. **Labeling Standards**:

   ○ **Content and Format**: Health claims must be presented clearly and accurately on food labels. The wording should be precise, and any qualifying statements or disclaimers must be prominently displayed.
   ○ **Nutrient Content Requirements**: For a product to bear a health claim, it must meet certain nutrient content criteria, such as being low in fat, saturated fat, cholesterol, and sodium.

3. **Compliance and Enforcement**:

   ○ **Monitoring and Audits**: Regulatory authorities monitor food labels and advertisements to ensure compliance with health claim regulations. This includes reviewing product labels, marketing materials, and supporting scientific documentation.
   ○ **Penalties for Non-Compliance**: Non-compliance with health claim regulations can result in enforcement actions, including warnings, fines, product recalls, and legal penalties.

Consumer Education and Awareness:

1. **Understanding Health Claims**:

   ○ **Educational Campaigns**: Regulatory authorities and health organizations often conduct educational campaigns to help consumers understand health claims and make informed dietary choices.
   ○ **Reading Labels**: Consumers should be encouraged to read and understand health claims on food labels to select products that meet their health needs and preferences.

2. **Identifying Misleading Claims**:

   ○ **Critical Evaluation**: Consumers should be aware of marketing tactics and critically evaluate health claims that seem too good to be true. Awareness of regulatory standards can help in identifying misleading or exaggerated claims.

- ○ **Reporting Concerns**: Consumers should report any suspicious or misleading health claims to regulatory authorities for investigation and action.

Health claims on food labels provide valuable information about the potential health benefits of food products. Ensuring the accuracy, truthfulness, and compliance of these claims with regulatory standards is crucial for maintaining transparency and consumer trust in the food industry. Consumer education and awareness are also vital for empowering individuals to make informed dietary choices and identify misleading claims. By adhering to regulatory requirements and promoting accurate labeling, the food industry can contribute to a healthier and more informed consumer base.

7.3.4 Dietary Supplements Claims

Introduction: Dietary supplements claims refer to the statements made on product labels that describe the benefits and functions of dietary supplements. These claims can highlight the nutritional content, potential health benefits, and role of the supplement in maintaining or improving overall health. It is essential that these claims are substantiated by scientific evidence and comply with regulatory standards to avoid misleading consumers.

Types of Dietary Supplements Claims:

1. **Nutrient Content Claims**:

   - ○ **Definition**: These claims describe the level of a nutrient or dietary substance in a supplement. They use terms such as "free," "low," "high," "reduced," and "good source of."
   - ○ **Examples**:

     - "**High in Vitamin C**": Indicates that the supplement contains a significant amount of vitamin C.
     - "**Low in Sodium**": Suggests that the supplement contains a minimal amount of sodium.

   - ○ **Regulatory Standards**: Nutrient content claims must meet specific criteria set by regulatory authorities to ensure they are accurate and not misleading.

2. **Health Claims**:

   - **Definition**: Health claims describe a relationship between a dietary supplement ingredient and reduced risk of a disease or health-related condition.
   - **Examples**:

     - **"Calcium and Osteoporosis"**: States that calcium supplements may reduce the risk of osteoporosis when taken as part of a well-balanced diet.
     - **"Folic Acid and Neural Tube Defects"**: Indicates that adequate folic acid intake may reduce the risk of neural tube defects in pregnancy.

   - **Regulatory Standards**: Health claims must be substantiated by significant scientific agreement and approved by regulatory authorities. They are subject to rigorous review and must be accompanied by disclaimers if the evidence is not conclusive.

3. **Structure/Function Claims**:

   - **Definition**: These claims describe the role of a nutrient or dietary ingredient in affecting or maintaining normal structure or function in the human body.
   - **Examples**:

     - **"Calcium Builds Strong Bones"**: Indicates that calcium contributes to the development and maintenance of strong bones.
     - **"Antioxidants Support Immune Health"**: Suggests that antioxidants help maintain a healthy immune system.

   - **Regulatory Standards**: Structure/function claims do not require pre-approval by regulatory authorities but must be truthful and not misleading. Manufacturers must notify regulatory authorities about the use of these claims and have substantiation on file.

4. **Qualified Health Claims**:

- ◦ **Definition**: These claims are based on emerging evidence suggesting a relationship between a supplement ingredient and a health benefit. They require a qualifying statement to indicate the level of scientific support.
- ◦ **Examples**:

  - ▪ **"Omega-3 Fatty Acids and Heart Disease"**: "Supportive but not conclusive research shows that consumption of EPA and DHA omega-3 fatty acids may reduce the risk of coronary heart disease."

- ◦ **Regulatory Standards**: Qualified health claims must include a disclaimer to ensure consumers understand the level of scientific evidence supporting the claim.

Regulatory Requirements and Compliance:

1. **Scientific Substantiation**:

   - ◦ **Evidence Requirements**: All dietary supplement claims must be supported by credible scientific evidence. This includes clinical studies, peer-reviewed research, and other reliable data.
   - ◦ **Review Process**: Regulatory authorities, such as the FDA, review the scientific evidence supporting health claims to ensure they are valid and not misleading.

2. **Labeling Standards**:

   - ◦ **Content and Format**: Dietary supplement claims must be clearly and accurately presented on labels. The wording should be precise, and any qualifying statements or disclaimers must be prominently displayed.
   - ◦ **Nutrient Analysis**: Supplements making nutrient content claims must undergo laboratory analysis to verify the nutrient levels. These analyses must be conducted using approved methods.

3. **Compliance and Enforcement**:

- **Monitoring and Audits**: Regulatory authorities conduct regular monitoring and audits of dietary supplement labels and advertisements to ensure compliance with claim regulations.
- **Penalties for Non-Compliance**: Non-compliance with dietary supplement claim regulations can result in enforcement actions, including warnings, fines, product recalls, and legal penalties.

Consumer Education and Awareness:

1. **Understanding Supplement Claims**:

   - **Educational Campaigns**: Regulatory authorities and health organizations often conduct educational campaigns to help consumers understand dietary supplement claims and make informed choices.
   - **Reading Labels**: Consumers should be encouraged to read and understand the claims on dietary supplement labels to select products that meet their health needs and preferences.

2. **Identifying Misleading Claims**:

   - **Critical Evaluation**: Consumers should be aware of marketing tactics and critically evaluate claims that seem too good to be true. Awareness of regulatory standards can help in identifying misleading or exaggerated claims.
   - **Reporting Concerns**: Consumers should report any suspicious or misleading dietary supplement claims to regulatory authorities for investigation and action.

Dietary supplement claims play a vital role in providing consumers with information about the potential benefits of supplements. Ensuring the accuracy, truthfulness, and compliance of these claims with regulatory standards is crucial for maintaining transparency and consumer trust in the supplement industry. Consumer education and awareness are also essential for empowering individuals to make informed choices and identify misleading claims. By adhering to regulatory requirements and promoting accurate labeling, the dietary supplement industry can contribute to a healthier and more informed consumer base.

EIGHT

ABOUT THE AUTHORS

Mr. Sudhakar Kommu

Mr. Sudhakar Kommu is an Associate Professor of Pharmacognosy at Anurag Pharmacy College, Ananthagiri, Kodad, affiliated with JNTU Hyderabad, Telangana, India. He completed his UG and PG from Osmania University, Hyderabad, in 2007 and 2010, respectively. With over 13 years of teaching and research experience, he has published more than 34 research and review articles in reputed national and international journals, holds 3 patent publications and 2 design patents, and has guided around 78 UG student projects. A life member of APTI, he has presented over 15 papers at conferences and attended more than 100 national and international events.

He authored a book and a book chapter, served as an evaluator in several national seminars, and is known for his dynamic and hardworking nature in the field of Pharmacognosy.

Mr. Thirumurugan R

Mr. Thirumurugan R is the Principal at Niveditha College of Pharmacy, Chintamani, Karnataka, India, with 19 years of teaching experience. He has published several papers in national and international journals and has presented numerous papers at conferences. He is an active researcher in Pharmaceutics.

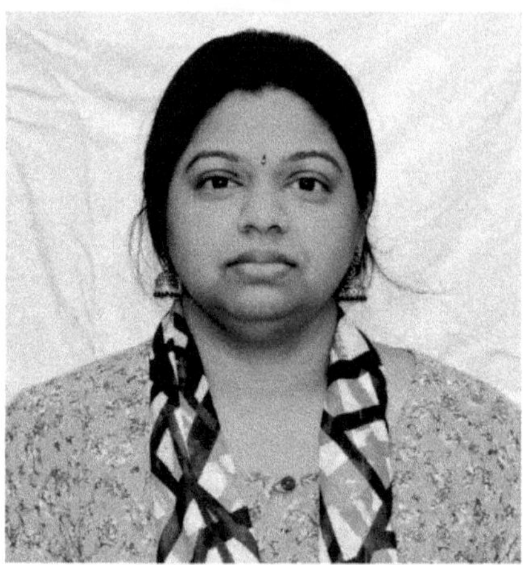

Mrs. Bhavana Madupoju

Mrs. Bhavana Madupoju is an Assistant Professor in the Department of Pharmaceutics at KL College of Pharmacy, KL Deemed to be University, Guntur, Andhra Pradesh, India. She completed her B.Pharm and M.Pharm from Nalanda College of Pharmacy, Nalgonda. With 11 years of academic experience, she has guided many graduate and postgraduate students and has published 6 research papers in national and international journals. Her research interests include Pharmaceutics, Pharmacology, and Nanotechnology.

NINE
GLOSSARY

Adulteration: The act of adding inferior or harmful substances to food or drink.

AGMARK: A certification mark employed on agricultural products in India, assuring that they conform to a set of standards.

Antioxidants: Compounds that inhibit oxidation, a chemical reaction that can produce free radicals and lead to cell damage.

Authorized Health Claims: Claims approved by regulatory authorities that describe a relationship between a food substance and a reduced risk of a disease.

Bioactive Compounds: Substances in foods that have biological effects in the body.

Biological Contaminants: Microorganisms such as bacteria, viruses, and fungi that can cause foodborne illnesses.

Blockchain Technology: A decentralized digital ledger used to record transactions across multiple computers.

Butylated Hydroxy Anisole (BHA): A synthetic antioxidant used to preserve fats and oils in food products.

Butylated Hydroxy Toluene (BHT): A synthetic antioxidant similar to BHA, used to prevent oxidation in foods.

Calcium: A mineral essential for bone health and various metabolic functions.

Carotenoids: Pigments found in plants that have antioxidant properties.

Case Study: An in-depth examination of a particular instance or event used for research or teaching purposes.

Certified Organic: A certification indicating that a product has been produced through approved organic farming methods.

Chemical Contaminants: Harmful chemicals that can enter the food supply through agricultural practices, industrial processes, or environmental pollution.

Chlorophyll: The green pigment in plants responsible for photosynthesis.

Codex Alimentarius Commission: An international organization that sets food safety and quality standards.

Consumer Awareness: The understanding and knowledge that a buyer should have about a product before buying it.

Contamination: The presence of harmful substances or microorganisms in food.

Critical Control Points (CCPs): Stages in the food production process where control can be applied to prevent or eliminate food safety hazards.

Deoxyribonucleic Acid (DNA): The molecule that carries genetic information in living organisms.

Dietary Fiber: The indigestible portion of plant foods that aids in digestion.

Dietary Supplements: Products taken orally that contain dietary ingredients intended to supplement the diet.

Essential Fatty Acids: Fatty acids that the body cannot produce and must be obtained from the diet.

Fat-Free: Contains less than 0.5 grams of fat per serving.

Flavonoids: A group of plant metabolites thought to provide health benefits through cell signaling pathways and antioxidant effects.

Food Additives: Substances added to food to preserve flavor or enhance its taste and appearance.

Foodborne Illness: Illnesses resulting from the ingestion of contaminated food.

Fortified Foods: Foods that have nutrients added to them that are not naturally present.

Fructooligosaccharides (FOS): A type of carbohydrate that acts as a prebiotic, promoting the growth of beneficial bacteria in the gut.

Functional Foods: Foods that have a potentially positive effect on health beyond basic nutrition.

Gas Chromatography (GC): An analytical method used to separate and analyze compounds that can be vaporized.

Genetically Modified Organisms (GMOs): Organisms whose genetic material has been altered using genetic engineering techniques.

Good Manufacturing Practices (GMP): Guidelines to ensure that products are consistently produced and controlled according to quality standards.

Hazard Analysis Critical Control Point (HACCP): A systematic preventive approach to food safety that addresses physical, chemical, and biological hazards.

Health Claims: Statements about the health benefits of a food or dietary supplement.

High-Performance Liquid Chromatography (HPLC): A technique in analytical chemistry used to separate, identify, and quantify each component in a mixture.

Hormones: Chemical messengers that regulate various functions in the body.

Hydrogenation: A process used to solidify liquid oils, often resulting in trans fats.

Immune System: The body's defense system against infections and diseases.

Indole-3-Carbinol: A compound found in cruciferous vegetables that may have cancer-preventive properties.

Isoflavones: A type of phytoestrogen found in soy products with potential health benefits.

Lactobacillus: A type of beneficial bacteria used in probiotics to promote gut health.

Lead Chromate: A toxic chemical sometimes used illegally to enhance the color of turmeric and other spices.

Lycopene: A red carotenoid pigment found in tomatoes and other red fruits and vegetables with antioxidant properties.

Malondialdehyde (MDA): A marker for oxidative stress and lipid peroxidation.

Melatonin: A hormone that regulates sleep-wake cycles and has antioxidant properties.

Micronutrients: Essential nutrients needed by the body in small amounts, such as vitamins and minerals.

Minerals: Inorganic elements required by the body for various functions, including building bones and producing hormones.

Misbranding: Providing false or misleading information on product labels.

Mitochondria: Organelles in cells responsible for energy production.

Naringin: A flavonoid found in citrus fruits that has antioxidant and anti-inflammatory properties.

Nuclear Magnetic Resonance (NMR) Spectroscopy: An analytical technique used to determine the content and purity of a sample.

Nutraceuticals: Products derived from food sources that offer health benefits beyond basic nutrition.

Nutrient Content Claims: Statements on food labels about the level of a nutrient in a product.

Nutritional Labeling: Information provided on food packaging about the nutritional content of the food.

Oligosaccharides: Carbohydrates composed of a small number of sugar molecules.

Omega-3 Fatty Acids: Essential fatty acids found in fish oils that have various health benefits.

Oxalic Acid: An organic compound found in plants that can bind to minerals and reduce their absorption.

Oxidative Stress: An imbalance between free radicals and antioxidants in the body.

Pesticide Residues: Traces of chemicals used in agriculture to protect crops from pests.

Phytochemicals: Chemical compounds produced by plants, often with beneficial health effects.

Phytoestrogens: Plant-derived compounds that mimic estrogen in the body.

Polyphenolics: A group of chemical substances found in plants, characterized by the presence of more than one phenol unit.

Polyunsaturated Fats: Fats found in plant and animal foods that are essential for health.

Potassium Permanganate: A chemical compound used in water treatment and sometimes in food adulteration detection.

Prebiotics: Non-digestible food ingredients that promote the growth of beneficial microorganisms in the intestines.

Probiotics: Live microorganisms that provide health benefits when consumed in adequate amounts.

Protein: A macronutrient essential for building muscle and repairing tissue.

Quality Control: Procedures implemented to ensure the quality and safety of products.

Qualified Health Claims: Health claims based on emerging evidence that require a qualifying statement.

Quercetin: A flavonoid with antioxidant and anti-inflammatory properties.

Random Errors: Errors in measurement that lead to inconsistent results.

Resveratrol: A polyphenolic compound found in red wine and grapes with potential health benefits.

Rutin: A flavonoid found in many plants that has antioxidant properties.

Significant Figures: The digits in a number that carry meaningful information about its precision.

Sodium Hydroxide: A strong base used in various chemical reactions and food processing.

Soluble Fiber: Fiber that dissolves in water and can help lower glucose levels and cholesterol.

Spirulina: A type of blue-green algae used as a dietary supplement for its high nutrient content.

Structure/Function Claims: Statements describing the role of a nutrient or dietary ingredient in normal body function.

Sulfides: Compounds containing sulfur, some of which have health benefits.

Superoxide Dismutase (SOD): An enzyme that helps break down potentially harmful oxygen molecules in cells.

Synthetic Antioxidants: Man-made substances that prevent oxidation in food products.

Tocopherols: A class of organic chemical compounds, many of which have vitamin E activity.

Traceability Systems: Systems that track the movement of food products through the supply chain.

Trans Fats: A type of unsaturated fat associated with increased health risks.

Ultraviolet-Visible (UV-Vis) Spectroscopy: A method used to measure the absorbance of UV or visible light by a sample.

Vitamins: Organic compounds that are essential for normal growth and nutrition.

Water Activity: The measure of the availability of water for biological reactions in a food product.

Xanthophylls: Yellow pigments found in plants that have antioxidant properties.

Zinc: A mineral essential for immune function, wound healing, and DNA synthesis.

Lutein: A carotenoid found in leafy greens that supports eye health.

Epicatechin: A type of flavonoid found in cocoa and green tea with antioxidant properties.

Saponins: Phytochemicals found in various plants that have potential health benefits.

Tannins: Polyphenolic compounds found in plants that have antioxidant properties.

Lectins: Proteins found in plants that can bind to carbohydrates and have various biological effects.

Mycotoxins: Toxic compounds produced by certain types of fungi.

Phytates: Compounds found in seeds and grains that can inhibit the absorption of minerals.

Alkaloids: Naturally occurring chemical compounds containing basic nitrogen atoms, many of which have medicinal properties.

Glycosides: Compounds formed from a sugar and another molecule, often with medicinal properties.

Terpenes: A large and diverse class of organic compounds produced by plants, known for their aromatic properties.

TEN

ACRONYMS AND THEIR MEANINGS